In this remarkable book, Adam Szumorek proposes th
theory can be used to good effect in preaching. He j
the analyses of many examples from the Bible, but he
this. He convincingly argues that the understanding of the word of God invites
reliance on conceptual metaphors, since the process of God's revelation unfolds through embodied (metaphorical) images, a major focus of attention by
cognitive linguists. But in a clear-headed way, he also points out that cognitive
linguistics cannot and should not be viewed as the only and ultimate tool of
biblical hermeneutics.

Zoltán Kövecses, PhD
Eötvös Loránd University, Hungary

There is a perennial challenge facing preachers. How can I communicate what
Scripture says in such a way as to allow listeners to enter the world of the text,
understand it, and come away not just with more information, but with their
view of the world transformed and their lives shaped by the gospel?

Adam Szumorek addresses this by making use of conceptual metaphor
theory (CMT) within cognitive linguistics. Though not without its critics, it
has the virtue of taking a holistic approach to meaning and Szumorek assesses
this well, demonstrating its relevance to our exposition of the biblical texts.

He not only connects CMT with key issues in hermeneutics but goes on to
show how, in practice, this can be used to open up Scripture in powerful and
effective ways. This is a great example of research bearing fruit in practical
approaches to preaching and ministry – a very worthwhile study.

Ian Paul, PhD
Adjunct Professor, Fuller Theological Seminary, California, USA
Associate Minister, St. Nicholas Church, Nottingham, UK

Dr. Szumorek provides a thoughtful and helpful roadmap for us to more holistically communicate God's word to God's world. He does this by helping us
better understand how we conceptualize ideas in order to understand biblical
metaphors and communicate them in ways that speak more effectively to the
minds, emotions, and imaginations of ourselves and others. His book is well
researched, insightful, and practical. Get your copy soon!

Tony Twist, PhD
President & Chief Executive Officer,
TCM International Institute

The question of how to understand the rich variety of imagery in the Bible and communicate it in meaningful ways today is a vital one for Christian preachers and teachers. In this book, Adam Szumorek draws on his expertise in the field of cognitive linguistics and his experience as a preacher and teacher of preaching to offer a carefully grounded theoretical basis for this process, leading to detailed practical suggestions. I commend it wholeheartedly to all those concerned to interpret and open up the Bible with faithfulness and creativity.

Stephen Wright, PhD
Formerly Vice Principal and Academic Director,
Spurgeon's College, UK

Seeing and Showing the Unseen

Using Cognitive Lingustics in Preaching
Images and Metaphors

Adam Szumorek

Langham

MONOGRAPHS

© 2023 Adam Szumorek

Published 2023 by Langham Monographs
An imprint of Langham Publishing
www.langhampublishing.org

Langham Publishing and its imprints are a ministry of Langham Partnership

Langham Partnership
PO Box 296, Carlisle, Cumbria, CA3 9WZ, UK
www.langham.org

ISBNs:
978-1-83973-793-0 Print
978-1-83973-906-4 ePub
978-1-83973-907-1 PDF

Scripture taken from the New American Standard Bible®, Copyright © 1960, 1962, 1963, 1968, 1971, 1972, 1973, 1975, 1977, 1995 by The Lockman Foundation. Used by permission.

British Library Cataloguing-in-Publication Data
A catalogue record for this book is available from the British Library

ISBN: 978-1-83973-793-0

Cover & Book Design: projectluz.com

Contents

List of Diagrams

Introduction

In this book, I present a methodology for employing Cognitive Linguistics in preaching that makes use of metaphors and images to convey the meaning of biblical texts with a special emphasis on biblical metaphors. This task is vital since God is unseen and invisible, and, therefore, the only reason preachers can talk about him is because of his self-revelation, which is largely metaphorical in nature. The Bible presents many abstract concepts in the form of concrete images and metaphors. Consequently, preachers, as communicators of God's word, are faced with the challenge of seeing and showing the unseen in ways that help others to see. My research was motivated by a desire to help preachers to employ Cognitive Linguistics in order to understand biblical metaphors, communicate these metaphors to their listeners, and create new metaphors that convey the meaning of the biblical text.

1. Interdisciplinary Character

This work is interdisciplinary because it combines four different areas of study: (1) Cognitive Linguistics, which is a secular and pragmatic science; (2) Christian theology, which is a normative science; (3) hermeneutics, which is a theory and a method of interpretation; and (4) homiletics, which is a theory and a method of communicating biblical texts to contemporary listeners that belongs to the realm of practical theology. This research was conducted from a broadly understood evangelical perspective in the Western culture. Thus, the homiletical scholars referred to in this study represent various currents of the evangelical movement, including mainline Protestant churches.

Cognitive Linguistics is also interdisciplinary in character since, generally speaking, it "integrates what is known about the mind with how humans use language."[1] Additionally, it needs to be stressed that this term "does not refer to a single well-articulated theory, but a loose family of models that affirm two key commitments," which are the Generalization Commitment and the Cognitive Commitment.[2] The Generalization Commitment seeks to "locate general principles applicable to all areas of language."[3] The Cognitive Commitment is based on the assumption that language does not function in isolation but that "the general principles of linguistic structure should be in accord with what we know about the mind and brain from a range of disciplines."[4] This means that cognitivists intend to integrate knowledge about language, perception, conceptualization of the world, neuroscience, and other areas of study into a coherent system to understand how people conceptualize the world and express it through the medium of language.[5]

Therefore, this research is interdisciplinary in character since it requires interacting with theology, hermeneutics, and homiletics, as well as with Cognitive Linguistics – which itself embraces numerous areas of study.

2. Cognitive Linguistic Perspective and Its Challenges

As stated above, two key commitments help to define the concept of Cognitive Linguistics, but there are also several assumptions that are fundamental to this theory.

First, cognitivists claim that the human mind is embodied and that human knowledge is perspectival.[6] Cognitive Linguistics challenges a traditional view of reason as transcendent, universal, and *disembodied*, and its proponents insist that there is no such entity as a disembodied mind. Humans are embodied minds, and our perception and conceptualization of the world are shaped, to

---

1. Sanders, *Theology in the Flesh*, loc. 67–68 of 5234, Kindle.

2. Sanders, loc. 219–220 of 5234.

3. Sanders, loc. 220–221 of 5234.

4. Sanders, loc. 234–235 of 5234.

5. In this thesis, the term Cognitive Linguistics will be spelled with capital letters because it refers to the group of theories that adhere to commitments presented above, as opposed to uncapitalized cognitive linguistics that refers to wider spectrum of cognitive sciences that focus on a broader study of language and its cognitive aspects. See Geeraerts, "Introduction: A Rough Guide," 1–28.

6. Lakoff and Johnson, *Philosophy in the Flesh*, 3.

a great extent, by our senses and bodily experiences. Thus, the only perspective that is accessible to human beings is limited to their embodied minds.

Second, "human thought is mostly unconscious," which means that these processes of perception and conceptualization often do not require any intentional mental effort.[7] As opposed to more traditional views that perceive metaphors as expressions of artistic talent and conscious effort, Lakoff and Johnson argue that people use metaphors naturally and, often, unconsciously.[8] Using the non-invasive recording of event-related brain potentials (ERPs), Seana Coulson proved that metaphors are comprehended in real time, which means that humans need the same amount of time to process metaphorical and non-metaphorical language.[9] Metaphorical thought processes taking place in human minds seem to be an unconscious, natural, and ubiquitous part of a human system of cognition.[10]

Third, cognitivists argue that since we conceptualize reality by understanding one concept in terms of another, human language is mostly metaphorical in nature. We talk about companies and organizations in terms of plants and living organisms. We conceptualize births as arrivals and deaths as departures, which shows that metaphors are not only conceptual in nature but also grounded in human experience. Therefore, metaphorical thinking becomes a dominant way of expressing our abstract thinking and, as such, is unavoidable and pervasive in language. Consequently, Lakoff and Johnson argue that abstract concepts "have a literal core but are extended by metaphors, often by many mutually inconsistent metaphors."[11] They claim that metaphors make these abstract concepts complete, as seen, for example, in the way that notions of madness, union, and nurturance complete the concept of love.[12] Thus, metaphors are not simply linguistic phenomena but are

---

7. Lakoff and Johnson, 3.

8. Lakoff and Johnson, 21. For a further discussion on differences in views on the disembodied and the embodied mind, and its influence on perception of morality, see Lakoff, "How the Body Shapes Thought," 49–53.

9. Coulson, "Metaphor Comprehension," 179.

10. For more on metaphorical thinking, creating new categories, and comparison between literal and metaphorical utterances, see Glucksberg, "How Metaphors Create Categories, " 17–38.

11. Lakoff and Johnson, *Metaphors We Live By*, 272.

12. Lakoff and Johnson, 272.

cognitive in nature because they embody our experience and understanding of the surrounding reality.

Fourth, even though meaning is encyclopedic in nature, it is "integrated with other cognitive processes" and "grounded in usage and experience."[13] Even though words have their dictionary meanings, they also evoke mental and emotional associations, and access knowledge accumulated through learning and experience.

Thus, Cognitive Linguistics views humans holistically and gives insights into their cognitive processes of conceptualizing the world. Within the broad scope of Cognitive Linguistics, in this research I engage with various theories such as conceptual metaphor theory, a theory of categories and prototypes, image schema theory, frame theory, and conceptual blending theory.

When applying Cognitive Linguistics to theology, hermeneutics, and preaching, it is necessary to identify both its limitations and its advantages. Thus, my research was aimed at finding out to what extent Cognitive Linguistics contributes to our theological understanding of language and how the key doctrines of Christianity – such as revelation, inspiration, and the incarnation – influence and modify our application of this theory and our understanding of its limits. My intention in this book is not only to explain the basic assumptions of Cognitive Linguistics but also to show the implications of perceiving language, even biblical language, in the context of human conceptualization for the purpose of applying this theory to biblical interpretation and, ultimately, to preaching.

In terms of limitations, Cognitive Linguistics as a secular and pragmatic science is anthropocentric in character. It is focused on analysis of human thinking and communication based on observable phenomena, such as ways people conceptualize the world and use language in the process of communication. It is not concerned with the notions about the existence of God, absolute truth, or transcendence since these notions are beyond the scope of this pragmatic approach. Consequently, as I discuss in chapter 1, some adherents of Cognitive Linguistics argue against the idea of the existence of any all-knowing mind and believe that the concept of God originated in human minds, whereas others claim that there are no limits to our conceptualizations of God as evidenced by the existence of numerous religions.

---

13. Sanders, *Theology in the Flesh*, loc. 316–337, Kindle.

However, the numerous advantages of utilizing Cognitive Linguistics make it a critical tool in discussing theology, in carrying out biblical interpretation, and in communicating Scripture. Cognitive Linguistics changes our understanding of language and communication. It helps us to understand the mechanisms behind the conceptualization of theological concepts.

Furthermore, Cognitive Linguistics supports the assertions of theology regarding the importance of the incarnation as an act of communication because it stresses the gravity of the idea of embodiment for human conceptualization of the world and for communication.[14] God's incarnation enables us to understand him better, to communicate with him, and to enter into a relationship with him. The idea of embodiment, from the perspective of Cognitive Linguistics, allows us to better understand the importance and meaning of abstract concepts such as baptism, washing away of sins, and the indwelling of the Holy Spirit.

When applied in the field of hermeneutics, Cognitive Linguistics provides the most holistic and comprehensive approach to metaphors and images because its scope of research extends beyond just literary study and linguistics. Conceptual metaphor theory, which is part of Cognitive Linguistics, allows us to describe biblical metaphors in the context of human cognitive processes because it argues that metaphors are not just a matter of words, sentences, or even discourse, but a matter of concepts and thoughts.

Cognitive Linguistics provides vital tools for thinking about and interpreting the Bible. In debates on biblical interpretation, various biblical scholars distinguish the world of the text, the world of the author, and the world of the reader as if these were separate realms, often stressing the importance of one of them over the others. Cognitive Linguistics allows us to bring these separate worlds back together, placing them within the coherent process of communication and stressing the value of each of them.

As far as homiletics is concerned, the act of communication is a phenomenon that can be better understood and analyzed from the perspective of Cognitive Linguistics, which helps us to appreciate more fully than other traditional theories the complexity of human conceptualization and

---

14. John Sanders stresses the importance of embodiment as the key factor in human conceptualization and also believes that God, in the incarnation, assumed "a human perspective in order to discuss truth with us." Sanders, loc. 207–212 of 5234.

communication that is shaped by our embodiment, experiences, and cultural universality and variation. Since communication is an encounter of minds, Cognitive Linguistics gives preachers tools to better understand the context of the implied author and, analogically, the context of the contemporary listener.

Cognitive Linguistics also enhances our methodology of developing sermon applications. Some scholars maintain that morality is about setting out principles of behaviour. Cognitive Linguistics challenges this idea and supports the claim that human morality is not rule-based but prototype-based. Prototype-based applications in preaching, instead of focusing on rules of behaviour, seek to create mental models to follow, and Christ is perceived as the most important prototype for his followers.

Applying conceptual metaphor theory to homiletics makes the whole endeavour of communicating biblical metaphors less intuitive and far more systematized. This requires that preachers perceive metaphors as the vehicles of meaning rather than as embellishments of meaning. Moreover, conceptual metaphor theory offers fresh insights into developing new ways of creating new metaphors and images in order to convey the meaning of the biblical texts.

This book seeks to test the assumption that Cognitive Linguistics – which is a vital tool among secular disciplines – can be used by Christians to articulate their theology, interpret the Bible, and express the rationale and methodology of preaching.

3. Main Research Question

Understanding the basic assumptions of Cognitive Linguistics leads to an awareness of its potential in terms of applying this theory to preaching. In order to preach effectively, preachers should understand how people conceptualize the world around and how this conceptualization is expressed in language. Moreover, they can benefit greatly from learning the key principles of applying this theory to the analysis and preaching of biblical texts and biblical metaphors, which may result in creating new metaphors where appropriate. Therefore, my main research question is this: In a theological context, how can Cognitive Linguistics be productive in biblical preaching that employs metaphors and images and seeks to convey the meaning and the mood of the biblical text by connecting with listeners' embodied minds, emotions, and imagination?

4. State of Research

The research question formulated above became even more vital and relevant once I analyzed the state of research on the subject of employing Cognitive Linguistics in preaching. Cognitive Linguistics is a growing area of study, and numerous books and articles have been devoted to this subject. George Lakoff and Mark Johnson are among the pioneers and most prominent proponents of this area of study. Their best known book, *Metaphors We Live By*, prompted more research and resulted in new findings that were applied to other areas of linguistics and other disciplines.[15] Ron Langacker identifies the notion of image schemas that are simple, highly schematic cognitive structures – for example, paths, containers, links, and spatial orientations. Image schemas reflect our physical experience of the world and are a universal basis for other metaphors.[16] In *More than Cool Reason*, Lakoff and Turner apply conceptual metaphor theory to poetic texts.[17] In his book *The Body in the Mind*, Mark Johnson elaborates on the embodied nature of a human conceptual system.[18] At the same time, further research that has been conducted shows that metaphors describing different emotions such as anger, love, happiness, sadness are conceptualized in a similar fashion in various cultures and that these conceptualizations have experiential bases rooted in human physiology. Zoltán Kövecses devoted a great deal of attention to studying both emotions and cultural variations of metaphors.[19]

Research on mental spaces – which are mental constructs organizing our knowledge – was initiated in 1977, and its first findings are captured in *Mental Spaces* by Gilles Fauconnier, Eve Sweetser, and George Lakoff.[20]

---

15. Lakoff and Johnson, *Metaphors We Live By*.

16. Langacker, *Foundations of Cognitive Grammar*. For a more detailed explanation of image schemas see section 3.3.2.1., 120–122.

17. Lakoff and Turner, *More than Cool Reason*.

18. Johnson, *Body in the Mind*.

19. Kövecses, *Language of Love*; *Metaphor and Emotion*; *Language, Mind, and Culture*; *Metaphor in Culture*; *Emotion Concepts*.

20. Fauconnier, Sweetser, and Lakoff, *Mental Spaces*. For a more detailed definition of mental spaces see section 3.3.9.

Further study was carried out by John Dinsmore, who focused on applying mental spaces to language phenomena such as tense and viewpoint.[21] Michelle Cutrer worked on mental spaces in the context of time and tense in narratives.[22] In the 1990s – on the basis of Fauconnier's work on mental spaces and early versions of conceptual metaphor theory – Fauconnier and Turner started their research on conceptual blending. At that time, several studies on this subject – such as "Blending and Metaphor" by Grady, Oakley, and Coulson[23] – were published. In 1997, Fauconnier published *Mappings in Thought and Language*.[24] One of the most important publications on the subject is Fauconnier and Turner's book *The Way We Think*.[25] Eve Sweetser applies conceptual blending theory to her analysis of performativity in language with a special emphasis on religious language.[26] Seana Coulson developed ERP (event-related potential) techniques to provide empirical evidence for theoretical research on conceptual blends and also worked on concepts of frame shifting and blending in developing new ideas and the construction of meaning.[27] Fauconnier and Turner also applied this theory to an analysis of the way concepts of time and space are used in linguistics.[28]

In 1988, Feldman and Lakoff began their studies on a neural theory of language (NLT), giving further support for the theory of Cognitive Linguistics and showing how conceptual metaphors reflect neural processes taking place in the human brain. This research was continued by Joseph Grady, Christopher Johnson, and Srinivas Narayanan, who showed that all metaphors, even complex ones, come from primary metaphors that originate from our earliest sensory-motor experiences. Narayanan, using modern technologies, showed how metaphors are processed in a human neural system, and this led to forming a neural theory of metaphor.[29] Lakoff presented his modified

---

21. Dinsmore, *Partitioned Representations*.

22. Cutrer, "Time and Tense."

23. Grady, Oakley, and Coulson, "Blending and Metaphor."

24. Fauconnier, *Mappings in Thought and Language*.

25. Fauconnier and Turner, *Way We Think*. See also Fauconnier, "Mental Spaces," 350–376.

26. Sweetser, "Blended Spaces," 305–333.

27. Coulson, *Semantic Leaps*.

28. Fauconnier and Turner, "Rethinking Metaphor," 53–66.

29. Joseph E. Grady, 'Metaphor', in The Oxford Handbook of Cognitive Linguistics, ed. by Dirk Geeraets and Hubert Cuyckens (Oxford; New York: Oxford University Press, 2010), 188–213; Joseph E. Grady, 'Foundation of Meaning: Primary Metaphors and Primary Scenes'

view on metaphors in his article "The Neural Theory of Metaphor," which was published in *The Cambridge Handbook of Metaphor and Thought*.[30] In the same collection, Fauconnier and Turner presented their papers on blending and their understanding of blending mechanisms. Even though they approach the subject from a perspective that is different to that of adherents of neural metaphor theory and utilize different theoretical paradigms, their outcomes seem to be compatible with the findings of Neural Linguistics.[31]

Not surprisingly, in recent years, numerous works on applying conceptual metaphor theory to analyzing biblical metaphors have been published. The earliest appropriation of Cognitive Linguistics to biblical studies took place in the 1990s and early 2000s. Marc Zvi Brettler applied Lakoff and Johnson's metaphor theory to analyzing Old Testament texts.[32] Laurence Erussard, in his article "From SALT to SALT: Cognitive Metaphor and Religious Language," conducts a cognitive analysis of the biblical image of Christ's followers being the salt of the earth.[33] Olaf Jäkel revisits the main hypotheses of cognitive metaphor theory and shows how to apply these to the study of religious texts.[34] Ellen van Wolde conducted her research on employing Cognitive Linguistics to the analysis of the Old Testament texts, as seen in her study of Job.[35] In 2006, the Society of Biblical Literature initiated a three-year consultation on the subject that resulted in the publication of a collection of essays entitled *Cognitive Linguistic Explorations in Biblical Studies*.[36] Among the contributors to this work are Eve Sweetser, Mary Therese DesCamp, and Hugo Lundhaug.

Job Y. Jindo, who shows how to apply Cognitive Linguistics to the analysis of biblical texts, emphasizes the significance of conducting cultural studies in order to understand the cognitive framework of the original audience.[37]

(unpublished PhD dissertation, University of California, 1997); Srini Narayanan, 'Karma: Knowledge-Based Action Representations for Metaphor and Aspect' (unpublished PhD dissertation, University of California, 1997).

30. Lakoff, "Neural Theory," 17–38.

31. Fauconnier and Lakoff, "On Metaphor and Blending," 393–399.

32. Brettler, *God Is King*.

33. Erussard, "From SALT to SALT," 197–212.

34. Jäkel, "Hypotheses Revisited," 20–42.

35. van Wolde, "Wisdom, Who Can Find It?," 1–36, and "Cognitive Grammar at Work," 193–221.

36. Howe and Green, *Cognitive Linguistic Explorations*.

37. Jindo, "Toward a Poetics," 222–243.

Yoon-Man Park applies frame theory to the analysis of the Gospel of Mark.[38] Zoltán Kövecses, in his numerous publications, refers to the Bible and gives examples of how Cognitive Linguistics can be utilized to study religious texts and biblical concepts.[39] Another important example of applying Cognitive Linguistics to theology, biblical interpretation, and ethics is the book *Theology in the Flesh* by John Sanders.

When I began studying homiletical literature, however, I discovered that even though some homileticians refer in their writings to conceptual metaphor theory, they do not usually show how to apply this theory to preaching or how it can enhance their communication of the word of God. There are, however, some exceptions, such as David Buttrick, who devotes a lot of attention to metaphors in his classic work *Homiletic: Moves and Structures*.[40] Taking advantage of studies in Cognitive Linguistics, Buttrick stresses the importance of using conceptual metaphors that are common in everyday language and are an essential means of conceptualization of the surrounding reality. He also adopts some elements of Lakoff and Johnson's theory in order to develop his idea of creating moves of consciousness. However, his methodology draws from various sources and is a combination of different approaches, including his own ideas. He does not show how to apply various elements of Cognitive Linguistics to hermeneutics and homiletics nor how they can influence both our analysis of the biblical text and preaching – for instance through presenting biblical metaphors in sermons, creating new metaphors, or developing sermon application.

There are two collections of papers at two different conferences of the Evangelical Homiletics Society in 2002 and 2005. They were devoted to interpretation and preaching images, metaphors, and finding sermon illustrations.[41] However, even though contributors did not limit themselves to very traditional approaches to metaphors but also referred to Cognitive Linguistics, they did not go beyond simply summarizing conceptual metaphor theory as the newest approach to metaphors.

---

38. Park, *Mark's Memory Resources*.

39. Kövecses, "Biblical Story Retold," 325–354 and *Where Metaphors Come From*.

40. Buttrick, *Homiletic: Moves and Structures*.

41. Among the presenters were Sackett, "Illusive Illustration," Radford, "Sermon as Illustration," Petersen, "Garden, Park, Glen," and Smith, "Rethinking the Value of Metaphors."

In their research, Daniel Sheard and Trygve David Johnson refer to conceptual metaphor theory and use some of its elements; however, they do not show how application of this theory can transform the whole process of sermon preparation including analysis of the text, conveying the meaning of a text, developing the sermon structure, and developing sermon imagery.[42]

5. Applying Cognitive Linguistics to Preaching

As I analyzed hermeneutical and homiletical literature on the application of Cognitive Linguistics to biblical interpretation and preaching, I identified an area that had not yet been investigated as far as applying Cognitive Linguistics to preaching is concerned. There is a need to show, in more workable and accessible ways, how utilizing Cognitive Linguistics can influence preachers' understanding of their task, as well as their methodology of interpretation of the biblical text. There is also the question of how this theory can reshape the manner in which metaphors and images are used in sermons as a means of conveying the meaning of the biblical texts and biblical metaphors, and how this can influence the ways in which sermons are structured and sermon applications developed.

Therefore, I aim to demonstrate how Cognitive Linguistics can contribute to conveying the meaning of biblical texts in general and biblical metaphors in particular through the use of metaphors in sermons. This would mean that sermons must not only take into consideration the need to understand the human cognitive processes that are verbalized in cognitive metaphors and images but must also reflect the holistic nature of God's revelation, the holistic nature of human beings as created in the image of God, and the holistic nature of preaching as modelled by the incarnation, and address the whole human person by speaking to listeners' embodied minds, emotions, and imagination.

Thus, in this book, I show how Cognitive Linguistics is productive in developing sermons that are rooted in both a cognitive view of humans as embodied minds, and in the nature of God's revelation through images as seen in the act of creation of people, written revelation, and the incarnation of Christ. I also show how the idea of God's revelation through images is foundational for developing a theology of preaching because it emphasizes

---

42. Sheard, "Preaching in the Hear and Now," and Johnson, "Preacher as Artist."

the Trinitarian nature of revelation and preaching. This Trinitarian nature of revelation is based on the fact that God revealed himself by creating people in his image, that Christ, who is our Saviour, is the perfect image of the Father, and that the Holy Spirit transforms us into the image of Christ. As preachers, we enjoy the privilege of participating both in this process of conveying God's revelation and in the process of transformation into the image of Christ.

Consequently, I show that even though Cognitive Linguistics is a secular science, it articulates many assumptions of a traditional theology of preaching. The primary goal of my book, however, is to demonstrate the usefulness of Cognitive Linguistics to the practice of preaching.

6. Research Objectives

My research was conducted with the aim of meeting the following objectives:

- Provide theological justification for using metaphors and images in sermons, with a special emphasis on utilizing Cognitive Linguistics in homiletics.
- Verbalize how Cognitive Linguistics can be productive both in giving preachers deeper understanding of the act of preaching and in enriching their practice of preaching.
- Analyze the unique contribution of Cognitive Linguistics to studies on metaphor.
- Explain how Cognitive Linguistics has been used in hermeneutics and homiletics.
- Identify the key elements of cognitive metaphor theory that are essential to the interpretation of biblical metaphors and preaching metaphors in general.
- Demonstrate, with examples, how biblical metaphors can be seen through the lens of Cognitive Linguistics.
- Explain how this theory can be utilized in creating new metaphors and images to convey the meaning of non-metaphorical texts of the Bible.
- Evaluate the usefulness of these findings.
- Show areas for further research.

7. Book Overview

Chapter One

Chapter 1 is divided into two parts. In the first part, I provide the theological justification for utilizing Cognitive Linguistics in preaching by referring to the idea of God's revelation that originated from God but comes to us in human terms. I argue for using metaphors and images in sermons by referring to the means of God's revelation as seen in the creation of people in God's image, written revelation that includes metaphors and images, and the incarnation of Christ who is the perfect image of the Father. I show that the idea of using images and metaphors in sermons is justified by the fact that God is the first image-maker and that images are an essential means of his self-revelation. Moreover, I show that Cognitive Linguistics is a helpful tool in the analysis of God's revelation and that it changes our perception of religious language.

The second part of this chapter deals with the preacher's role and authority in using images and metaphors in sermons. I seek to answer to the question whether the preacher's task is merely explaining biblical metaphors, translating them into contemporary ones, or creating new ones that convey biblical revelation.

The final sections of this chapter are devoted to explaining some key presuppositions of a theology of preaching that is Trinitarian in character and seeks to employ Cognitive Linguistics while remaining faithful to the goal of conveying God's revelation.

Chapter Two

The main goal of chapter 2 is to give linguistic justification for using Cognitive Linguistics in general and conceptual metaphor theory in particular to biblical metaphors and images. This chapter has two parts. In the first, I present major developments in metaphor theory, paying special attention to three aspects: a definition of metaphor, the relationships between elements creating metaphor, and the meaning of metaphor. In the second part, I explain the main presuppositions of conceptual metaphor theory and give reasons why this theory and Cognitive Linguistics enrich our understanding of metaphor studies.

Chapter Three

In this chapter, I present the basic elements of Cognitive Linguistics and conceptual metaphor theory that are essential for biblical interpretation and show

how these concepts can be utilized in the analysis of biblical texts. Elements of this theory – such as categories, frames, prototypes, image schemas, domains, and blends – are discussed in greater detail in this section.

Chapter Four

Chapter 4 is devoted to applying Cognitive Linguistics to hermeneutics, and the issue of the relationship between the author, the text, and the reader is discussed from a cognitive perspective. The topic of universality and variation in human conceptualization is discussed in the light of analysis of the cultural setting of the text and the possibility of identifying the timeless truth of the text.

In this chapter, I also present some key principles of the analysis of metaphors as a part of discourse, and I conclude with a summary of a hermeneutical method that is applicable to preaching.

Chapter Five

The purpose of chapter 5 is to show practical ways of applying Cognitive Linguistics to preaching metaphors and images. This chapter is divided into two main parts. The first focuses on a cognitive perspective on the imagination and the task of bridging the world of the Bible and the world of the listeners. In this section, I explain how notions taken from Cognitive Linguistics – such as universality and variation, and prototype theory – can be useful both in understanding the world of the listeners and in developing a new approach to application, which is known as prototype-based application.

The second part of the chapter is devoted to presenting various strategies of reworking existing metaphors and showing how these are applicable to biblical metaphors and images. Additionally, I present a methodology for creating new metaphors and images to convey the meaning of biblical texts. This section concludes with a practical application of the notion of levels of schematicity to a sermon structure on a macro level and sermon imagery on a micro level.

8. Novelty of the Research

This book is the first attempt at a more systematic and coherent application of Cognitive Linguistics and conceptual metaphor theory to preaching. As pointed out earlier, there have been some homileticians who have made various references to these theories, but there is lack of a coherent methodology in employing these theories in homiletics.

While applying Cognitive Linguistics to preaching, I show not only how it impacts the shape of a sermon, but also how it can be utilized in studying the text and in sermon preparation. I have enhanced the application of this theory to hermeneutics by developing a notion of category operations and applying it to biblical texts. I propose a method of studying the text from the perspective of Cognitive Linguistics that can enhance more traditional approaches.

In the area of homiletics, I introduce the idea of using prototypes as means of understanding the listeners and transforming their values by employing a prototype-based application. Even though the concept of reworking existing metaphors into more creative ones is well established in Cognitive Linguistics, Cognitive Linguistics methodology has never been applied to preaching. In explaining how this methodology can be used in the area of preaching, I expand the scope of application by proposing new ways of reworking and conveying biblical metaphors. Furthermore I also introduce a novel methodology for conveying the meaning of biblical texts by creating new metaphors and images. Finally, I show how Kövecses's idea of levels of schematicity can be applied to developing sermon structures on a macro level and sermon imagery on a micro level.

9. Limitations of the Research

This book is only a step towards developing a methodology for utilizing Cognitive Linguistics in preaching. Therefore, it does not deal with all possible areas of application. This same limitation applies to the application of this theory to hermeneutics. The area of hermeneutics is already well researched, and my intention is to show the relevance of Cognitive Linguistics to biblical interpretation and highlight only those aspects that are vital for understanding the text and sermon preparation.

Given that the aim of this research was to develop a coherent methodology for using metaphors and images in sermons to convey biblical metaphors and the meaning of biblical texts, it was impossible to analyze all examples of metaphors or even all biblical genres. Even though I was conducting an inquiry into a wide and general topic, I had to use a narrow set of examples to define some general principles. This does not mean that my conclusions are inaccurate or superficial because even a general study of biblical metaphors may result in identifying universal coherent patterns of using metaphors, patterns that are not limited to any particular genre.

In the process of developing the idea of a prototype-based application and methods of reworking existing metaphors and creating new ones, I became aware that each of these issues were possible topics for a whole new research project.

CHAPTER 1

The Theological Framework for Utilizing Cognitive Linguistics in Preaching

People say, "A picture is worth a thousand words," but preachers – while attempting to convey word pictures and biblical images in their preaching – find pictures puzzling in a number of ways. While recognizing that pictures are worth a thousand words, they often have more than a thousand problems with communicating pictures of the unseen – which involves preaching about the invisible and incomprehensible God, as well as numerous other abstract biblical concepts that are often conveyed through metaphors and images. Thus, preachers face the challenge of seeing the unseen – which involves understanding biblical images and metaphors – and showing the unseen – which involves using images and metaphors to talk about God and convey the meaning of biblical texts.

In this book, I argue that since Cognitive Linguistics changes our understanding of language and communication, it also changes our perception of religious language and ways in which we communicate about God. However, when we try to apply Cognitive Linguistics to theology, we encounter several types of difficulties in defining the interrelationship between these two disciplines.

Therefore, in this chapter, I will establish a theological foundation for preaching metaphors and images, which requires providing both the theological context for utilizing Cognitive Linguistics as the means of analyzing these biblical images and communicating theological concepts and theological justification for using metaphors and images in preaching. Both these objectives will be accomplished by referring to the doctrine of God's revelation, and this will be done from the perspective of classical, mainstream Western evangelical theology. I will not spend time on proving ideas such as the existence of God, his revelation, or the inspiration of God's word since these concepts are the presuppositions underlying my study and verifying their truthfulness is not the purpose of this book. Instead, I will define these terms to avoid misunderstandings as far as their meaning is concerned.

The second part of this chapter will focus on the preacher's role and authority in communicating biblical metaphors and images, as well as in creating new metaphors and images. Some preachers define their role as merely repeating and explaining biblical metaphors and images to help people to understand their content. Others argue that metaphors cannot or should not be narrowed down to propositional statements because, in doing so, their rhetorical impact is lost. They maintain that metaphors and images are best conveyed as metaphors and images and, consequently, see the preacher's role as that of a translator who translates ancient images into modern ones. Other homileticians would go even further and insist that the preacher is more of an artist, who has both the right and the authority to create new images and metaphors to effectively communicate even non-metaphorical texts of the Bible.

The final section of this chapter are devoted to presenting some basic assumptions of a theology of preaching that utilizes Cognitive Linguistics and aims at reflecting the Trinitarian nature of God's revelation in images. These sections are meant to be a theological framework for the practical applications of Cognitive Linguistics to hermeneutics and homiletics which are presented in the chapters that follow.

1.1 Revelation of the Unseen God: The Image-Maker as the Context for Utilizing Cognitive Linguistics and as the Foundation for Preaching Metaphors and Images

A discussion about applying Cognitive Linguistics to preaching needs to start with a theological framework both for employing Cognitive Linguistics to communicate theological and biblical concepts and for using metaphors and images in sermons. I will first present some advantages and disadvantages of using Cognitive Linguistics to talk about theology. I will then show how the idea of God's revelation changes our perspective on Cognitive Linguistics, both setting some limits on it and broadening its perspective. Next, I will discuss the ways in which God's revelation involved metaphors and images and show why this means that preachers can also use metaphors and images to convey God's revelation.

1.1.1 Cognitive Linguistics and Theology

I became interested in Cognitive Linguistics after taking a class on conceptual metaphor theory. My tutor, Dr. Monika Cichmińska, warned us that after just one semester we would see metaphors everywhere, and she was right! Taking this class was a transformative experience that influenced my perception of language and communication. Being a preacher, I could not help thinking about possible applications of conceptual metaphor theory and Cognitive Linguistics to preaching in general. What especially appealed to me about this approach was the fact that Cognitive Linguistics, since it describes patterns people use to conceptualize the world and communicate in everyday life, is very intuitive. These patterns are rooted in our bodily structure, experiences, and cultural influences. For instance, we think about an argument as a war. When we refer to arguing, we talk about taking sides. There are allies and opponents. During the argument, we can attack or defend. We fight. We sometimes describe our conflicts as real battles even though, typically, we do not use any physical weapons and nobody usually dies. We can win or lose. But what if we conceptualized an argument as a dance? How might this change the ways people argue?

As a preacher, I often ask myself how people think and communicate because I believe that answering this question could change the way I think about my listeners and the ways I communicate with them. Although Cognitive Linguistics opens up a new field for reflection and research, when we decide to enter this field, we encounter numerous difficulties. Thus, before explaining my views on applying Cognitive Linguistics to hermeneutics and homiletics in a theological context, I consider two categories of difficulties. The first set of difficulties come from those who oppose applying any kind of linguistics to reading of the Bible, the second from adherents of Cognitive Linguistics.

Some opponents of linguistics do not see any value in studying Cognitive Linguistics and applying its concepts to preaching because they believe that reading and interpreting the Bible requires no special tools and only takes common sense. However, these well-meaning Christians often ignore the fact that the nature of communication is very complex, especially when we are talking about reading a biblical text that is thousands of years old.

Relying purely on a common-sense basis when reading and interpreting the Bible is insufficient when it comes to crossing a wide historical and cultural gap. As we read the Bible, we encounter a whole spectrum of metaphors that seem distant from our experience – for example, God as king or warrior, offering our bodies as living sacrifices, and so on. Even if contemporary readers are able to comprehend these metaphors, these metaphors depict a reality that is radically different from ours. Hence, in preaching, it is possible to impose contemporary concepts on ancient ideas – for example, we may perceive God as king in terms of modern kings or kings from European history.

Those who perceive linguistics as redundant in biblical interpretation and preaching also face the challenge of determining which statements should be taken metaphorically and which ones literally. C. S. Lewis rightly says, "People who take symbols literally might as well think that when Christ told us to be like doves, He meant that we were to lay eggs."[1] It is not always easy to distinguish the metaphorical from the non-metaphorical. What did Jesus really mean when he urged his followers to gouge their own eye if it caused them to stumble (Matt 5:29) or to turn the other cheek if someone attacked them (Matt 5:39)? Over the centuries, there have been ongoing debates about the meaning of the words Jesus spoke at the Last Supper: "This is my body" (1 Cor 11:24). These debates have resulted in a whole array of interpretations and doctrines, beginning with the most literal, which is transubstantiation, through consubstantiation, the idea of spiritual presence, and, at the other end of the spectrum, purely symbolic approaches. It becomes apparent from these examples relating to historical distance and literal interpretation that readers need more tools than just their common sense when approaching biblical texts and that linguistics is among the most helpful of such tools. Cognitive Linguistics, with its novel approach to understanding metaphorical language, sheds new light on this topic.

The second set of challenges involved in applying Cognitive Linguistics to biblical interpretation and preaching come from some of the adherents of this theory. Some linguists argue against the existence of an all-knowing mind

---

1. Lewis, *Mere Christianity*, 122.

that is the source of our cognition and that provides us with an objective view of reality. Instead, they claim that the only view of reality that is accessible to us is the one that comes from the perception of our individual minds that are incapable of any other perspectives. Consequently, not only do they give up the quest for any hints of the objective truth or an objective vision of the world, but they also discard the whole notion of objective truth itself. Lakoff and Johnson do not believe that "there is such a thing as *objective* (absolute and unconditional) *truth*" and reject the idea of objective truth as "not only mistaken but dangerous".[2] The only kind of truth they are concerned with is the truth that is necessary for functioning in the world, which is based on accumulated knowledge and experiences about the human body, the environment, people, and situations.

In Lakoff's view, our "moral concepts too are embodied and metaphorical," and so he insists that "to understand this in full detail is to give up forever on the idea that there is transcendent morality based on transcendent universal reason."[3] He also directly questions the existence of God, pointing out that all conceptualizations of God are metaphorical and that, moreover, different religions form diverse and even antagonistic conceptions of God. He finds the question about the existence of God strange and pointless since to "recognize that the question is inherently metaphorical is to know that no answer can be literal."[4] Thus, Cognitive Linguistics is often used to question the idea of objective truth and even the existence of God. Cognitivists say that even if there is a God, we, as people, cannot see the world as God does and cannot even validate if this vision is correct. Therefore, according to some cognitivists, questions about the existence of God or about absolute non-perspective truth are meaningless.

John Sanders, one of the authors often cited in this book, is an adherent of open theism, and he uses Cognitive Linguistics to support his theological convictions. He also argues against the idea of finding timeless truth in the text or having non-perspectival truth, which he also calls "God's-eye" truth, that is not limited by our human bodies and conceptualization.[5] He believes

---

2. Lakoff and Johnson, *Metaphors We Live By*, 159 (emphasis original).

3. Lakoff, "How the Body Shapes Thought," 52.

4. Lakoff, 53.

5. Sanders, *Theology in the Flesh*, loc. 5055–5059 of 5234, Kindle.

that there are numerous ways to conceptualize God, as evidenced by the existence of different religions and Christian denominations. For him, the real question is which human categories "we deem appropriate for God" and, in his view, the answer depends on many factors, including our cultural upbringing, values, philosophical convictions, religious traditions, and experiences.[6] As an open theist he redefines the idea of the transcendence of God, stressing that this does not mean that God is above us but only that he is ahead of us in our journey.[7]

Along similar lines, the John Templeton Foundation supports a research project on applying Cognitive Linguistics to theology to discuss topics such as God, salvation, and morality. The goal of the research is "to show that there are no definitive ways of conceptualizing these topics but only ways that are better or worse depending upon what one is attempting to achieve."[8] Consequently, it appears that Cognitive Linguistics may be used to promote relativism since there are numerous ways of conceptualizing God and key Christian doctrines, and since it appears that we can never say anything about God with certainty. Every believer may have a different conception of God and, since we do not have access to knowledge coming from the all-knowing mind, we are left with our limited minds and have no way of determining which conceptions are accurate. Going a step further, why should we stop with Christian conceptualizations? Why should we not embrace conceptualizations of other religions as well?

Moreover, Sanders states that biblical language is anthropogenic, which means that it is "based on human embodied cognition," and even "if God communicates with us, such communication will employ concepts that we can understand, which means that God will make use of human conceptual structures that depend upon human bodies and cultural thought forms."[9] Sanders's understanding of anthropogenic makes me wonder whether he means that our knowledge of God is conveyed through human cognition in human terms or that our knowledge of God actually originates from human cognition and that God is a figment of our imagination. Sanders is clear

---

6. Sanders, loc. 54 of 5234.

7. Sanders, loc. 47 of 5234.

8. John Templeton Foundation, "Cognitive Linguistics and Theology," <https://www.templeton.org/grant/cognitive-linguistics-and-theology> [Accessed 5 March 2018].

9. Sanders, *Theology in the Flesh*, loc. 196, 5059 of 5234, Kindle.

that our knowledge of God is conveyed through human thought in human terms, but in his book he also engages in a lengthy discussion on reasons why the idea of one personal God seems to be the most natural for human cognition.[10] He says that certain conceptions of God can be widespread if they have "features that make them memorable, interesting, and useful to explain life events and phenomena," and the idea of one God meets these criteria.[11] It seems that our knowledge of God is the result of our human perception and imagination. Thus, the real question here is about the source of these conceptions about God: Is it God himself? Or is it humans? Maybe some other human-divine explanation is also possible.

However, it must be noted that Cognitive Linguistics, as a secular and pragmatic science that focuses on studying human cognition, simply does not have any tools to answer questions of transcendence, the existence of God, or the absolute truths that are beyond its reach. Cognitivists can only study individual human brains and perception that is available to human beings, but they do not have the means to prove or disprove the existence of any greater mind than ours and are unable to see the world from such a perspective. In this respect, Cognitive Linguistics can be an effective tool in studying the Bible on a linguistic level, but it is inadequate when it comes to answering questions about the existence of God.

Consequently, in order to effectively apply Cognitive Linguistics to hermeneutics and preaching of biblical metaphors and images, it is necessary to perceive it in a theological context that sets some limits on possible applications of this theory but also widens our perspective beyond the human mind. Instead of arguing that everything that exists is limited to what we can perceive with our senses, classical theology frees us to use Cognitive Linguistics as a useful tool while still maintaining both that there is a greater mind and a greater perspective on the world than our minds and that our conceptualization is the result of God's conceptualization. Therefore, while the doctrines of God's creation and revelation set theological boundaries on the application of this theory to preaching, these boundaries actually broaden the scope and perspective of this theory.

---

10. Sanders, loc. 4843–4849 of 5234.

11. Sanders, loc. 4802–4804 of 5234.

In the next few sections, I show how the doctrine of God's revelation changes our perspective and possible range of applications of Cognitive Linguistics to preaching and how the means of God's revelation provide theological justification for using metaphors and images in sermons.

1.1.2 God's Revelation as the Context for Applying Cognitive Linguistics

As pointed out earlier, in attempting to apply Cognitive Linguistics to conveying theological concepts, we must recognize that Cognitive Linguistics, as a human and pragmatic science, does not take into consideration the existence of God because it cannot verify it. In this respect, it reflects the general human predicament – confirmed by theology – that people, by their own efforts, are not able to know God. As Karl Barth claims, "God is the hidden one."[12] God is transcendent, which Barth defines as being "separate from and independent of nature and humanity."[13] Erickson, summarizing Barth's view, elaborates on this issue by saying, "God is not an aspect of man or the best of human nature. He is separated from man by *infinite* qualitative distinction."[14] So, the difference between God and humans is not merely a matter of degree but one of quality and essence. As a result, God is beyond the human capacity of comprehension or description.[15] Erickson stresses that "God can never be completely captured in human concepts"[16] and adds that God is infinite, which means "not only that God is unlimited, but that he is illimitable."[17]

Thus, we need to ask how humans can get to know God if he is beyond their ability to understand. Cognitive Linguistics will not help to verify God's existence. Thus, how can we preach about God who is completely beyond our reach and understanding since no image, description, or comparison can describe him fully?

---

12. Barth, *Doctrine of the Word of God*, 188–190.

13. Erickson, *Christian Theology*, 312.

14. Erickson, 314 (Emphasis original).

15. Grenz, *Created for Community*, 38.

16. Erickson, *Christian Theology*, 317. Karl Rahner devotes a lot of attention to the doctrine of the incomprehensibility of God. See Rahner, *God and Revelation*, 89–104.

17. Erickson, 272.

1.1.2.1 God's Images of Himself or Human Images of God?

Cognitivists claim that any metaphors and images found in the Bible are the fruit of the human mind and human conceptualization as they convey the human conception of God. To be more precise, not only do people talk about God using language and metaphors that are human, but even the idea of God has a human origin. As opposed to Cognitive Linguistics, Christian theology provides the answer to the human inability to get to know God by stating that God took the initiative and revealed himself and his perspective using human terms. Classical Christian theology argues that since people could not get to know God, he made himself known in an act of self-revelation that includes metaphors and images.

Millard Erickson, reflecting on God's special revelation, says that this revelation was personal, anthropic, and analogical. It is personal because "the personal God presents himself to persons."[18] He unveils some information about himself in order to enter a relationship with human beings. Its anthropic character can be seen in the fact that God, who is transcendent, revealed himself in human categories, using human languages as they were used at that time. It is also analogical because "God draws upon those elements in man's universe of knowledge that can serve as likeness of or partially convey the truth in the divine realm."[19] Since we cannot access and comprehend God directly, he decided to use analogy to introduce himself to people. Therefore, we can say that God's revelation is metaphorical in nature since it is based on the idea of explaining one concept in terms of another.

This doctrine of God's revelation asserts that God, who is the all-knowing mind, took the initiative and introduced himself to human beings using our human conceptual system so that we could get to know him and enter into a relationship with him. Consequently, even though we as humans are limited by our embodied minds that are incapable of acquiring non-perspectival truths, we can learn about ideas that were not invented by us and which are naturally beyond our limits. We can learn about the existence of God, the notion of salvation, eternal life, our accountability for our sins, and the possibility of forgiveness. Knowing that our lives are a part of God's larger story

---

18. Erickson, 177.
19. Erickson, 179.

of salvation gives us a new perspective on the world and our existence since we start perceiving our daily struggles in the context of eternity.

A word of clarification is in order. The fact that God reveals himself to human beings and provides them with some knowledge that is not naturally accessible to their minds does not mean that we cease to be limited by our human perspective and our embodied minds. Moreover, the existence of an all-knowing God does not imply that human beings have direct access to his mind any time or are always able to look at the world from God's perspective. We can only know as much about God and his perspective as he chooses to reveal about himself.

The whole issue of God's revelation – which has been broadly addressed in a number of publications on systematic theology – is not free from debate, and numerous scholars propose various approaches to understanding biblical revelation.[20] Some emphasize the importance of God's words, whereas others lay greater stress on God's deeds and his involvement in history. Some argue that when God revealed himself to the writers of the Scriptures, he disclosed certain truths and facts about his nature, his will, and his plan of salvation. They conclude, therefore, that God's revelation consists of facts about God that come from God himself and can be comprehended by humans and enable them to acquire knowledge about him. However, others claim that the revelation found in the Bible does not convey facts about God but is a record of people's experiences of God at different times in history, which they articulated in their own human terms.[21]

---

20. For a further dissuasion, see Akin, *Theology for the Church*, 71–176. Brian Hebblethwaite also tries to show possible ways of reconciling the discrepancies between natural and revealed theology. Hebblethwaite, *Philosophical Theology*, 16–18. For further reading, see Mavrodes, *Revelation in Religious Belief*, and Alister McGrath, who summarizes four major models of revelation that represent various emphases within Christian theology, namely, revelation as doctrine, presence, experience, and history. McGrath, *Christian Theology*, 184–187. For more information on the relationship between revelation and history, see Wright, *God Who Acts*, 107. Wright views the Bible as a record of historical events remembered and believed by Israel and the church, rather than as a set of doctrinal propositions. Wolfhart Pannenberg discusses different ways of God's revelation and states that the events through which God acted in history actually became his revelation. Erickson, *Christian Theology*, 186. See also Runia, "Hermeneutics of the Reformers," 150. Similarly, Sidney Greidanus defines God's revelation as interpreted facts or events. Greidanus, *Modern Preacher*, 88. More on the issue of revelation by deeds and words can be found in Pinnock, *Biblical Revelation*, 31–34.

21. Hick, *Philosophy of Religion*, 64. Among the most prominent proponents of the idea that God reveals himself through religious experience are Friedrich Schleiermacher, Rudolf Otto, and Martin Buber. Schleiermacher emphasizes the importance of intuition of the infinite

Nevertheless, the Bible itself bears witness to the holistic nature of God's revelation since it shows God revealing himself in direct propositional statements, in historical events – which, when accompanied by interpretation, become his revelation – and in people's experiences of God. This notion of the holistic nature of God's revelation becomes even more evident when we take into consideration the holistic nature of the image of God in humans, the holistic nature of God's revelation in Christ – who is God embodied – the holistic nature of Christ's redemption of the world, and the holistic nature of the Holy Spirit's transformation of believers. These notions, which will be explained in more detail in later parts of this chapter, will help to shape our understanding of the nature of preaching.

However, the most important question raised in this dialogue with cognitive linguists is about the origin and role of biblical metaphors and images: Are these metaphors and images given by God? Or should these be perceived merely as human constructs that express people's conception of a God who is their own invention? Do these metaphors and images convey knowledge about the God who used these to reveal himself? Or are they just the biblical writers' vision of God, which originated in their own minds? Is it possible to show that they convey authoritative revelation of God while maintaining their human nature and frequently human origin?

1.1.2.2 Importance of Biblical Inspiration

Traditional, conservative theology assumes that biblical images and metaphors are a means of God's self-revelation. As indicated above, biblical scholars seem unable to resolve the dilemma of the origin and nature of biblical metaphors and images, and the Bible itself appears to testify to their divine-human nature and origin. Therefore, it seems necessary to take a step further and move on from the doctrine of revelation to the doctrine of inspiration.

John Webster, explaining the origin and nature of Scripture, talks about three elements: revelation, sanctification, and inspiration. God not only revealed himself through Scripture, he also sanctified it and inspired it. Sanctification "refers to the work of the Spirit of Christ through which

---

within the finite. Schleiermacher, *Christian Faith*, 5–18. Otto talks about the feeling of God's transcendence, whereas Buber suggests knowing God through encounters with other people. Otto, *Idea of the Holy*, 5–18; Buber, *I and Thou*, 75–83.

creaturely realities are elected, shaped and preserved to undertake a role in the economy of salvation: creaturely realities are sanctified by divine use."[22] Hence, God sanctifies human language, words, and efforts by using them to convey his revelation. Inspiration, in Webster's view, is "the specific textual application of the broader notion of sanctification as the hallowing of creaturely realities to serve revelation's taking form."[23]

Millard Erickson defines inspiration as the "supernatural influence of the Holy Spirit upon the Scripture writers, which rendered their writings an accurate record of the revelation or which resulted in what they wrote actually being the Word of God."[24] Stanley Grenz differentiates between plenary and verbal inspiration and argues that both apply to the Bible. Plenary inspiration means that the Holy Spirit's oversight of the writing process embraces the whole Bible, whereas verbal inspiration assumes that the Spirit "superintended the process of word selection and word order to the extent that they are capable of communicating the intended meaning of the text."[25]

Peter Enns, in the context of a discussion about some of the difficulties Christians have with the interpretation of the Old Testament, addresses the issue of the inspiration of the Bible. In his study, Enns wrestles with the notion of the uniqueness of the Old Testament as God's revelation by comparing numerous Old Testament texts with other ancient writings. For instance, he points out evident similarities between the creation account of Genesis and Enuma Elish, the biblical flood narrative and stories from Atrahasis and Gilgamesh, the Law and the Code of Hammurabi, and the book of Proverbs and the Instruction of Amenemope.[26] A comparison of these texts leads some scholars to conclude that the Bible is just a human product and, as such, that it reflects the myths, moral standards, and wisdom of its time. However, while stressing the similarities, they often tend to minimize the differences between these writings and the Bible.[27]

---

22. Webster, *Holy Scripture*, 26.

23. Webster, 30.

24. Erickson, *Christian Theology*, 199.

25. Grenz, *Theology for the Community of God*, 398.

26. Enns, Inspiration and Incarnation, 30–48. On the issue of inspiration, literary forms, and similarities of the biblical texts to other ancient writings, see Feinberg, "Literary Forms and Inspiration," 29–67.

27. While talking about the similarities, it is also in order to show the uniqueness of the biblical creation account and the privileged role of humans. In Enuma Elish, people were

Enns also discusses the issue of diversity within the Old Testament, where different perspectives can be seen and different voices can be heard, especially when studying Wisdom Literature, the Law, and Chronicles, and particularly when these are studied in comparison to the books of Samuel and Kings.[28] There are several proverbs and laws that seem to be differing and contradictory accounts of the same event [29] This diversity exists because the Old Testament often presents complex ideas that require numerous portrayals, and there are tensions between these portrayals. Its authors represent different traditions, and their ways of recording history do not adhere to our modern standards since biblical historiography "is not the mere statement of facts but the shaping of these facts for a particular purpose" in order "to relay to someone the significance of history."[30]

Finally, Enns examines the ways in which New Testament writers use the Old Testament and finds these questionable according to modern hermeneutical standards since they seem to violate the original context of these texts.[31] Enns notes that the New Testament writers, who functioned in the Second Temple context, employed Second Temple interpretive methods and interpretive traditions in their interpretation of the Old Testament.[32] However, while using these methods and traditions, their purpose was Christotelic, and they read the Old Testament "knowing that Christ is somehow the end to which the Old Testament story is heading," which shaped their perspective on the Old Testament texts.[33]

For Enns, these findings do not undermine the notions of the inspiration and authority of the Bible but, rather, allow Christians to gain a deeper understanding of these notions. Instead of trying to minimize potential problems caused by similarities to other ancient texts, diversity of voices, or interpretive methods and traditions that come from the Second Temple

---

created from the blood of a murdered god, and their task was to maintain the earth because other gods found this duty overly humiliating and offensive. Contrary to *Enuma Elish*, we read in the book of Genesis that God created people in his image and that their task was to rule over the earth on his behalf. See also Hamilton, *Book of Genesis*, 140.

28. Enns, *Inspiration and Incarnation*, 104–138.

29. For proverbs, see Enns, 104–106; for laws, 121–122, 127–129; for Chronicles, 117–120.

30. Enns, 83.

31. As an example, see the discussion on Luke 20:27–40 in Enns, 163–165.

32. Enns, 220–221.

33. Enns, 223.

period, Enns fully embraces the fact that "the human marks of the Bible are everywhere, thoroughly integrated into the nature of Scripture itself."[34] He believes that "Christianity is a historical religion" and that, for this reason, "God's word reflects the various historical moments in which Scripture was written."[35] However, he also emphasizes that the fact that "the Bible bears an unmistakable human stamp" does not mean "that it is merely the words of humans rather than the word of God."[36]

To explain this phenomenon, Enns introduces the concept of incarnational analogy, which means that "Christ's incarnation is analogous to Scripture's 'incarnation.'"[37] He points out that "*as Christ is both God and human, so is the Bible*" (emphasis original).[38] Therefore, just as Christians believe that Christ has both a divine and human nature and is both fully divine and fully human, the same can also be said about the Bible. It is a mystery, and just as "we can speak of the incarnate Christ meaningfully, but never fully," we can speak of the nature of the Bible meaningfully but never fully.[39]

Even though the Bible is the word of God, it is also a human work that was conditioned by its authors and their cultures. Thus, the uniqueness of the biblical narratives, laws, history, and wisdom is not to be found in the fact that they differ in terms of their form from other ancient writings or moral codes but in the fact that they point to the God who revealed himself to Israel through these texts "in order to form Israel into a godlike community."[40] Therefore, God uses human speech, human norms, and human forms shaped by human cultures to introduce himself to human beings on their terms.

Even though Enns sometimes overemphasizes the similarities between the Bible and other ancient texts and downplays the striking differences – and despite the fact that some of his exegetical examples of apparent contradictions or taking the Old Testament texts out of context by New Testament

---

34. Enns, 20.

35. Enns, 19.

36. Enns, 24.

37. Enns, 19.

38. Enns, 18.

39. Enns, 243.

40. Enns, 78. Enns, speaking about similarities between ancient moral codes, also claims that "Proverbs, the Code of Hammurabi and the Instruction of Amenemope, and others, reflect a deeper reality, that God has set up the world in a certain way and that way is imprinted on all people." See Enns, 81.

writers are not very convincing – his notion of incarnational analogy is very helpful in explaining biblical inspiration in terms of the divine and human nature of the Bible. Moreover, as Enns emphasizes, there is great value in perceiving the Bible in its cultural context and understanding the influences that shaped its form and the mindset of its writers.

In conclusion, it seems that the whole dispute about the origin of biblical metaphors and images loses its edge when viewed in the light of an idea of inspiration of the Bible. This doctrine of inspiration assumes that God allowed some extent of human freedom in expression of his concepts and thoughts. However, it needs to be stressed that the Holy Spirit supervised the process and takes ownership over the final product. As Mary Hilkert emphasizes "the word of God is available only in and through the limits – including the sinful limits – of human words."[41] Thus, it could be said that even though human concepts about God, as expressed in the Bible through the use of language, cannot be equated with God himself, God still chose human language and these concepts to reveal himself. Therefore, the origin of images and metaphors is not as important as their function and authority as the means of God's revelation. The doctrine of God's inspiration allows us to overcome the polarity between human conceptualization and God's revelation and the consequent dichotomy between the human and divine origin of biblical images. It also shows that these images – even though some of them might have been chosen by people, borrowed from other sources, or reflect cultural influences of their times – were inspired by God as the means of his self-revelation and all of them are filtered through human conceptual system.

1.1.2.3 Conclusion on Cognitive Linguistics and God's Revelation

While discussing in previous paragraphs the issue of Cognitive Linguistics in a theological context, I stressed that this pragmatic science is not capable of proving or denying the existence of God. Thus, Cognitive Linguistics actually confirms what theology has already stated – that human beings are not able to get to know God on the basis of their own abilities. Therefore, according to classical theology, God revealed himself to us using a variety of forms so that we could have a relationship with him and start perceiving our lives through the lens of this revelation we cannot access using our natural human means.

---

41. Hilkert, *Naming Grace*, 74.

The idea of God's revelation limits some of the claims made by adherents of Cognitive Linguistics regarding any possibility of the existence of objective truth and, at the same time, should encourage them to broaden their perspective by reminding them that their view of reality is not restricted to human minds. Even though many conservative Christian theologians believe in the idea of God's revelation, this does not mean that we, as humans, possess constant and direct access to the mind of God or that we can see reality as God sees it. However, God's revelation equips us with knowledge that is beyond the reach of our natural human cognitive capacities, enabling us to know some aspects of non-perspectival truth as revealed by God in his word.

Moreover, the doctrine of God's revelation and inspiration changes our view of biblical metaphors and images, enabling us to see that these are not merely human ideas about God. Even though we may not be able to determine whether a given metaphor or image originated from God or from a biblical writer, all these images, as part of God's revelation, convey knowledge about God and were inspired by God as part of the word of God.

The idea that God revealed himself in human language and that his revelation is transmitted though human minds justifies using Cognitive Linguistics – which deals with understanding human conceptualization – to study biblical revelation that has both divine and human dimensions. Thus, Cognitive Linguistics provides preachers with practical tools to study and articulate God's revelation.

The idea of God's revelation has implications for preaching because it gives preachers the confidence that when they preach biblical metaphors and images they are actually communicating God's revelation and not merely ideas that humans have invented about God. However, this doctrine also sets some limits on preaching because preachers, as communicators of God's revelation, are restricted in their sermons by the content of this divine revelation.

1.1.3 God's Revelation in Images

Having discussed how the doctrine of God's revelation influences the scope of the application of Cognitive Linguistics to theology and preaching, I will now demonstrate how the manner of God's revelation through images justifies using metaphors and images in sermons. This topic is controversial because many Christians wonder if it is permissible to create metaphors and images to present the one who explicitly forbade making any visual representations of himself (Exod 20:1–4). Therefore, in order to justify using metaphors and images in sermons, I will examine the manner of God's revelation as seen in the creation of people in his image, in images and metaphors in the Bible, and in the incarnation of Christ, who is the image of the Father. I will also demonstrate how Cognitive Linguistics can be productive in understanding and describing these key events of God's revelation, and I will then explore further implications of the correlation between Cognitive Linguistics and theology.

1.1.3.1 Creation: The Image of God as Seen in Humans

Theologians point to numerous reasons for the existence of the commandment that forbids making any visual representations of God. For instance, since God created everything and is above the whole created order, there is nothing that he can be compared to. Moreover, in some pagan religions, making an image of a god was a way of exercising control over that deity.[42] However, the idea of using metaphors and images is strongly rooted in the manner of biblical revelation. Even though the Old Testament clearly forbids making any images or visual representations of God for cultic purposes, God himself was the first image-maker. When God created the animals, he created them "according to their kinds" (Gen 1:21, 24–25 NIV), but God created people in his own "image" and "likeness" (Gen 1:26–27). The phrase "the image of God" or equivalent is found only four times in the Old Testament (Gen 1:26–27; 9:6). Its usage in Genesis 9:6 is especially instructive. The creation of human beings in God's image is what invests them with great value, and this image of God, even though impacted by sin, was not lost as a result of the fall.[43]

There are a further fifteen instances where the Old Testament uses the word "image" (צֶלֶם).[44] Adam "had a son in his own likeness, in his own image" (Gen 5:3 NIV).[45] Six times, the word for "images" is used to refer to idols that were physical representations of other gods (Num 33:52; 2 Kgs 11:18;

---

42. For an overview of the topic, see also von Rad, "Prohibition of Images," TDNT 2:381–383, and "εἰκών," NIDNTTE 2:102–105.

43. Christopher Wright enumerates the impact of sin on the image of God in humans by showing how sin affects people spiritually, rationally, physically, and socially. See Wright, *Mission of God*, 421–433.

44. Kohlenberger and Swanson, "צֶלֶם" 1370. On the meaning of צֶלֶם, see Stendebach, "צֶלֶם," TDOT: 386–396.

45. For a further discussion on the relationship between image and likeness, see Hamilton, *Book of Genesis*, NICOT 1:135–136.

2 Chron 23:17; Ezek 7:20; 16:17; Amos 5:26). In three instances, "images" refer to representations of rats and tumours (1 Sam 6:5, 11), and in two other places, the word is used in a metaphorical sense (Ps 39:6; 73:20). Thus, in a majority of cases, "image" denotes a physical representation of something. According to von Rad, an image in the Old Testament "means predominantly an actual plastic work, a duplicate, sometimes an idol; only on occasion does it mean a duplicate in the diminished sense of a semblance when compared with the original."[46] Yet, this term is especially intriguing when used to describe humans as being created in the image of God. Bruce Waltke, commenting on the Old Testament uses of the term, stresses that "a human being is not said *to have* or *to bear* the image of God, such as God's immaterial essence, but each is said *to be* in his or her entirety be the image of God".[47] Therefore, the image of God in people is something intrinsic to human nature.

There are also numerous New Testament passages that refer either to the idea of the image of God in humans or to the likeness of God.[48] Two texts use this idea in the context of creation (1 Cor 11:7; Jas 3:9). A few other passages deal with the notion of believers being transformed into the image or likeness of God or Christ in the process of salvation. In Romans 8:29, Paul says that Christians are being conformed to the image of the Son, and the similar idea of being changed into Christ's likeness is also found in 2 Corinthians 3:18. In Ephesians 4:23–24, Paul writes about believers putting on the new nature "created after the likeness of God" (ESV). Similarly, in Colossians 3:10, Christians are admonished to put on the new nature that is being "renewed in knowledge after the image of the creator" (ESV). Therefore, it appears that there is not any clear statement in the Bible that the image of God was lost in humans, but the New Testament indicates that God's image is on the one hand an intrinsic element of human nature, but on the other hand, it is something Christians are to grow into.

Janet Soskice believes that in the New Testament "the image becomes dynamic." She points out that the image "is not something we wholly and simply possess for it is Christ who is truly the image of the invisible God.

---

46. von Rad, *Genesis*, 56.

47. Waltke, *Old Testament Theology*, 215 (emphasis original). For a more detailed analysis of New Testament texts on the image of God, see Kuhli, "εἰκών," EDNT 2:388–391.

48. For a more detailed study of New Testament texts on the image of God, see Wright, "Phrase 'Image of God,'" 31–44.

The faithful are in the process of being 'conformed to the image' of the Son."[49] Accordingly, it seems that, through faith in Christ, people can resemble Christ more closely and the image of God can become more visible in them as they fulfil the function they were created to fulfil.[50] Christians are to grow into the image of Christ, who is the perfect image of God.[51]

As Henry Wansbrough puts it, we are "made in the image of God and remade in the image of Christ."[52] This is possible because Christ proved to be faithful where humans failed. Wansbrough makes an important connection between the Genesis narrative and the New Testament teaching on the incarnation. In comparing Adam as described in Genesis and Christ as depicted in Philippians 2, he points out that while Adam and Christ were both in the image of God, there were significant differences between them:

> Adam tried to be like God, Christ did not count the equality
> with God a thing to be grasped (or perhaps "exploited"). Adam
> tried to exalt himself, but Christ humbled himself. Adam tried
> to evade death, but Christ accepted death.[53]

Therefore, even though humans never lost the image of God, only through Christ can they be transformed and remade in the image of Christ, which is a much more privileged position compared with the one they had in the garden of Eden.

It is important at this stage to investigate further the meaning of the concept that humans are created in God's image and likeness so that we can make sure that using this concept as a justification for the use of metaphors and images in sermons informed by Cognitive Lingustics is firmly rooted.

1.1.3.1.1 Different Views on the Image of God

Defining the image or likeness of God is a challenging task since, as Barth rightly emphasizes, "the text speaks less of the nature of God's image than of its purpose. There is less said about the gift itself than about the task."[54] There

---

49. Soskice, *Kindness of God*, 38.

50. For a more detailed discussion on the relationship between the image of God and salvation see Piper, "Image of God."

51. Valeš, "Wolfhart Pannenberg's imago Dei Doctrine," 44.

52. Wansbrough, "Made and Remade," 45.

53. Wansbrough, 46.

54. Barth, *Doctrine of Creation*, 197.

are several views on the meaning of the image of God, and Millard Erickson divides these views into three groups: substantive, relational, and functional.

A substantive view assumes that the image of God is an inherent feature of some aspect of being a human.[55] Depending on the particular variants of this view, this feature might be physical, psychological, or spiritual, or it might include all these elements. The church fathers emphasized spiritual and moral characteristics as those elements reflect people's likeness to God and enable them to relate to him. But theologians such as Thomas Aquinas, being influenced by Greek thought, perceived human reason and cognitive capabilities as the qualities that constitute the image of God.[56]

Adherents of a relational view believe that the Triune God, who is relational, created people to have a relationship with him and with each other and that it is only through this relationship with God that people can experience being in the image of God.[57] For Garrett Green, there is a "family resemblance" between God and human beings.[58] Green argues that the image of God is "the point of similarity between Creator and creature" and, as a result, it "made God accessible to the human imagination: Adam in the garden could imagine God as he truly is."[59] People sinned because, even though they were created into the image of God, they wanted to become like God (Gen 3:5). As a consequence of sin, they lost both access to God and their ability to know him.

Accordingly, if the image of God is understood in terms of having a relationship with God, the loss of this relationship implies not only a distorted image of God but also the loss of the ability to have the right image of God, which means knowing God. Having the wrong image or understanding of God leads to one of the most common sins of the Old Testament – namely, idolatry, which is worshipping other gods or having an understanding of God that is different from the one that he has revealed. God revealed himself as the invisible Creator of everything, the one who – as the omniscient,

---

55. Erickson, *Christian Theology*, 498–517.

56. Aquinas, Summa Theologica 1.93.

57. Berkouwer, *Man: The Image of God*, 71. See also Kern, "Our Knowledge of God," 329–341.

58. Green, *Imagining God*, 87.

59. Green, 87. Referring to Michelangelo's vision of creation as depicted on the ceiling of the Sistine Chapel, Green says that this is not an anthropomorphic rendering of God but a theomorphic rendering of man, who is a reflection of God.

omnipotent, and omnipresent God – is beyond human comprehension. As people lose their relationship with this God, they may begin to imagine God in their own human terms. For this reason, Green defines idolatry as "the misuse of the religious imagination."[60]

Adherents of a functional view claim that the image of God is not found in substantive qualities of human beings or in their relationship with God but, rather, in the role assigned to human beings by their creator to exercise dominion on his behalf over the whole of creation.[61] By looking at human beings and the authority they exercised, the whole creation would see the authority of God who had ordered people to rule over his creation on his behalf.

Stanley Grenz presents a fourth view, which he calls the dynamic view. According to Grenz, the idea of the image of God refers to the eschatological future. "The divine image is the goal or destiny that God intends for his creatures."[62] Through Christ, God restores his image in believers, and this restoration will not be completed until Christ returns.[63]

As I analyzed these views on the issue of the *imago Dei*, I found them insufficient since they all focused on just one aspect of human beings – such as rationality, spirituality, ability to make moral choices, or immortality – or one ability, such as a relationship with God, or one task, such as exercising dominion, or one goal, such as the future resemblance to Christ. A substantive view ignores the idea of the unity and completeness of human beings. It does not give a satisfactory answer to the question of which particular human feature is actually the image of God, and it ignores elements from the relational and functional views. A relational view does not answer the question of what constitutes the human ability to enter into a relationship with God and what happened to the image of God when this relationship was broken because of the fall. A functional view is also debatable since the Bible itself does not make clear the nature of humanity's dominion over the creation and its correlation with the notion of the image of God. Consequently, it is

---

60. Green, 92.

61. Silva, "εἰκών," NIDNTTE 2:103. See also Middleton, "Liberating Image?," 12; Hamilton, *Book of Genesis*, 140; and Wright, "Phrase 'Image of God,'" 32–33.

62. Grenz, *Theology for the Community of God*, 173.

63. Since Grenz develops his approach drawing on Wolfhart Pannenberg, see also Pannenberg and Priebe, *What Is Man?*, 3. For a more detailed discussion on consequences of Pannenberg's perception of the image of God, see Valeš, "Wolfhart Pannenberg's *imago Dei* Doctrine," 43–56.

unclear whether exercising dominion should be equated with being the image of God or whether the idea of dominion is a separate privilege God bestowed on the people he created in his image.[64] Even if dominion is equated with the image of God, this approach, like the others, seems to be overly limiting by narrowing the image of God simply to one aspect while ignoring others. Finally, a dynamic view does not really explain the meaning of Old and New Testament passages that suggest that the image of God is an inherent quality of all humans, not just followers of Christ.

Numerous modern readers of the Old Testament, especially those living in the Western hemisphere, often feel compelled to try to define the exact nature of the image of God in humans. However, the Old Testament writers, who did not think in terms of precise definitions, accepted much more ambiguity in their thinking about God and his works. Thus, when studying the narratives of Genesis 1–2, both creation accounts seem to focus on the creation of humans and show their uniqueness in relation to the rest of creation. People are distinct and unique because, in the first account, they were created as the climax of God's work and, in the second account, they are the main focus of the narrative. The first account stresses that the manner of their creation was different to that of the rest of the world and that they were made in the image of God. The Hebrew writers did not feel compelled to explain the nature of this image or likeness but, instead, left their readers with the simple statement that God created people in his own image, which suggests that a human being as a whole, in their totality, is the reflection of God.

Hence, it does not seem justifiable to emphasize or give prominence to just one aspect of humanity. I agree with Victor Hamilton, Bruce Waltke, Moisés Silva, and others who believe that we bear the image of God in our total being.[65] Even though God does not have a body, he has reason, will, and emotions. He is a personal and spiritual being with an ability to enter into relationships and engage in social interactions. He also rules over his creation.[66] Human beings reflect these same qualities.

---

64. Berkouwer, *Man: Image of God*, 71. See also Piper, "Image of God."

65. Hamilton, *Book of Genesis*, 137; Waltke, *Old Testament Theology*, 215–219; Silva, "εἰκών," NIDNTTE 2:103.

66. Waltke, *Old Testament Theology*, 215–219.

Thus, God is the first image-maker in history, and he chose images to reveal himself. In the case of creation, he chose people to be his image. This idea is significant for a number of reasons. First, contrary to objections voiced by some theologians who claim that God cannot be expressed in human terms because he is ineffable, God chose to create limited human beings in his image to reflect the illimitable God. Second, the fact that God made humans in his image indicates that they are part of his general revelation. Hence, it is possible to learn something about God by looking at people. Since images are means of God's revelation, it is also justified to perceive them as a valid manner of conveying God's revelation in preaching.

1.1.3.1.2 Image of God and Cognitive Linguistics

These reflections on the concept of God creating people in his image strongly suggest that this biblical doctrine validates applying Cognitive Linguistics to communicating theological concepts. As we investigate further, we will see that Cognitive Linguistics helps us describe the idea of the image of God and gives preachers a deeper understanding in the context of human cognition and embodiment.

Some people argue that it was purely natural processes that resulted in the origin of humankind. But the biblical view that God created humankind in his image changes our perception and does not allow us to secularize our view of the humankind. It also changes our perspective on Cognitive Linguistics because, according to Genesis, God is the source of his revelation through his image in humans, which means that the idea of the image of God did not originate in the human mind; instead, this conceptualization took place in the mind of the Creator and was expressed in the act of creation. Since people are created in the image of God, this image is a quality that is given to them rather than one invented by them.

Moreover, Cognitive Linguistics is productive in analyzing and conveying God's revelation because of the nature of humanity as created in the image of God. The image of God in people establishes a connection between human beings, human language, human cognition, and God who chose to reveal himself through imperfect humans. Therefore, the act of creation not only justifies using human terms to talk about God but also allows us to analyze God's revelation from the point of view of human cognition. The fact that God made people in his image is not only one of the reasons to hold to a theistic vision of the world, it also stresses the human aspect of God's revelation that allows us to embrace Cognitive Linguistics as a helpful tool in understanding it.

Cognitive Linguistics is helpful because it neither separates the mind from the body nor stresses just one aspect of humanity but is based on the idea of embodied minds and describes the human being as a psychosomatic unity. Therefore, it confirms the theological perspective of scholars such as Hamilton, Waltke, and Silva, who, instead of seeing the image of God as only one aspect of humanity, perceive human beings in their totality as being made in the image of God.

Cognitive Linguistics also provides preachers with effective tools to describe the "image of God" metaphor. Since human beings are made in the image of God, it is possible to perceive this image in terms of a conceptual metaphor that is based on the idea that one concept is described in terms of another – an idea that will be elaborated on later. In this case, the more abstract concept of God is understood in terms of the more concrete concept of human beings. In Genesis, since people, as the image of God, are an element of God's self-revelation, they also convey some information about God's character. Of course, God is not a human being, but he chose to reveal some aspects of his nature by creating people in his likeness. The image of God is a metaphor depicting humanity's role, origin, characteristics, and their relationship with God; but in the act of creation, humans became, in a sense, a metaphor of God. From the perspective of the rest of creation, people are like God, they represent God, and they exercise dominion over creation on his behalf. In fact, they are the only physical image of God available for the rest of creation to see.

1.1.3.2 Written Revelation: God as Seen in Biblical Images

In the sections that follow, I continue my argument on how the manner of God's written revelation justifies employing metaphors and images in preaching. I also explore how Cognitive Linguistics transforms our understanding of religious language.

The abundance of images in the Bible indicates that God does not oppose every kind of image but, rather, uses these to communicate with his creation. DesCamp and Sweetser conducted research on conceptual metaphors of God in the Bible and identified forty-four such metaphors that depict various attributes of God and ways in which he relates to his creation.[67] The biblical writers make frequent use of images that can be defined as "words that evoke a sensory experience in our imagination" and, according to modern literary theories, their purpose was not purely artistic.[68] Even though biblical texts that include metaphors have great literary value, significant studies have shown that biblical imagery was used predominantly as a vehicle to convey ideas in a manner that was familiar to the audience and would captivate their minds. The topic of biblical interpretation, with a special emphasis on interpretation of metaphors, has been addressed broadly by numerous scholars, and there are a variety of approaches to studying the Bible and metaphors. However, the methodology presented in this research is based on the modern theory of literary interpretation of the Bible, and the principles presented reflect a mainstream conservative evangelical approach.[69] Despite numerous views on metaphors and images in history, modern metaphor theories stress the fact that the images in the Bible are not just decorations of the message but are the message itself. It appears that the biblical writers, in conveying God's revelation, utilized images and metaphors in order to express in words ideas that could hardly be expressed in other ways. The most important doctrines of Christianity – such as salvation, redemption, becoming the children of God, or even the concept of God as Father – are presented in a metaphorical fashion.

Therefore, it is worth stressing that if preachers are communicators of God's revelation, using metaphors and images is not only unavoidable but, given that metaphors are the key vehicles of conveying God's revelation, essential We could even say that metaphors and images become our primary preaching material. When we consider biblical metaphors and images from the perspective of Cognitive Linguistics, there are even more arguments for employing them in sermons since, as cognitivists say, language is largely metaphorical and metaphors are the dominant manner in which we conceptualize

---

67. Sweetser and DesCamp, "Motivating Biblical Metaphors," 7–23; DesCamp and Sweetser, "Metaphors for God," 207–238.

68. Ryken, *How to Read the Bible*, 90.

69. See Sweetser and DesCamp, "Motivating Biblical Metaphors," 7–23; Paul, "Metaphor," 507–510. Thiselton, *Hermeneutics*, 43–44, 52–53, 235–237; Paul, "Metaphor and Exegesis," 387–402. For more about the application of metaphor theory to preaching, see Radford, "Sermon as Illustration," and Smith, "Rethinking the Value of Metaphors."

life and communicate concepts, especially abstract ones. If this is indeed the case, preachers cannot communicate about God without using metaphorical language.

1.1.3.2.1 Biblical Revelation and Religious Language

When discussing the manner of biblical revelation as the justification for employing metaphors in sermons, one of the issues that needs to be addressed is the concept of religious language and its meaning. For centuries, scholars have debated the nature and function of language as a vehicle of God's revelation. These debates led to the emergence of the idea of religious language. This religious language is the language that we preachers find in the Bible, but it is also the theological language we use to explain theological ideas. In the following section, I present a few approaches to religious language and show how Cognitive Linguistics transforms our understanding of this concept.

Historically, theologians have debated whether language about God is metaphorical or literal and how to distinguish these two. At times, this task seems easy since statements such as "God is a warrior" appear to be metaphorical. But how are we to understand phrases such as "God is love"? Are such statements metaphorical or literal? If literal, what does "love" as a descriptor of God really mean? Is God more loving than us or is he loving in a completely different manner?

From medieval times, there have been four traditional ways of speaking about God: univocal, equivocal, negative (*via negativa*), and analogical.[70] Univocal language assumes that a given word has the same meaning in different contexts, but equivocal language assumes different meanings. For example, words such as "be" or "wise" can be used to describe both God and humans. As Michael Nevin puts it:

> It might be that God and humanity *are* in the same way – that we therefore use the word *be* univocally. It might be that God and humanity *are* in irreconcilably different ways – that therefore we use the word *be* equivocally.[71]

Some scholars perceive the word "wise" in a similar fashion. God is wise, and a human being can be wise and, in their opinion, the only difference is

---

70. Stiver, *Philosophy of Religious Language*, 15–29.

71. Nevin, "Analogy: Aquinas and Pannenberg," 201(emphasis original).

the matter of degree.[72] Duns Scotus argues that when such terms are applied to God, they are used "in a most perfect degree," without any of the imperfections or limitations that are characteristic of creatures.[73] In Scotus's view, since God's revelation was given in a clear and meaningful manner, religious language must be univocal so that there is no question about the meaning of our statements about God.[74]

The univocal approach was criticized by Thomas Aquinas, who claims that God is transcendent and immanent in the universe and, as the ultimate cause of everything, is not in the same way as the universe is.[75] Aquinas also stresses the fact that the word "wise" has different meanings when used to describe human beings and when applied to God since God is wise in a completely different way to humans. Aquinas states: "What it signifies in God is not confined by the meaning of our word but goes beyond it."[76] Jeff Astley takes this discussion further and points out that using univocal language to talk about God may result in very anthropomorphic theology.[77]

Thus, some theologians choose to follow the negative way (*via negativa*) and reach the conclusion that all language about God is equivocal and, therefore, needs to be negated. Considering that God is beyond all knowing, it is easier and more reliable to say who he is not than to say who he is because God is unseen, incomprehensible, indescribable, immutable, unfillable, and illimitable. Dan Stiver defines the goal of the negative way as to move "beyond words and concepts by denying them, which is not to lead to scepticism or unbelief, but precisely to the truth, to insight, and actual experience that God is beyond all such words."[78] Thus, language does not carry any descriptive information, but it has an evocative function. Among proponents of the negative way were Moses Maimonides, Pseudo-Dionysius, and numerous mystics such as Meister Eckhart. Critics of the negative way, even though they stress that this approach has some value, hold that it might be overly

---

72. Davies, *Introduction to the Philosophy*, 142.

73. Scotus, *Duns Scotus*, 25.

74. Stiver, *Philosophy of Religious Language*, 20–21.

75. Nevin, "Analogy: Aquinas and Pannenberg," 201.

76. Aquinas, Summa Theologiae, 1.13.5 in Davies, *Introduction to the Philosophy*, 142.

77. Astley, *Exploring God-Talk*, 57.

78. Stiver, *Philosophy of Religious Language*, 18.

limiting, not allowing people to make any positive statements about God who is a complete mystery.[79]

For these reasons, another approach was introduced, which is based on analogical predication. Astley explains that this notion "involves applying concrete positive terms to God with a similar meaning to that which those words and phrases normally have when they are applied to us."[80] However, it is essential to emphasize that the meanings of these words when used to talk about God are neither completely the same nor totally different than when these same words are used to talk about people. "Hence the idea of analogical language as language that is attributed to God in a way that is *at the same time* like and unlike. Thus God is like us in that we both exist, but unlike us in that his existence transcends ours".[81]

Aquinas and his followers defined two kinds of analogy: *analogy of attribution* and *analogy of proportionality*. In analogy of attribution, certain characteristics are attributed to somebody or something. For example, only a person can be healthy, but we say that food is healthy or that exercising is healthy because these things cause or help to maintain health. In the same way, it is possible to talk about God as being wise or to say that God is love because he is the source of all wisdom and love. Analogy of proportionality applies the same words to beings belonging to different categories and, consequently, the meanings of these words change. For example, while people often call their pets friendly, intelligent, loyal, funny, and faithful, it is assumed that the word friendly when applied to a dog has a different meaning than when applied to a friendly person and that there is also a difference of proportion. The same is true when we talk about God. It appears that human love, loyalty, and faithfulness are only faint echoes of God's attributes.[82] Thus, analogy, as defined by Aquinas, is based on the idea of similarity and dissimilarity of compared elements, and Aquinas perceived it as a more suitable way to talk about God.[83]

---

79. Astley, *Exploring God-Talk*, 57.

80. Astley, 58.

81. Nevin, "Analogy: Aquinas and Pannenberg," 201 (emphasis original).

82. Stiver, *Philosophy of Religious Language*, 21, and Astley, *Exploring God-Talk*, 59.

83. Stiver, 127.

In concluding this discussion about the historical views on religious language, it is worth noting that even though the proponents of the views presented above all agree that God revealed himself in human language and human terms, they treat human language with some measure of mistrust when applied to God since it seems inadequate and overly limited.[84] They also struggle with understanding and explaining the meaning of human terms when used to talk about God because they seem to find equivocal and polysemous language perplexing. This is due, in part, to the difficulty in distinguishing between literal and figurative ways of speaking about God. On the one hand, they do not deny that God revealed himself using metaphors and that God saw metaphors as being necessary in communicating about himself; on the other hand, they perceive metaphors with mistrust, valuing more literal language that can present reality in more accurate ways. In their understanding of language "each word is assumed directly to signify an entity in the real world."[85] Thus, Aquinas's view on utilizing analogy to speak about God is based on an Aristotelian understanding of language, where metaphors are seen as improper or deviant uses of words. Therefore, the difficulty of defining how religious language functions and how people can talk about God remained unresolved, and there was a need for a different and more comprehensive view of language and metaphors.

One way of resolving some of the issues that medieval scholars tried to address is to overcome the dichotomy between religious and non-religious language. Thus, Gregory J. Laughery presents a different and more unified approach. While wrestling with the nature of religious language and trying to answer the question whether it is different from other kinds of language, Laughery stresses the importance of unifying language without ignoring its diversity. He argues that God is both transcendent and immanent, which means that "God is outside, *beyond* language, but can be said inside, *within* language. . . . God in Scripture is revealed by language, although never confused with it".[86] Laughery insists that God's relationship with language is the same as his relationship with the rest of creation – namely, he is both related to it and distinct from it. Consequently, for Laughery, the word of

---

84. Howe, *Because You Bear This Name*, 38.

85. Howe, 40.

86. Laughery, "Language at the Frontiers," 179(emphasis original).

God addresses the whole of life, and there is no need for a division between religious language and other types of language. He confirms that "whether scientific, ordinary or religious, all language has a capacity, in a meaningful, referential, dynamic manner, to point back to the Creator."[87] This unified understanding of all language as capable of conveying the truth about God brings a new perspective to the discussion on metaphors as vehicles of God's revelation. However, it needs to be said that Cognitive Linguistics moves the discussion even further, not only eliminating the distinctions between religious and secular language but also explaining how people conceptualize abstract concepts such as God.

1.1.3.2.1 Religious Language and Cognitive Linguistics
Cognitive Linguistics provides further arguments against distinguishing between religious language and other types of language since it argues that human cognition and language are perspectival, dependent on embodiment, and species-specific. As mentioned before, John Sanders argues that the human brain does not have any special conceptual apparatus designed to talk about God but that, instead, "we use our everyday conceptual structures to think about God and religion."[88] His insights are especially vital for understanding the nature of God's written revelation in metaphors and images since, as he points out, God in communicating with people utilizes the "normal human-embodied perceptual system."[89] This means that even biblical metaphors and images that are created by the unique inspiration of God are based on human conceptual system, which means that God presents himself using human terms.

Therefore, from the perspective of Cognitive Linguistics, there is no difference between comprehending and describing the concept of God and other abstract concepts. This process is based on the same mechanism of understanding one conceptual domain in terms of another; and since our domain of experience is located in our physical world, this is the domain from which our comparisons are drawn Numerous Christians, arguing against using metaphorical language to talk about God, cite the prophet Isaiah's words,

---

87. Laughery, 179.

88. Sanders, *Theology in the Flesh*, loc. 72–75 of 5234, Kindle.

89. Sanders, loc. 1648 of 5234.

"To whom then will you liken God? Or what likeness will you compare with Him?" (Isa 40:18), which point out that God is unlike idols made by people.

However, as humans, we have no other way to conceptualize reality except by using our perception shaped by our embodiment. Even Isaiah, in this chapter, uses numerous metaphors for God, presenting him as a ruler (40:10), a shepherd (40:11), and as the one who "sits above the circle of the earth" and "stretches out the heavens like a curtain" (40:22). In the following chapters, he depicts God as "a king, master, warrior, father, husband, and mother."[90] Each of these metaphors presents different characteristics of God but presents them in human terms. Moreover, in the Bible, God is portrayed in anthropomorphic ways as the one who speaks, sees, hears, sits on the throne, and whose hand is not too short to help us.

Cognitivists also point out that attempts to develop a separate category of religious language are insufficient. They say that even the traditional negative way of speaking about God is based on human concepts. When theologians define God's transcendence as being beyond or outside, they actually prove that they conceptualize God from their own human perspective and use spatial concepts of transcendence. They perceive the world they live in as a container and God, since he is greater, as being beyond their known boundaries or outside of this world.[91]

As I will demonstrate later, conceptual metaphor theory allows the use of human concepts to talk about God while retaining the similarity and dissimilarity of the two concepts, whereas blending theory explains how bringing together two concepts like God and king results in emergence of a new concept while respecting the integrity of each of them.

Thus, in conclusion, it must be said that applying Cognitive Linguistics to articulating biblical and theological concepts disproves the claim that there is a distinction between religious and non-religious language and demonstrates that our human conceptual system and human language are the only tools we have to talk about God. Therefore, it also justifies using metaphors and images in sermons because such metaphors and images are the means of God's revelation and the primary means of human communication.

---

90. For a further discussion on the subject, see Brettler, "Incompatible Metaphors," 97–120.

91. Sanders, *Theology in the Flesh*, loc. 4487–4514 of 5234, Kindle.

1.1.3.3 The Incarnation: God as Seen in Christ

The next stage of our argument concerning the manner of God's revelation justifies using metaphors and images in sermons and how Cognitive Linguistics contributes to communicating biblical and theological concepts, is the discussion of another instance of God's revelation through images – namely, the incarnation of Christ.

1.1.3.3.1 Christ as the Image of God

God revealed himself through images by creating people in his image, in the images in the Bible, and in the incarnation of Christ – the perfect image of the Father.[92] By becoming a man, Jesus not only entered this broken world but also revealed God in a way that humankind could understand. In the apostle John's words, "No one has ever seen God, but the one and only Son . . . has made him known" (John 1:18 NIV). Thus, in the act of incarnation, Christ revealed himself by taking human nature and communicating in human terms.

Paul, in the Epistle to the Colossians, makes an even more striking statement when he says that "the Son is the image of the invisible God" and that "God was pleased to have all his fullness dwell in him" (Col 1:15, 19 NIV). The invisible becomes visible in Christ since he is the one who allows people to see the unseen. Gerhard von Rad lists possible ways the word image (εἰκών) was used in Greek and also includes more metaphorical examples, such as a mental image, similitude, living image, likeness, embodiment, and manifestation.[93] Von Rad, while commenting on image (εἰκών) in Colossians 1:15, stresses the equality of Christ as the image of God with the original – that is, with God himself – and perceives Christ as the perfect revelation of God, the one in whom God's fullness bodily dwells.[94]

In *Preaching the Incarnation*, Peter Stevenson and Stephen Wright provide their readers with important insights regarding Christ being the image of God. First, they argue that the Pauline words about the Son being the image of the invisible God do not refer to "the eternal pre-existent Word, but to the human Jesus of Nazareth."[95] Second, referring to the literary context of

---

92. Garrett Green provides a helpful discussion on the issue of *imago Dei*, the incarnation, and, specifically, Christ as the image of God. Green, *Imagining God*, 83–88.

93. von Rad, "εἰκών," TDNT 2:388.

94. von Rad, TDNT 2:395.

95. Stevenson and Wright, *Preaching the Incarnation*, 149.

these words, they observe echoes of the creation narrative in the description of Christ as

> the firstborn over all creation. For in him all things were created: things in heaven and on earth, visible and invisible, whether thrones or powers or rulers or authorities; all things have been created through him and for him. He is before all things, and in him all things hold together (Col 1:15–17 NIV).[96]

This text indicates that Christ, as simultaneously the image of God and the true human being, fulfils the role that the first humans forfeited. He rules over the whole creation, which he himself had created. Hence, Stevenson and Wright conclude that Christ being the image of the invisible God means that *"Jesus Christ is the end-time fulfilment of humanity's destiny to rule over the earth"*.[97]

Earlier in the chapter, I argued that humans reflect the image of God in their total being – and not just in one aspect or one function – now I also argue that an analogical observation can be made regarding Christ being the image of God. Paul, in Colossians, places this idea in the context of creation and ruling over the earth; but Christ's role as the one who perfectly reveals God cannot be forgotten.

The fact that Christ is the image of God has significant implications for developing a theology of preaching, and these implications will be discussed later in this chapter. At this point, I simply stress that Christ's incarnation as an example of God's revelation in images is yet another argument justifying using metaphors and images in sermons since metaphors and images are suitable tools to talk about God.

This idea of reflecting the form and manner of God's revelation goes even further when we consider the role of the Holy Spirit. The Holy Spirit is the one who conforms believers to the image of Christ, and several biblical texts present this idea of being changed into the likeness of Christ or God (Rom 8:29; 2 Cor 3:18; Eph 4:23–24). As humans, we are created in the image of

---

96. For a detailed analysis of this text and its Christology, see Fee, *Pauline Christology*, 298–307.

97. Stevenson and Wright, *Preaching the Incarnation*, 150 (emphasis original). While I agree with Stevenson and Wright's analysis of the text, I disagree with their understanding of the image of God as being limited to the privilege of ruling over the creation.

God, but as believers redeemed by Christ, we are being transformed by the Holy Spirit into the likeness of Christ – that is, we are being conformed to the image of God who became a human. Hence, the revelation of God in the incarnation of Christ – who is the image of God – is both preached by Christians in their sermons and visible in Christians in their lives as they are becoming living images of Christ. As a result, their bodies are the temple of the Holy Spirit and they live striving to embody Christ's character and his example. Thus, the embodied God allows us to embody his character and his way of living.

1.1.3.3.2 The Incarnation and Cognitive Linguistics

The act of incarnation establishes another link between theology and Cognitive Linguistics, justifying its use and also showing its usefulness in conveying theological concepts. The incarnation not only reinforces the idea that we are not limited to our human perspective and that there is a God who wants to have a relationship with people, it also crosses over the boundaries between divine and human and shows the lengths to which God went to enter the human conceptual system and communicate in human language.

The fact that God became a human is the strongest argument for theistic theology and engaging Cognitive Linguistics in the examination and communication of biblical concepts. It is a foundational belief of Christianity that God entered our world as a historical character in the person of Jesus of Nazareth, and the fact that this act of revelation took place in the form of a human being with human perception allows us to employ Cognitive Linguistics as a means of examining Christ's incarnation and his words.

An example of a productive application of Cognitive Linguistics in theology is Zoltán Kövecses's attempt to apply it to interpreting and explaining the doctrine of the incarnation of Christ. In his analysis, Kövecses refers to the prologue to the Gospel of John, stressing that God is the Word and that the essence of Christ's coming is to become an embodiment of God's Word. He explains that "as such, Jesus metonymically also stands for God, the metonymic chain being EMBODIMENT OF INSTRUMENT stands for the INSTRUMENT itself that stands for the AGENT. That is, we have the EMBODIMENT OF THE WORD OF GOD FOR THE WORD OF GOD FOR GOD HIMSELF."[98]

---

98. Kövecses, "Biblical Story Retold," 336. Following the accepted convention, I use small capitals for indicating conceptual metaphors, metonymies, and domains.

Thereafter, referring to various passages from the Gospels, Kövecses identifies a series of metaphors related to the incarnation. Based on the Gospel texts, he perceives the birth of Jesus as the coming of God's Word to people, which is based on the metaphor BIRTH IS ARRIVAL ("The baby will come soon"). By living among people, Jesus embodied the Word and God himself. Through Christ, God was physically present among people and this fact reflects the metaphor EXISTENCE IS PRESENCE HERE ("Christ was born," "the Word became flesh, and dwelt among us"). Finally, Christ as the perfect image of God and embodiment of God's Word allowed people to get to know God. God revealed himself and communicated with people by sending his Son since COMMUNICATION IS SENDING.[99]

Kövecses's analysis is compelling as an example of employing conventional conceptual metaphors and metonymies to explain the biblical texts about the coming of Christ and to describe the biblical concept of the incarnation. In the chapters that follow, I will discuss more practical aspects of conducting this kind of analysis.

To summarize this part of the chapter, the notion of preaching images and metaphors is rooted in God's revelation in images – when he created the humans in his own image, when he revealed himself through the biblical images, and, finally, when he revealed himself in Christ who is the image of the Father. God's use of metaphors and images as an essential means of his self-revelation provides the theological justification for using metaphors and images in sermons that convey God's revelation. Considering the fact that God's revelation took place in human terms – which includes human beings in their totality, the written revelation expressed in human language, and the incarnation when God became a human – it is helpful to utilize Cognitive Linguistics as a tool for examining this revelation. This set of theories provides both a theoretical framework and a practical approach to understanding human cognition as expressed in language.

The idea of God's revelation is important when applying Cognitive Linguistics to preaching because it brings in a theistic perspective that widens the view advocated by this theory, which is limited only to the perspective of human minds. If our perception of reality is merely a product of our embodiment and experiences, how did ideas of God, afterlife, eternity, spirituality,

---

99. Kövecses, 336.

or a soul even appear in our minds? All these point beyond our experience to our Creator.[100]

1.2 Implications of God's Revelation for Developing a Theological Framework for Showing the Unseen by Using Metaphors and Images in Preaching

In the previous sections I argued that using metaphors and images in sermons is justified because of the manner of God's revelation in images. Preachers, as recipients of God's revelation, are able to see images in themselves since they are created in the image of God, in the Bible since it is filled with imagery, and in Christ since he is the image of God. Therefore, they have to use images in sermons because when they preach, they inevitably bring themselves to the pulpit as people created in the image of God. They also preach biblical metaphors and images. Finally, they proclaim the message about Christ, the image of God. These images seem to be an indisputable means of conveying God's revelation in their sermons.

However, when trying to find the best ways of presenting biblical revelation, preachers have to define their role and the limits of their authority. Should preachers only repeat and explain biblical metaphors? Can they convey the meaning of biblical texts by creating new metaphors? The first part of this section addresses these issues, although its purpose is not to resolve all those serious hermeneutical, theological, and linguistic problems but, rather, to depict the scope of the challenges preachers face and to define the preacher's role and authority when it comes to preaching metaphors. In order to define the preacher's role and authority, three different approaches

---

100. Cognitivists, in attempting to explain the origin of ideas such as God, the afterlife, eternity, soul, and truth, perceive humans as outcomes of evolutionary processes. In their opinion, some of these ideas might have survival value, whereas others seem to be the most intuitive for human beings or have resulted from the forming of societies and social relationships. See Lakoff and Johnson, *Metaphors We Live By*, 159–184. See also Barrett, *Why Would Anyone Believe in God?* and Boyer, *Religion Explained*. For more information on how religious beliefs are natural for children and how they are formed from the early years by our perceptions, see Barrett, *Born Believers*.

to preaching will be presented and discussed: cognitive-propositional, experiential-expressivist, and cultural-linguistic.[101]

In the next part of this section, I show how God's revelation through images serves as a theological framework for understanding preaching, which also utilizes metaphors and images I will also demonstrate that the notion of God's revelation understood in terms of embodiment of God's speech that is expressed in images leads to the development of a Trinitarian theology of preaching. Thus, before examining how Cognitive Linguistics may enrich and transform our methodology of interpreting the biblical text and preaching, it is helpful to give some insights regarding a theology of preaching that is based on some concepts already presented in this chapter. The principles presented in the following sections, even though rooted in the idea of God's revelation in images, apply to all preaching, not only to preaching that utilizes Cognitive Linguistics. However, in this latter kind of preaching, these principles play an especially important role in showing how a theological context and the boundaries set on the claims of some cognitivists can be articulated in preaching practice.

1.2.1 Views on Preaching

Since various scholars perceive preaching differently, this section presents three major views on preaching: cognitive-propositional, experiential-expressivist, and cultural-linguistic.

Scholars like Haddon Robinson, who adhere to a cognitive-propositional approach to preaching, understand preaching as "the communication of a biblical concept."[102] For Robinson, preaching is propositional in nature and is about discovering the biblical concept through the process of exegesis and then communicating it to the listeners. However, before this concept can become the sermon idea that is communicated, it has to go through a series of transformations. In a modified version of Robinson's approach, there are three steps. First, as preachers study the text, they identify the exegetical idea which captures what the text says. Then, using the exegetical idea,

---

101. This terminology originates from George Lindbeck. His ideas were further developed by Hans Frei and applied to preaching by Charles Campbell, who devoted his book to the analysis of Hans Frei's approach and its influence on preaching. See Campbell, *Preaching Jesus*, 65–82, 122, 141.

102. Robinson, *Biblical Preaching*, 21.

they formulate the theological idea that conveys the purpose of the text and its timeless truth. Finally, they create the homiletical idea, which becomes the main idea or dominant thought of the sermon. This homiletical idea is a sermon in a nutshell.[103] The purpose of preaching is to communicate the biblical concept in a way that reaches and impacts contemporary listeners.

The notion of identifying the main controlling idea of a text that then becomes the main idea of the sermon has been widely discussed among homileticians. Eugene Lowry believes that the Bible is largely "non-propositional" and argues that any attempt to reduce the text to propositional statements distorts its experiential meaning.[104] Instead of identifying the dominant idea of a sermon, Lowry insists on naming a sermon focus, which is understood not as the thesis of a sermon but, rather, as the main issue, conflict, or, in Lowry's terminology, the "itch."[105] Thomas Long, instead of finding a sermon's "Big Idea", writes that preachers should state the claim of a text upon the hearers and identify its intention, and then proceed to define the focus and function of a sermon. "What the sermon aims to say can be called the 'focus', and what the sermon aims to do can be called its 'function.'"[106]

It is significant that even those who criticize the notion of defining a sermon's main idea or dominant thought in a single sentence cannot escape it completely, and they also have some way of expressing the text by narrowing the sermon to some kind of statement. Critics argue that if a single sentence can capture the meaning of the whole text, then there is no further need for a text. When preachers focus on giving their audience just the main idea, the text may sometimes be neglected. In some traditional sermons, preachers tend to focus more on explaining and analyzing the dominant thought than on actually expositing the text and following its flow. Propositional preaching has been often accused of flattening the text, losing much of the richness of its content, and failing to reflect its genre, form, mood, and conflicts.[107]

Therefore, it can be argued that biblical preaching is more than just communicating the biblical concept, but it is rather communicating the biblical

---

103. Szumorek, *Spotkanie z Wszechmocnym*, 125–134.
104. Lowry, *Doing Time in the Pulpit*, 79–80.
105. Lowry, *Dancing the Edge*, 107–109.
106. Long, *Witness of Preaching*, 108.
107. Long, 101–105.

text that can be expressed in a form of the concept.[108] Even Robinson's preaching practice goes beyond just communicating the main idea of the text. After reading and listening to many of Robinson's sermons, I observed that even though he always identifies the main idea, his preaching is very textually focused. Consequently, from my perspective, preaching biblical concepts should supplement exposition of the text rather than be a substitute for it.

Utilizing George Lindbeck's terminology, there is a turn in homiletics from cognitive-propositional preaching to its experiential-expressivist understanding.[109] Proponents of the experiential-expressivist approach – Charles Rice, Fred Craddock, Eugene Lowry, and others – argue that a sermon should have narrative qualities and must connect the Bible story with the listeners' stories and experiences.[110] Listeners should not only understand the text but also experience its meaning and mood. Such sermons begin with a problem or a depiction of a contemporary situation and move towards the biblical resolution or to the point where the audience can interpret the problem from a biblical perspective. Supporters of this approach understand a sermon as a "Word event" that is supposed to be revelatory, experiential, and transformational. Preachers like Rice, Craddock, and Lowry frequently use non-biblical stories to convey biblical ideas, trying to relate these biblical concepts to human experience. They not only strive to communicate what the text says but also what it does, which means that they attempt to capture its mood and rhetorical function in their preaching.

Charles Campbell, however, critiques experiential preaching and argues that neither the option of starting with a contemporary situation nor the "idea of evoking something that is already within" listeners is a good strategy for preaching since preaching should not be based on the analysis of contemporary situations, human needs, or experiences but on the word of God as its only starting point. Preachers are not to evoke hidden thoughts and emotions but must present the biblical message.[111] Thomas Long, whose approach to preaching differs from that of Campbell's, is also critical of experiential

---

108. These other approaches also include a broad category of exegetical expositional sermons.

109. Campbell, *Preaching Jesus*, 122.

110. In Craddock, *Craft of Preaching* half the book is devoted to preaching as a story; see also Lowry, *Homiletical Beat*.

111. Campbell, *Preaching Jesus*, 128.

preaching and warns against preaching that seeks to generate emotions. His point is that even if preaching creates an experience, this does not necessarily mean that people actually experience God.[112]

In developing his understanding of religion, theology, and preaching, Charles Campbell builds on the work of both Lindbeck and Frei, which results in his articulation of a cultural-linguistic approach to preaching. George Lindbeck, questions a propositional understanding of religion that claims that religions are based on a set of propositional truths, while opposing an experiential-expressivist model of religion that assumes that religions are products of an experience. For Lindbeck, religion is not based on a body of doctrines or beliefs to adhere to but, rather, functions like an idiom "that makes possible the description of reality, the formulation of beliefs, and the experiencing of inner attitudes, feelings, and sentiments."[113] He compares religions to a language and culture because they are communal phenomena that shape those who belong to the community. Lindbeck argues that to become a religious person "involves becoming skilled in the language, the symbol system of a given religion. To become a Christian involves learning the story of Israel and of Jesus well enough to interpret and experience oneself and one's world in its terms."[114]

Hans Frei develops his approach along similar lines. For Frei, theology "is a practical discipline; it is in effect part of learning the grammar of a linguistic symbol system; it is a Christian self-description under some norm for its specific language use."[115] Charles Campbell, in discussing implications of Hans Frei's cultural-linguistic approach to biblical interpretation, stresses that for Frei the text is more than just the written Scripture and is also the "enacted text" of a given culture with its symbolic system, performative language, community practices, and traditions.[116]

Stephen Wright provides a balanced criticism of Frei's approach, stressing that even though Frei emphasizes the need to protect the integrity of Scripture and take it on its own terms, he unduly limits its imaginative application to the

---

112. Long, *Witness of Preaching*, 40–41.
113. Lindbeck, *Nature of Doctrine*, 19.
114. Lindbeck, 21.
115. Frei, *Types of Christian Theology*, 126.
116. Campbell, *Preaching Jesus*, 79.

life of the community of faith and its conversation with the world.[117] It must also be said that such an approach may result in preaching sermons which overlook the emotive dimensions of the text and only focus on its content.

As seen above in their attempts to define preaching, various scholars stress different elements as being central to the preacher's task – for example, communicating a biblical concept, evoking an experience of the biblical text, or helping listeners to become more skilled in using the language of the Bible as a way of re-describing their vision of the world and expressing their deepest convictions. All these views influence the way preachers define their task and understand their authority to create new metaphors and images.

1.2.2 Defining the Preacher's Role and Authority

In the context of such diverse views about preaching, the question about the preacher's role and authority in using non-biblical images and metaphors or creating new ones becomes even more urgent.

Haddon Robinson, while a proponent of a cognitive-propositional approach to preaching, is also known for using numerous metaphors, images, and stories that illustrate the meaning of the biblical text and help listeners to experience biblical truth. Robinson does not limit his task to explaining biblical metaphors but feels free to create his own. In his view, these images and sermon illustrations serve the purpose of communicating textual ideas and the text itself must limit their selection. Such a sermon is a combination of explanation, illustration, and application. Therefore, according to Robinson, preachers have authority to create new metaphors and images to convey the meaning of the text.

As mentioned before, adherents of experiential preaching believe that preachers must convey in their sermons both the content of the text and its mood in ways that effectively reach contemporary listeners. Therefore, they can use images, metaphors, and stories that will help them achieve this purpose and communicate, in modern terms, what the text says and what it does in terms of its rhetorical function and its impact on the reader.

However, Campbell criticizes the idea of preachers being translators of the biblical message into contemporary language or using other stories to

---

117. Wright, "Inhabiting the Story," 495–498.

convey the biblical story.[118] He challenges the idea that a non-biblical story can convey the same content and evoke the same emotion as the biblical one. In his view, introducing different content – in the form of a different story – creates an experience that is different to the one created by the biblical text.[119] Instead of focusing on finding more relevant stories or wondering about the life situations of the listeners, he follows Hans Frei and opts for acquainting listeners with the biblical story and its language in such a way that they are able to "hear the story truthfully and use the language rightly."[120]

For Frei, it is not the narrative form that is the key to biblical revelation but, rather, the identity of Jesus, who is the main character of these narratives and the one who saves us. Thus, instead of focusing on a plot and story form, he focuses on the character of Christ and his identity as revealed in the New Testament. Hans Frei even rejects the idea of referring to Jesus as providing a model of preaching in his telling of the parables. Instead of concentrating on individual parables, he analyzes them in the wider context of the Gospels and emphasizes that they must be read "in the light of the story identifying Jesus of Nazareth."[121] In Frei's view, Jesus is not the model of preaching but the one the parables preach about.

Thus, according to proponents of this view, preachers should not violate the biblical text by adding any contemporary images or stories that introduce a different form or different content. Instead, they should focus on educating listeners about the biblical story and its language, remembering that biblical images and metaphors are a new language that Christians need to learn to talk about God and themselves, and to live as God's people.

As I reflected on these various views on the preacher's role from the perspective of my earlier theological discussion on God's revelation and Cognitive Linguistics, I observed that the different views on God's revelation and the image of God tend to emphasize just one aspect of God's revelation and that the same applies to the preaching theories presented above. The approaches to preaching that were described above usually focus on just one facet of revelation and communication, which may be perceived as

---

118. Campbell, *Preaching Jesus*, 148–152.

119. Campbell, 169–172.

120. Campbell, 153.

121. Frei, "Theology and the Interpretation," 104. See also Campbell, *Preaching Jesus*, 153, 177–178.

propositional, experiential or cultural-linguistic. However, while reflecting on the mode of revelation, I observed its richness and its diverse nature that includes propositional statements about God and his character, God's actions and people's experiences of him, and, finally, cultural-linguistic dimensions that allow forming a new community of faith. God's revelation also encompasses a whole variety of forms, of which metaphors and images are among the most prominent.

As described in the earlier sections of this chapter, even God's revelation in images – as seen in the act of creating people, God's revelation in biblical images, and Christ's incarnation – is holistic in nature. The image of God in people refers to the whole of a human being, not just one aspect of human nature. This is also true of biblical metaphors, which are vehicles of God's revelation, and, therefore, they not only help us to understand the concept of God but also have emotive dimensions. Finally, this richness and the holistic nature of God's revelation is seen in Christ, the perfect image of God, who is both fully God and fully human.

Therefore, using Lindbeck's terminology, we can say that preaching by employing metaphors should have a cognitive-propositional dimension because metaphors, as a part of God's revelation, convey knowledge about God. As suggested by proponents of experiential preaching, metaphors and images have an evocative character because they involve our emotions and imagination. Finally, as proposed by adherents of the cultural-linguistic model, such metaphors and images are also community-forming devices that give a sense of identity, common language, and purpose. Consequently, if preaching is to reflect the nature of God's revelation, it should employ metaphors and images and aim to convey propositional knowledge, touching on experience and creating a cultural-linguistic community that knows its own language. Thus, images and metaphors play a vital role in conveying God's revelation.

Accordingly, while seeking an answer to the question of the preacher's authority to create new metaphors to convey biblical revelation, it must be said that the Bible does not limit the use of new metaphors to proclaim God's revelation; on the contrary, there are numerous examples of biblical writers creating new metaphors and images. As pointed out earlier, many metaphors used in the Bible have human origin. The apostle Paul, writing after the death and resurrection of Jesus, did not restrict himself to using only Old Testament images but created new images to present his message more clearly. Some of his metaphors and images were rooted in the Old Testament and also had resonance with the Roman culture as images drawn from or relating to slavery and armour (Rom 1:1; 6:15–23; Eph 6:11–17), whereas others were based solely on his cultural experiences – for instance soldiers, and sports (2 Tim 2:3–5; 1 Cor 9:24–24).

Furthermore, while analyzing biblical revelation through images and metaphors, we observe that, over the centuries, these images change and that different biblical writers use different metaphors depending on the time, place, and their readers.[122] From our perspective, metaphors and images that were close to the cultural experiences of biblical writers and their readers often are remote and unclear to us. Some other non-metaphorical biblical texts seem to be ambiguous to modern readers, which means that they either require explanation or creation of new metaphors to convey their meanings. As preachers, we still face the same challenge of proclaiming God's revelation in a way that people can understand it, making the unknown known.

While it may be true that Jesus is the most important subject of at least some of his parables, he used everyday images to convey theological meaning, and we can learn from him by listening not only to what he said but also to how he communicated his message. Jesus did not only preach the word, he is the Word incarnate. The next section will explain how Christ's incarnation serves as a great model for preaching.

Thus, David Buttrick – who developed the idea of phenomenological preaching with its sermonic moves – sees "preaching as a work of metaphor" and argues that preachers have to reach for the language of analogy and metaphors because God is mysterious. While he warns against creating idols and false images of God, he encourages utilizing a rich stock of biblical images.[123] Moreover, he explains how to use non-biblical illustrations and examples which "bring together images from different realms of experience" and calls these "the native tongue of faith."[124]

Craig Ott, discussing the issue of metaphors from a missiological perspective, points out that "finding a common frame of reference or shared

---

122. See section 5.2.1.4 for how Jesus uses and elaborates on Old Testament images.
123. Buttrick, *Homiletic*, 113–116.
124. Buttrick, 128.

experience is essential to effective cross-cultural communication."[125] He supports the idea of "redemptive analogies" by recalling Don Richardson's story of the "Peace Child." In a culture where betrayal was a virtue, Judas was considered a hero since he betrayed Christ. The perception of the story changed when the Sawi people finally saw an analogy between Christ's coming and their own ritual of peacemaking, which took place when one chief have up his son to be brought up by an enemy chief. In that culture, killing the peace child was viewed as the worse possible crime. This new image of God sending his peace child and people killing this child opened the door for the Sawi people to understand and accept the gospel.

Hence, using images in preaching can be defended on theological grounds, on the basis of the doctrines of revelation and the incarnation of Christ as a model for preaching. This concept has a biblical basis since the Bible is filled with images and metaphors that seem to be the primary means by which God communicates with humans. It is also valid linguistically because a significant proportion of human communication is metaphorical in nature.

1.2.3 Trinitarian Understanding of Preaching

Mike Pasquarello III convincingly argues that theology is our grammar of faith that "enables us, in certain, definable ways, to see, to understand, to hear, and to speak of God."[126] Therefore, in while attempting to define preaching, it is necessary to place the whole discussion in a theological context that is Trinitarian in nature.

Christian preaching does not exist without God's revelation, which can be understood as God's speaking. Preachers can speak about God only because God first spoke about himself. The idea of God's revelation viewed as God's speech is not new in Christian theology. Pasquarello analyzes the history of the theology of preaching and points to Augustine who, in his preaching, "attributed special status to Christian revelation, the Word of God speaking through Scripture and human speech to God's people, *verbum dei* in *sermo dei*."[127] Pasquarello also gives the example of Luther, who "considered

---

125. Ott, "Power of Biblical Metaphors," 360.

126. Pasquarello, *Sacred Rhetoric*, 135.

127. Pasquarello, 26.

Holy Scripture to be an emergency measure provide by God the Speaker."[128] Therefore, Pasquarello defines God's revelation as the "speaking of God" and states:

> Speaking of God is ecstatic speech, the self-emptying or giving away that opens us to yield ourselves and our words to the Word of the Father, which is the revelation of the Son in whom we delight and to whom we are drawn by the Spirit's movement of self-giving love.[129]

Pasquarello introduces an important concept of God's revelation as "Trinitarian speaking of God," and this idea transforms our perception of preaching. Consequently, for Pasquarello, the notion of speaking of God is also "a shorthand definition of Christian preaching since the source, means, and goal of all we are and all we do is the Word spoken by the Father in the power of the Holy Spirit."[130] This means that when preachers faithfully proclaim the word of God, God speaks through their human speaking, and their preaching becomes the speech of God himself, which is always Trinitarian in nature. Therefore, the doctrine of the Trinity is not only fundamental for Christian theology – as expressed by Karl Barth, who says that "Trinity is the Christian name for God"[131] – but also vital to our understanding of the task of preaching.

When the church fathers were trying to depict the communion and cooperation of the divine persons, they used the term περιχώρησις (perichoresis). This term "comes from the prefix *peri* ('around') and the verb *choreo* ('to go' or 'to contain')" and describes "the Father and the Son being in one another, and the Holy Spirit in both," which results in "the Trinitarian persons 'containing' one another."[132] This means that divine persons "cannot be separated as though they are different from each other," and they are all involved in every activity of the Trinity as seen in the acts of creation, revelation, redemption,

---

128. Pasquarello, 111.

129. Pasquarello, *Christian Preaching*, 215.

130. Pasquarello, 10.

131. Quoted in Fee, *Listening to the Spirit*, 27.

132. Kilby, "Perichoresis," 238. See also Hilary of Poitiers, Concerning the Trinity, 3:1. where he talks about the persons of Trinity mutually enveloping each other and being enveloped.

and many other actions of God.[133] Therefore, it is also not surprising that they cooperate with each other in the act of preaching and that truly Christian preaching grows out of dependence on the persons of the Trinity and through understanding both their unity and the uniqueness of their different roles.

Numerous theologians have attempted to provide their own definition of Trinitarian preaching. Even though they come from different traditions, present diverse preaching styles, and place different emphases in their explanation of the idea of Trinitarian preaching, all these theologians agree that this doctrine is fundamental to understanding the task of preaching. For instance, Steve Holmes claims that in order to comprehend the significance of a church ministry such as preaching, Christians have to realize that "the Church participates through the Spirit in ministry of Christ which was given to him by the Father."[134] Michael Quicke says, "The Father who speaks forth his Word in creation and revelation, the Son is the eternally spoken Word, and the Spirit causes the Word to be heard and preached."[135] In his "360-Degree Preaching" model, Quicke explains that preaching "involves movement through 360 degrees of eventfulness as God – Father, Son, and the Holy Spirit – speaks through his Word *and* empowers the preacher *and* convicts the listeners *and* transforms the lives of the preacher and the listeners".[136]

Pasquarello, in reflecting on the Trinitarian theology of preaching, points out that since Christian preaching "takes place in, with, and through the initiative of and activity of the Triune God," human speakers and listeners respond and participate "in the prior gift of God's speech, the Word spoken by the Father in the power of the Spirit."[137] Therefore, he gives the following definition of preaching:

> *Christian preaching, then, is theological rhetoric,* a gift of the Spirit, in which Christ, the Incarnate Word spoken by the Father,

---

133. Quicke, *360-Degree Preaching*, 58.

134. Steve Holmes, "Toward a Baptist Theology of Ordained Ministry," unpublished paper, 5, quoted in Quicke, *360-Degree Preaching*, 56.

135. Quicke, *360-Degree Preaching*, 55. Albrecht Mohler presents a Trinitarian perspective on preaching, saying that we preach because of the God who speaks, the Son who saves, and the Spirit who illuminates. Duduit, *Handbook of Contemporary Preaching*, 13–15.

136. Quicke, *360-Degree Preaching*, 49 (emphasis original). For ways of teaching about the Trinity in preaching, see MacKey, "Preacher," 347–366.

137. Pasquarello, *Christian Preaching*, 13.

condescends to indwell Scripture and the Church, himself speaking the restoration and fulfillment of creation by confessing the praise of the Creator.[138]

In understanding God's revelation and preaching in terms of God's speech, it is essential to bear in mind that this speech is embodied and expressed in images. Such an understanding is the foundation for developing a Trinitarian theology of preaching that utilizes metaphors and images.

Speaking of God always takes a tangible form. When God created the world by speaking, his speech was embodied in the form of the whole creation, but this embodiment was seen most clearly in the creation of human beings made in his image. God spoke, and his word took the form of a human person who became an image of God. Then, in the act of the incarnation, the word of God was embodied and became a human – the Son, who is the perfect image of the Father. Finally, the Holy Spirit is the one who works in believers, conforming them to the image of the Son, which is an ongoing process. The Holy Spirit makes it possible for God's speech to become embodied in humans, transforming them into the likeness of Christ.

In this whole process, the notion of embodiment is significant since, as humans, we came into existence as a result of the embodiment of God's speaking. Jesus Christ – as the Word who became flesh – is the perfect embodiment of God's speaking. Finally, as Christians, we are to embody the word of God by the power of the Holy Spirit who, through God's speaking, made us children of God and transforms us into the likeness of Christ.

Furthermore, we have an example here of the perfect unity and cooperation of the three persons of the Trinity – God, who makes people in his image; Christ, who makes the image of the Father visible and accessible to people and redeems them from their sins; and, finally, the Holy Spirit, who forms the image of the Son in Christ's followers so that they can grow into the likeness of Christ and be his visible images in the world.

Therefore, Christian preaching is Trinitarian in nature, which means that while it uses biblical and non-biblical metaphors and images that expound biblical revelation, its aim is to proclaim the God who created people in his image and offers them redemption in Christ, who is the perfect image of

---

138. Pasquarello, 56 (emphasis original).

God, so that they can be transformed by the Holy Spirit and conformed to the image of Christ by growing in his likeness.

In the sections that follow, I will discuss this concept of Trinitarian preaching that grows out of God's revelation – understood as the embodied speech of God in images – and show that it aspires to be biblical in its content, theocentric in its context, incarnational in its focus, and pastoral in its purpose.

1.2.4 Content of Preaching: The Bible as the Revealed Word of God

Pasquarello observes that "a living God speaks a living Word, Jesus Christ, and the Holy Scriptures are the written representation of that Word, which creates a conversation or 'sermon' between God and God's people."[139] Since the speaking of God became embodied in the form of Scripture and scriptural images, Christian preaching employs biblical and non-biblical images that expound biblical revelation, which means that Christian preaching seeks to be committed to the faithful communication of Scripture.

John Stott makes two fundamental statements about Scripture: "Scripture is God's Word written" and "God still speaks through what he has spoken."[140] Consequently, Stott believes that "to expound Scripture is to open up the inspired text with such faithfulness and sensitivity that God's voice is heard and his people obey him."[141] Therefore, preaching needs to be rooted in biblical revelation and convey biblical revelation.

Pasquarello also emphasizes the importance of the Bible in preaching, saying that preaching is "an instrument of the active and real presence of God, divine address mediated through scriptural speech to accomplish God's purpose."[142] Thus, through proclamation of the word of God, listeners can experience the presence of God and hear him speaking to them.

Considering that images and metaphors play a crucial role in God's revelation, Christian preaching seeks to use metaphors and images to expound biblical texts in general and metaphorical texts in particular. Hence, on the one hand, preachers need to find images and metaphors for concepts they

---

139. Pasquarello, 135–136.
140. Stott, *I Believe in Preaching*, 96, 100.
141. Stott, "Definition of Biblical Preaching," 24.
142. Pasquarello, Christian Preaching, 139.

have identified in biblical texts that might be non-metaphorical. On the other hand, they must attempt to understand biblical images and metaphors and to communicate these to their listeners. Cognitive Linguistics is helpful in both these tasks.

1.2.5 Context of Preaching: Preachers and Listeners Created in the Image of God

Trinitarian preaching focuses at proclaiming about God who created people in his image. Since God created humans, and since he is the beginning of everything, the Trinitarian understanding of preaching presupposes that biblical preaching must be theocentric. As pointed out earlier, since the Bible is the written record of God's self-revelation, God is its main character and should, therefore, be the main character of Christian sermons.

As we read the Bible, we discover that the great overarching narrative it presents is the story of salvation – the story of God fulfilling his redemptive plan in the history of the world – which means that all biblical passages should be viewed in the larger context of the history of salvation. It is apparent, when reading the Old Testament narratives, that "Jews wrote history because they were convinced that God acted through historical events, namely, they perceived it as God's history."[143] Leland Ryken, while arguing for the uniqueness of the Bible, states that "it is pervaded by a consciousness of God" and "constantly affirms a God-centered world view," where "God is not only the supreme value but also gives identity to all other aspects of experience."[144] Sidney Greidanus asserts that "the Bible reveals his theocentric nature" because, in the Bible, everything "is viewed in relationship to God: the world is God's creation; human beings are image-bearers of God; salvation belongs to God," which means that "all of life belongs and is governed by God."[145] Greidanus also confirms this God-centred character of the Bible by analyzing its various literary genres and showing, convincingly, that their focus is theocentric even in those passages where God seems to be invisible or even absent.[146] Finally, Pasquarello asserts that "the Bible is God-centered just as

---

143. Szumorek, *Spotkanie z Wszechmocnym*, 33.
144. Ryken, Literature of the Bible, 16.
145. Greidanus, *Modern Preacher*, 114.
146. Greidanus, 115–116.

the worship assembly is God-centered in its prayer, praise, and proclamation."[147] Therefore, God's character and his actions are to be the content of Christian preaching, which can be seen as both "a divine and human activity, and as a theological and pastoral activity that locates us in God's story."[148]

Reflecting on the theocentric nature of preaching, Haddon Robinson expresses his conviction that since "the Bible is a book about God," every biblical text presents a certain vision of God.[149] Hence, the most important question preachers can ask is what the text says about God. A second question – "What in humanity rebels against that vision?" – then allows the preacher to move from the theocentric text to the theocentric sermon application, which offers answers to our human predicament in the nature and actions of God.[150] If God had not spoken first, we would not be able to speak about him at all. If it had not been for Christ's death and resurrection, there would be no message about salvation. If the Holy Spirit did not convict, convince, and continue our transformation, we would not be able to get to know God and change.

As pointed out earlier, the idea that God created us in his image is another example of God's speech being embodied and taking physical form, which transforms our perception of God, the world, and also ourselves. Consequently, as humans, we are embodied expressions of God's speaking and we live before the Creator God who defines the difference between good and evil. Understanding the fact that we are created by God results in recognition of God's authority over the whole of creation in general and our lives in particular.

In his discussion of creation from a Trinitarian perspective, Stanley Grenz observes that "the divine goal in creating the universe is to bring creation to share in the eternal love within the heart of the Trinitarian God and to evoke a loving response from God's creatures, especially human beings."[151] The Triune God, who is love, and who shares this love within the Trinity, wants to extend this love to his creatures by inviting them to enter a relationship

---

147. Pasquarello, *Christian Preaching*. 138.

148. Pasquarello, *Sacred Rhetoric*, 135.

149. Robinson, "Convictions of Biblical Preaching," 23.

150. Robinson, "Heresy of Application," 308.

151. Grenz, *Moral Quest*, 261.

with him. Therefore, the assertion that God is the creator is foundational for developing a theocentric world view.

Additionally, the idea of creation in the image of God implies that, despite cultural and ideological differences, there is common ground between preachers and listeners. Christopher Wright explains that all human beings are addressable by God, are accountable to God, have dignity and equality, and need the same gospel.[152] Thus, even when preaching takes place in an adverse environment – where there are key differences in their world views and beliefs – preachers and listeners share the fact that they are made in the likeness of God. Therefore, issues that people value and care about, such as justice, the environment, animals, protecting human rights, helping the poor, and advancing social equality, are expressions of being made in the image of God even though some of those who hold these convictions may not realize or accept this fact. This point is further explained by Timothy Keller, who argues that people "still have strong moral convictions, but unlike people in other times, they do not have any visible basis for *why* they find some things to be evil and other to be good."[153]

Therefore, preaching that is built on the presupposition that both preachers and listeners are created in the image of God seeks to find ways to answer this "why" question by pointing to the Creator. Since the image of God is a shared quality, it can serve as a starting point for establishing a common ground of understanding and developing common language shared by preachers and listeners. This common ground in preaching finds its expression in sermons dealing with issues that people universally care about and identify with. It also creates a space for shared action, whereby both Christians and non-Christians can get involved in projects that are universally perceived as good.

However, it is important to stress that Christian preaching must always be theologically informed. Therefore, while preachers may start with common universal moral issues, they must not fall into the trap of moralism or social activism by failing to point to the ultimate source and judge of our values – God.[154] Keller, having studied the apostle Paul's methodology of presenting

---

152. Wright, *Mission of God*, 421–425.

153. Keller, *Reason for God*, 145 (emphasis original).

154. For Keller's discussion on preaching truth instead of pragmatism, see Keller, "Preaching Morality," 167–169.

the gospel to different cultures, says that Paul contextualized his message and adopted some elements of those cultures and their language in order to confront them by showing that only Christ was able to change them and that only in him could real value be found.[155] In his sermon in Athens, for instance, Paul pointed to the worship of the unknown God and stated that he had come to preach about this God whom the Athenians did not know about. However, in the same sermon, Paul also questioned the way the Athenians had conceptualized God by making statues and building temples, and he focused their attention on the fact that the God who created the world does not live in temples made by human hands.

Lesslie Newbigin defines his task of preaching along similar lines when he claims that "my task is to make clear to myself and (if possible) to others the word which is spoken in the Gospel in such a way that it may be heard in the language of this culture of which I am a part with all its power to question that culture."[156] Thus, he stresses the importance of both speaking the language of the culture and confronting that culture.

In the next few chapters, I present a Cognitive Linguistics perspective on cultural universality and variation. I will show how this perspective can be applied to biblical exegesis and preaching because, despite considerable cultural differences between them, the original audience and contemporary readers share numerous characteristics that are rooted in embodiment of their minds, emotions, perception, and human nature. The same factors that help to build bridges between modern readers and ancient recipients are essential in establishing common ground between communicators and listeners.

1.2.6 Focus of Preaching: Redeemed by Christ – the Incarnate Image of God

The key focus of preaching is the act of redemption in Christ – who is the perfect image of God – which is yet another expression of the embodied speech of God expressed in images. This redemptive and Christological focus in preaching is to be expressed by developing an incarnational perspective and a holistic understanding of preaching in a soteriological context.

---

155. Keller, *Preaching: Communicating Faith*, 19, 96–103.

156. Newbigin, *Light Has Come*, ix.

In the earlier part of this chapter, I explained the notion of Jesus being the perfect image of the Father. The incarnation of Christ is holistic in nature since Christ, while being fully divine, took on every aspect of human nature to redeem it in its wholeness, and not only that but the whole of creation as well. As such, the incarnation is the most personal and perfect way of God's revelation.

The idea that the incarnation of Christ is not only the climax of God's revelation but can also serve as a model of preaching has been widely presented in homiletical literature. For example, Michael Quicke says that just as Jesus entered history at a particular time and place, preachers need to speak to people living in a particular time and place, using methods of communication that are appropriate for them.[157] In a similar fashion, Roger Standing defines preaching as a mediated discipline since it always seeks to communicate the word of God to specific people living in a specific time and place.[158]

Therefore, incarnational preaching finds its expression not only in the way we think of preaching but also in the form of the sermon. Not only does the sermon enter the world of the listeners, it also speaks their language. Hence, Pasquarello notes:

> Thus in popular preaching, the lowly, earthly style incarnate in Christ embodied in Scripture, which was favored by the Fathers – *sermo humilis* – was capable of overcoming barriers that might impede hearing, evoking a world of the divine accommodating itself to the lowly in the plain, humble Word through preachers who exemplified its character.[159]

Consequently, Christ's humility and his ability to accommodate his style to that of his listeners serve as an example for preachers who aspire to preach truly incarnational sermons that help to overcome barriers their listeners face while listening to the word of God.

David Day explains this idea by stating that preaching that "embodies the Word also makes heavy use of images, pictures, analogies, similes and metaphors." Day also provides biblical examples of this visual communication and

---

157. Quicke, *360-Degree Preaching*, 24–25.

158. Standing, "Mediated Preaching," 10–25.

159. Pasquarello, *Sacred Rhetoric*, 103–104.

notes that "the great doctrines of Christianity began life as pictures: redemption, justification, election, repentance – bought out of slavery, pronounced not guilty, picked out of the crowd, changing our outlook."[160] Hence, incarnational preaching does not dwell on abstractions but involves the concrete, the physical, and the visual.

Additionally, it must be stressed that Christ in his incarnation is not only an example of a methodology of preaching that is understood as entering the world of listeners and using language they understand, but he is also an example of an embodied content of preaching since he embodied what he taught. As the Word who became flesh, he not only taught about loving our enemies and about forgiveness but also showed how we should love our enemies and forgive them; he talked about prayer but also showed his disciples how to pray. Christ embodied in his actions the message presented in his words.

Christ in his incarnation is also an example of the right attitude and motivation in preaching. As Darrell Johnson notes, "The Word made flesh submits all his speaking to the word of the One who sent him. This suggests to me that the most basic motive in preaching is not to win the hearer (as crucial as that is) but to please the Sender."[161] Therefore, Christ's incarnation not only models a preaching method but also shows that truly incarnational preaching should always be done in an attitude of complete submission to God, with the aim of bringing glory to God alone.

Consequently, our preaching should be incarnational in the sense that it enters the world of our listeners, takes into consideration their ways of conceptualizing the world and their communication patterns, and uses images familiar to them. In order to be effective, preaching has to present messages about the holy God in terms that are comprehensible for humans by showing them the biblical image of God. In the process, preachers' lives become sermons as well since, as they follow Christ, they are called to embody what they preach by growing in Christlikeness in their characters.

---

160. Day, *Embodying the Word*, 63.
161. Johnson, Glory of Preaching, loc. 791 of 5481, Kindle.

1.2.7 Purpose of Preaching: Conformed by the Holy Spirit to the Image of Christ

The desired result of Trinitarian preaching is to see preachers and listeners who are being transformed by the Holy Spirit and conformed to the image of Christ by growing in his likeness, thereby showing that the speaking of God has become embodied in their lives. This conviction is deeply rooted in the nature of the word of God. As Johnson emphasizes, the word of God "is living and active, powerful and creative" and, as such, it "not only informs, it performs, it transforms."[162] Therefore, preaching should be characterized by a pastoral approach to listeners and a holistic understanding of God's transformation.

However, some authors – by suggesting practical methods of application which are not supported by proper theological reflection – create the impression that it is preachers who bring about this change through their use of various techniques.[163] Pasquarello, going even further in his analysis of modern trends in preaching, claims that there has been a shift from theological to technological preaching. In his opinion, contemporary preaching is largely deprived of its theological content and driven by a desire to improve its form and delivery through the use of innovative techniques and the use of multimedia.[164] The use of modern technology, to the extent that it helps listeners to better understand the word of God, may serve as an example of incarnational preaching that seeks to speak the language of the audience. However, preachers must always remember that true transformation is the work of the Holy Spirit, who acts through both the word of God and the preacher. Hence, according to Paul Wilson, preaching is "an event in which the congregation hears from God's Word, meets their Saviour, and is transformed by the power of the Holy Spirit to be the kind of community God intended."[165]

This transformative approach to preaching allows us to see our lives from the perspective of their ultimate purpose. This idea is well expressed by Grenz,

---

162. Johnson, loc. 280 of 5481.

163. For example, see Galli and Larson, *Preaching That Connects*, and Stanley and Lane, *Communicating for a Change*. In the Polish context, numerous preachers follow methods presented in books about public speaking for business presentations, where the presented methodology does not have any theological foundation. See Stączek, *Prezentacja Publiczna*.

164. Pasquarello, *Christian Preaching*, 41–49.

165. Wilson, *Practice of Preaching*, 5.

who says that "God created us a unity" and, as a result, "God's design for us is holistic," which means that his "intentions for each person extend to the totality of his or her being."[166] In their everyday lives, Christians are called to be living, visible examples of the embodiment of the speech of God. When Christ returns, we will see redemption completed, with not only every aspect of human nature but also the whole of creation transformed.

It is worth stressing that the Holy Spirit is the one who produces this transformation in people. Johnson believes that "expository preaching is not about getting a message out of the text; it is about inviting people into the text so that the text can do what only the text can do."[167] Therefore, preaching is not about increasing people's knowledge about God or the Bible but, mostly, about helping them in the process of transformation, which takes place when they listen and submit to the word of God. The ultimate purpose of this transformation is to be like Jesus, which is also the ultimate form of glorifying God.[168] Thus, God's revelation is ongoing since people being transformed by the Spirit become images of Christ to others and, one day, when Christ returns and their transformation is complete, they will become all that God intended.

Johnson, reflecting on this transformative dimension of preaching, grounds it in the transformative nature of God's speaking:

> When the living God speaks something happens . . . always.
> When the preacher speaks God's speech, God speaks . . . always.
> When the preacher speaks God's speech, something happens . . .
> always. For when the preacher speaks, the preacher is participating in the speaking of the great Preacher.[169]

Thus, preaching understood as participating in the speaking of God is only effective when preachers speak God's speech by faithfully proclaiming the word of God.

Hence, preaching is grounded in the understanding of God's Trinitarian nature. As such, it is biblical in its content because it conveys biblical

---

166. Grenz, *Moral Quest*, 263.

167. Johnson, Glory of Preaching, loc. 17.

168. This idea of the Holy Spirit using biblical preaching to transform believers supports the emphasis of Cognitive Linguistics on the cognitive and emotive power of language.

169. Johnson, Glory of Preaching, loc. 3904.

metaphors and images; it is theocentric in its context because people are created by God in his image and can find their place in God's redemptive history; it is incarnational in its focus because Christ is the perfect image of God; and it is pastoral in its purpose because the Holy Spirit uses the word of God to transform listeners into the likeness of the image of Christ. This means that Christians, as they are being transformed by the Holy Spirit into the image of Christ, are, in a sense, the means of God's revelation to the rest of creation through displaying Christlikeness. Since God's revelation can be understood as God's speech embodied in the creation of humans, in the incarnation of Christ, preaching, thanks to the work of the Holy Spirit, is the vehicle that makes it possible to embody the word of God in the lives of believers.

1.3 Chapter Summary

In conclusion, the notion of applying Cognitive Linguistics to preaching that uses biblical and non-biblical metaphors and images requires establishing a theological context that is rooted in God's revelation, which includes both the act of revelation and the means of revelation. For cognitivists, for whom the human being's embodied mind is the only tool of perception and conceptualization, the human perspective is the only perspective available. However, the idea of God's revelation challenges this concept, both expanding our human perspective and setting some boundaries on cognitivists' claims regarding the existence of an all-knowing mind. In fact, Cognitive Linguistics confirms the claims of Christian theology that people are incapable of verifying the existence of God and are unable to know him by relying on their own minds.

This chapter has demonstrated that even though Cognitive Linguistics, as a pragmatic approach, has its limitations, it is productive in understanding language and communication, including biblical language. Cognitive Linguistics is also helpful in articulating theological concepts, and this conviction is grounded in the fact that even though God's revelation originated in God, it took human form – for instance, God's creation of people in his image, the use of images in the Bible, and Christ who is the perfect image of the Father. Since all these acts of God's revelation convey God's truth in human terms, they can be studied and discussed using Cognitive Linguistics as a systematized theoretical framework for such an analysis.

Moreover, the means of God's revelation – as seen in the image of God, in biblical images, and in Christ – justify employing metaphors and images in sermons. Since God employed metaphors and images to reveal himself, we, as preachers, cannot escape using them in our sermons. Thus, in my discussion of the issue of the preacher's role and authority, I argued that preachers have the right to create metaphors and images to convey biblical revelation. This conviction is rooted in my understanding of preaching as being shaped by a holistic and Trinitarian understanding of God's revelation and also by Cognitive Linguistics' holistic perception of human beings that overcomes the distinctions between the rational, the emotional, and the physical. Thus, preachers are not merely to explain the ideas presented in the text, convey the emotions of the text, and use the text to create a sense of community, but they must also try to communicate the text in its entirety to human beings in their psychosomatic totality.

This chapter concluded with the presentation of a theological framework for preaching metaphors and images that is Trinitarian in nature. This Trinitarian character of preaching is based on the idea of God's embodied speech that is expressed in images. This was seen when God spoke his Word and created the world and made humans in his image, in the incarnation of Christ who is the perfect image of God and the Word embodied, and in the work of the Holy Spirit who conforms believers into the image of Christ, allowing them to become living embodiments of the word of God.

CHAPTER 2

Attempts to See the Unseen: Different Views on Metaphor and Conceptual Metaphor Theory

"We are in the midst of metaphormania. Only three decades ago the situation was just the opposite: poets created metaphors, everybody used them, and philosophers (linguists, psychologists, etc.) ignored them," observes Mark Johnson.[1] The perception of metaphor has changed – from metaphor being seen as pure embellishment that has illustrative and decorative value but carries no weight in an argument to being "pervasive in everyday life, not just in language but in thought and action."[2] In order to develop a coherent methodology of interpreting metaphors, preaching them, and using them in sermons, it is important to trace a process of forming metaphor theories and understanding the basic assumptions of Cognitive Linguistics in general and conceptual metaphor theory in particular.

Therefore, the purpose of this chapter is to present a linguistic justification for employing Cognitive Linguistics and, especially, conceptual metaphor theory for analyzing metaphors and images. This chapter has two parts. The first part is devoted to understanding the main developments in metaphor theory and, while surveying major approaches to metaphors, I will focus on three issues: a definition of metaphor, the relationship between the elements creating metaphor, and the meaning of metaphor. In the second part of this

---

1. Johnson, "Metaphor in the Philosophical Tradition," 3.
2. Lakoff and Johnson, *Metaphors We Live By*, 4.

chapter, these three issues will be used as signposts in the discussion about linguistic reasons why Cognitive Linguistics and especially conceptual metaphor theory – in comparison with other theories – enrich our understanding of metaphors.

2.1 Understanding Developments of Metaphor Theory

Before analyzing the main theories of metaphor and showing the unique contribution of Cognitive Linguistics and conceptual metaphor theory, it is helpful to survey historical developments in metaphor studies. The issue of metaphors has been discussed since as far back as Aristotle, who claimed that "if one wants to master speech, one must master metaphor."[3] Aristotle believed that metaphors play a vital role in both poetics and rhetoric since, in poetry, they give insights through artistic imitation (mimesis), while in rhetoric, they are needed to make arguments more persuasive.[4] Even though Aristotle valued metaphor as an important rhetorical device, he understood it as functioning on the level of words and "giving the thing a name that belongs to something else."[5] However, as pointed out by Ian Paul, Aristotle did not take into consideration the nature of language as diachronic, with both language and meaning undergo changes over time.[6]

Cicero, who had a similar perception of metaphor, claimed that "a metaphor is a brief similitude contracted into a single word."[7] He insisted that this was based on the idea of replacing one word with another and that there was some degree of resemblance between these two words. For Cicero, metaphor moved even further away from philosophy, becoming just a stylistic device.

Latin rhetoricians and medieval scholars such as Bede went even further than Aristotle in diminishing the role of metaphors by questioning their usefulness in serious philosophical arguments and claiming that they were merely illustrative and lacked the ability to convey facts. The tendency to stress the

---

3. Aristotle, cited in Paul, "Metaphor," 507. For more on Aristotle's views on metaphor, see Aristotle, *Poetics*.

4. Johnson, "Metaphor in the Philosophical Tradition," 5.

5. Aristotle, *Poetics*, 1457 b 7.

6. Paul, *Metaphor in Revelation*, 63.

7. Cicero, "On the Character of the Orator", 3.38.156–39.157.

significance of direct and univocal language is also evident in the approach of Thomas Hobbes, who argued that words used in their metaphorical meaning are unclear and unreliable and, consequently, tend to deceive instead of bringing clarity.[8] Hobbes believed that only literal language – as opposed to metaphorical language – is a proper vehicle for conveying thoughts and arguments precisely. According to this perspective, metaphor is considered a linguistic deviation which, if it is to be understood, needs to be paraphrased into literal language.[9]

Perception of metaphor changed further with the introduction of Kant's idea of dividing knowledge into two exclusive realms: "aesthetic" and "useful." Metaphor, which was seen as belonging to the first realm, was perceived as a mere decoration of the message, and its ability to convey a message was seriously questioned. However, Kant also points out that the uniqueness of metaphors lies in their capacity to evoke more ideas and meanings than literal statements could express. Thus, his contribution lies in his attempts to explain the originality of language that is based on the fact that people are able to use their creativity to conceive aesthetic ideas.[10] Later, Romantic poets – such as Johann Wolfgang von Goethe, Samuel Taylor Coleridge, and William Wordsworth – and the creator of psychoanalysis Sigmund Freud questioned the dominant role of human reason, shifting the focus from the intellectual to emotive dimensions.[11] Their findings paved the way for future research, both into human cognition and into the role of metaphor.

The attitude towards metaphors changed in the twentieth century, with the emergence of scholars such as Philip Wheelwright, Monroe Beardsley, Max Black, and Paul Ricoeur, who started analyzing metaphors on the level of whole sentences rather than words.[12] They did not perceive metaphors as decorations of literary language but, rather, as the dominant principle of thought that permeates all language. Richards and Black claimed that

---

8. Hobbes, *Leviathan*, 1.5.22 in Johnson, "Metaphor in the Philosophical Tradition," 12.

9. Johnson, "Metaphor in the Philosophical Tradition," 12.

10. Kant, *Critique of Judgment*, 157. For more on Kant's understanding of metaphor see Cazeaux, *Metaphor and Continental Philosophy*, 35–55.

11. Wilson-Kastner, *Imagery for Preaching*, 22–24. Wilson-Kastner describes, in more detail, the changes that took place during the eighteenth century in views about human beings, their mental processes, and their perceptions of the world.

12. Wheelwright, *Metaphor and Reality*; Black, "Metaphor," 63–82; Beardsley, "Metaphorical Twist," 105–122; Ricoeur, *Rule of Metaphor*.

metaphors often convey ideas that cannot be conveyed using any other ways of expression.[13] In their opinion, therefore, metaphors could not be paraphrased and reduced to literal statements. Paul Ricoeur, in particular, emphasized that a cognitive approach to metaphors was necessary since their comprehension takes place in the sphere of thoughts and ideas. He pointed out that the essence of a metaphor is a juxtaposition of the concepts based on the dissimilarity between them. Therefore, using Dan Stiver's description, there was a shift in perception from metaphor as ornamental to metaphor as cognitive.[14]

Bonnie Howe conducted a survey on traditional views of metaphors and found that failure to take into consideration the newest findings in human psychology and neurology – which change our perception of human cognition and language – resulted in theoretical, pragmatic, and linguistic deficiencies in these traditional approaches.[15] She gives a number of reasons, drawn from linguistics, that demonstrate the need for a new and more comprehensive approach. For instance, she points out that if metaphors were indeed examples of deviant uses of words that occur in the realm of linguistic expressions instead of thoughts, each metaphorical expression should convey a different metaphor. However, cognitivists have shown that one metaphor may lie behind a number of metaphorical expressions that are based on a single concept. For example, we use the idea of a journey to talk about life, marriage, career, education, and other important life events. Moreover, if metaphors are to be considered only as poetic or rhetorical devices, they should be rare in everyday communication and difficult to understand, which is not the case.[16]

Consequently, cognitive linguists such as Gilles Fauconnier, Mark Turner, Zoltán Kövecses, and Mark Johnson introduced a new approach to metaphor study.[17] In their opinion, metaphor is a result of a cognitive process, and human communication is largely metaphorical in nature. People think in images, and the choice of images they use reveals some aspects of their perception of reality, which is embodied and perspectival. Metaphors are not deviant elements of language or embellishments but, rather, an important

---

13. Stiver, *Philosophy of Religious Language*, 115.

14. Stiver, 113–115.

15. Howe, *Because You Bear This Name*, 55.

16. Howe, 55–58.

17. Fauconnier and Turner, *Way We Think*; Kövecses, *Metaphor: A Practical Introduction*; Johnson, *Body in the Mind*.

part of language and everyday communication, which is often understood intuitively and instantly.

While reflecting on the advantages of conceptual metaphor theory in comparison to other approaches, Kövecses stresses the fact that it is comprehensive, generalized in nature, and empirically tested. This theory is comprehensive since it takes into consideration a wide spectrum of issues related to metaphors, such as its relation to other figures of speech, acquisition of metaphors, cultural universality and variation, teaching metaphors, language acquisition, and metaphors in different forms of discourse. Even though other metaphor theories also touch upon these issues, only Cognitive Linguistics and conceptual metaphor theory do so in such a comprehensive manner.[18]

Conceptual metaphor theory is also generalized in nature because it "attempts to connect what we know about conceptual metaphor with what we know about the working of language, the working of human conceptual system, and the working of culture."[19] This theory considers findings in fields of science such as linguistics, philosophy, sociology, psychology, and neuroscience. As such, it provides new perspectives on the ways in which metaphorical meaning emerges and "challenges the traditional view that metaphorical language and thought is arbitrary and unmotivated."[20] Cognitivists assert that the idea of embodiment is one of the key distinctions between conceptual metaphor theory and traditional approaches.

Finally, conceptual metaphor theory has been empirically tested in various experiments that "have shown that conceptual view of metaphors is a psychologically viable one: that is, it has psychological reality" and, therefore, "can be seen as a key instrument not only in producing new words, but also in organizing human thought."[21] The newest neurological research has confirmed numerous notions that have been proposed by Cognitive Linguistics and conceptual metaphor theory, and these will be described in more detail in this book.

At this point, it is relevant to introduce the main metaphor theories – which include substitution theory, comparison theory, and interaction

---

18. Kövecses, *Metaphor: A Practical Introduction*, xii.
19. Kövecses, xii.
20. Kövecses, xii.
21. Kövecses, xii.

theory – and to discuss the contributions of scholars such as Ricoeur, Austin, and Searle. In this section, special emphasis will be placed on the definition of metaphor, the relationship between elements creating the metaphor, and its meaning. The purpose of this section is not only to provide an overview of key approaches to metaphor but also to show how conceptual metaphor theory advances our understanding of the definition of metaphors, the relationship between elements creating the metaphor, and the emergence of metaphorical meaning.

2.1.1 Substitution Theory

Substitution theory can be described as a model of metaphor that can be presented in the form A is B where A is C. For instance, in the metaphor "John is a fox," "John" is A, "fox" is B, and, since this metaphor actually means that "John is cunning," "cunning" is C. Thus, we have "John is cunning," which means that A is C. To understand this metaphor, it has to be paraphrased into literal language, and the word "fox" has to be substituted with the word "cunning." Max Black, in explaining this theory, says that "the focus of a metaphor, the word or expression having distinctly metaphorical use within a literal frame, is used to communicate a meaning that might have been expressed literally."[22] Even though Aristotle did not call his metaphor theory substitution theory, Black, analyzing Aristotle's approach, identifies it as a substitution since Aristotle defines metaphor as a borrowing based on using an improper or deviant word in place of the proper one. In order to understand the given metaphor, one has to find a set of similarities between the two elements creating the metaphor and find the proper word that allows reducing the meaning of metaphor to a literal phrase.

Consequently, according to this theory, metaphors serve a decorative purpose by adding variety to a discourse or making an argument more appealing and evocative. Black emphasizes that some metaphors may also function as "a species of catachresis," which he defines as "the use of a word in some new sense in order to remedy a gap in the vocabulary." He states that catachresis is "putting of new senses into old words."[23] During the communication pro-

---

22. Black, "Metaphor," 69.

23. Black, 69. Black points out that numerous metaphors cannot be identified as "catachresis" since they have their literal equivalents.

cess, when speakers discover a lack of suitable literal words or expressions and need to create a word for this purpose, they tend to use some words metaphorically. As this communication need is successfully fulfilled, this newly created metaphorical sense becomes literal.

Janet Soskice, criticizing substitution theory, points out that the insistence on reducing metaphors to literal meanings results in ignoring "a cognitive content not provided equally by the literal term for which the metaphor is the figurative replacement."[24] She observes that if this theory was accurate, it would mean that a process of creating new metaphors is nothing more than translating words and replacing them with another. She points out that the opposite is true since metaphors are often created and used when the presented ideas are impossible to describe or reduce to literal statements.[25]

2.1.2 Comparison Theory

If, according to a substitution theory, the metaphor A is B means that A is C, using a comparison theory, we would get A is like B in being C. Therefore, the metaphor "John is a fox" could be reduced to a literal statement, such as "John is like a fox in being cunning." Max Black states that according to a comparison view of metaphor, "a metaphor consists in the presentation of the underlying analogy or similarity."[26] It is based on identifying similarities between two entities that are supposed to be "alike" in some respects. In his opinion, this theory presents metaphors as "condensed or elliptical similes" and is "a special case of a substitution view.'"[27] Thus, again, the meaning of metaphors emerges when the similarity between two compared elements is identified and understood.

However, there are several weaknesses of this theory. For instance, Janet Soskice points out that this approach based on identifying similarities "fails to mark the fact that the good metaphor does not merely compare two antecedently similar entities but enables one to see similarities in what previously had been regarded as dissimilarities."[28] Richards, while making a similar

---

24. Soskice, Metaphor, 25.

25. Soskice, 25.

26. Black, "Metaphor," 71.

27. Black, 71. Soskice also agrees with Black in this respect. See Soskice, Metaphor, 26.

28. Soskice, Metaphor, 26.

observation, emphasizes the role of differences in metaphors that transform our understanding and give us new insights.[29]

One of the main problems of a comparison theory is the fact that similarity cannot always be easily or clearly identified. Black highlights that a comparison theory "suffers from vagueness that borders upon vacuity" since similarities between a metaphorical expression and a literal one are not "objectively given," but there are always some degrees of similarity.[30] Moreover, two entities can be similar in a number of ways, but this theory does not explain how to determine which similarity is relevant for understanding the metaphor.

At times, finding similarities is even more complicated and intuitive. John Searle questions the idea that metaphors are based on a comparison of two actually existing objects because, in the case of some metaphors, the entities compared do not exist, as in the statement "Sally is a dragon." In Searle's opinion, "though similarity often plays a role in the *comprehension* of metaphor, the metaphorical assertion is not necessarily an *assertion* of similarity".[31] He argues that a relationship between these two objects is not based on actual similarities but, often, on similarities that are believed to be true.

Similarly, I. A. Richards makes a distinction between sense metaphors and emotive metaphors, indicating that the former are based on similarity between sensations, whereas the latter focus on similarity between feelings.[32] Richards believes that the same statement, depending on its context, could be considered either a sense metaphor or an emotive metaphor. If somebody is called a pig, it may be because there is something in this person's appearance or behaviour that resembles pigs, in which case this is a sense metaphor. However, it is also possible that that even though there is no such resemblance, the person called a pig evokes emotions that are conventionally felt towards pigs.[33]

---

29. Richards, "Philosophy of Rhetoric," 48–62.
30. Black, "Metaphor," 72.
31. Searle, "Metaphor," 259 (emphasis original).
32. Bilsky, "I. A. Richards' Theory of Metaphor," 132.
33. Johnson, "Metaphor in the Philosophical Tradition," 26–27.

2.1.3 Interaction Theory

Adherents of an interaction theory of metaphor claim that if we have a metaphor in the form A is B, the meaning emerges as an interaction between A and B. Even though Max Black is considered the pioneer of interaction theory, he developed this theory standing on the shoulders of his predecessor, I. A. Richards. Therefore, before analyzing Black's approach, it is essential to touch upon the key aspects of Richards's theory.

Richards believes that "metaphor is the omnipresent principle of language."[34] Therefore, metaphor cannot be treated as ornamental or as a deviation of language. As human beings, we think in metaphors, and the more abstract the subject of our thinking, the more we reach for metaphors. In his theory of metaphor, Richards shows that in order to understand metaphor, one has to go beyond analyzing a literary utterance and how it works and see the utterance in relation to thoughts, emotions, and other activities of the mind, which is a step towards conceptual metaphor theory.

Richards defines metaphor as "two thoughts of different things active together and supported by a single word, or phrase, whose meaning is a resultant of their interaction." Metaphors are not to be seen in terms of "displacement of words" but as "a borrowing between and intercourse of *thoughts*, a transaction between contexts".[35] In order to systematize metaphor study, he introduces the terms "tenor" and "vehicle," which refer to the two halves of a metaphor. "The tenor is the main subject of a metaphor, while the vehicle is that to which the tenor is compared."[36] Consequently, he states that "co-presence of the vehicle and tenor results in a meaning (to be clearly distinguished from the tenor) which is not attainable without their interaction."[37] Therefore, the meaning of metaphor does not emerge as a result of finding similarities between the tenor and the vehicle but, rather, is an effect of the interaction between them.

Max Black, in developing his interaction theory, adopted some of I. A. Richards's conclusions. Black speaks of a metaphor as having two subjects: the principal subject and the subsidiary subject. For instance, in the metaphor

---

34. Richards, "Philosophy of Rhetoric," 50.
35. Richards, 51 (emphasis original).
36. Bilsky, "I. A. Richards' Theory of Metaphor," 132.
37. Richards, "Philosophy of Rhetoric," 55.

"man is a wolf," man is considered the principal subject, while wolf is the subsidiary subject. Each of these subjects has its own set of characteristics that do not necessarily reflect dictionary definitions about men and wolves and do not even have to be true. Instead, they express what the speaker believes to be true about men and wolves. Black argues that "for the metaphor's effectiveness is not that the commonplaces shall be true, but that they should be readily and freely evoked."[38] These systems of associated commonplaces make a metaphor function as a filter.

Consequently, Black explains, "The principal subject is 'seen through' the metaphorical expression – or, if we prefer, the principal subject is 'projected upon' the field of the subsidiary subject."[39] Thus, we use one system of commonplaces to organize our perception of another system. This interaction between two systems of associated commonplaces, depicted as filtering or projecting, results in the extension of meaning or "shifts in meaning of words belonging to the same family or system as the metaphorical expression."[40] This projection of two systems cannot be reduced to any literal comparison or paraphrase.

Black's theory, even though considered a landmark in the study of metaphors, was criticized and amended by other scholars. Some critics point out that metaphors are not only based on existing associated commonplaces but may allow seeing connotations that were not previously noticed. Further research by Lakoff, Johnson, Turner, and others offers a new perspective on metaphors.

2.1.4 Paul Ricoeur's Understanding of Metaphors and Imagination

Paul Ricoeur's research shed new light on the existing understanding of metaphors, and his approach was a significant step in the process that resulted in the view of metaphors presently held by Cognitive Linguists. In this section, I present the most important elements of Ricoeur's approach.

Paul Ricoeur developed his own approach to metaphors. Even though he stresses a great value of his predecessors' work and theories, he also points

---

38. Black, "Metaphor," 74.
39. Black, 75.
40. Black, 78.

out existing gaps in their proposals. He believed that these gaps could not be filled unless the whole study of metaphors moved into a new field of psychology and that, in order to understand how metaphors work, it was necessary to take into consideration issues such as imagination and feelings, which, in his opinion, were hinted at in many approaches but not emphasized as they should be.

Clarifying the importance of the imagination in understanding metaphors, Ricoeur's work builds on Kant's concept of "productive imagination as schematizing a synthetic operation" and identifies three steps in supplementing a semantic theory with a psychology of imagination.[41] The first step is "seeing" or gaining insight, which involves perceiving proximity and likeness of two ideas that used to be distant and unlike.[42] The second step is "the pictorial dimension" that reflects the figurative aspect of metaphor. In this step Ricoeur proposes "the development from schematization to iconic presentation," explaining that the aim of this iconic presentation is not to create mental pictures but to "display relations in depicting mode."[43] The third step, which is called "suspension," is "the moment of negativity brought by the image in the metaphorical process,"[44] and Mark Johnson calls this a "negative step" in which "primary reference to the everyday world is suspended, in order to make possible a new creative reference, a "remaking" of reality."[45] Old connections have to be lost to allow new connections to be established. Therefore, metaphors change our perception of reality and our way of seeing the world.

Ricoeur notes that even Aristotle's theory has some elements of what Ricoeur calls "the semantic role of imagination" because Aristotle describes metaphors as a work of resemblance based on contemplating similarities and, as a result, metaphors have the unique capacity of displaying their meaning before our eyes. Therefore, using Ricoeur's terminology, there is a suggestion of picturing function of metaphorical meaning.[46]

For Paul Ricoeur, the idea of semantic innovation is essential in explaining how metaphors function. He asserts:

---

41. Ricoeur, "Metaphorical Process," 147.
42. Ricoeur, 147–149.
43. Ricoeur, 150.
44. Ricoeur, 151.
45. Johnson, "Metaphor in the Philosophical Tradition," 40.
46. Ricoeur, "Metaphorical Process," 144.

> Metaphorical meaning does not merely consist of a semantic clash but of the *new* predicative meaning which emerges from the collapse of the literal meaning, that is, from the collapse of the meaning which obtains if we rely only on the common or usual lexical values of our words.[47]

In Ricoeur's opinion, the key factors to consider in understanding the whole process of collapse of meaning and the emergence of a new meaning are semantic distance and proximity – as he puts it, "things or ideas which were remote appear now as close."[48] According to Ricoeur, the element of the distance and closeness of two ideas in metaphors makes them deviant in some ways and grabs our attention so that we perceive a given statement as distinctive and metaphorical. He calls this deviance "semantic impertinence".[49]

In conclusion, it must be said that Ricoeur's contribution to metaphor theory lies in the fact that he perceives metaphors as cognitive phenomena. Ricoeur emphasizes it is not sufficient to rely only on philosophy or linguistics to explain how metaphors function. His belief that metaphors must be perceived in the context of human psychology, emotions, and imagination closely aligns his proposal with the Cognitive Linguistics approach. Moreover, he is not satisfied with the traditional understanding of metaphors that was based on similarity and stresses both similarity and dissimilarity.

2.1.5 Metaphors and the Performative Nature of Language

In this presentation of a historical overview of various understandings of metaphors, I now touch upon the issue of the performative nature of metaphors, which is yet another dimension of metaphors that plays a vital role in understanding metaphors and is especially important in the analysis of biblical metaphors and images. I begin with a brief explanation of the idea of the performative character of language.

As already observed, language does not only serve the purpose of exchanging information, but among its many other functions, it is performative in its

---

47. Ricoeur, 146 (emphasis original).

48. Ricoeur, 147.

49. Ricoeur explains semantic impertinence by referring to the notion of "spilt reference," which assumes that "language is opened up by metaphor, and the phrase or sentence now has two meanings, the literal and the metaphorical, and these each have a corresponding reference, the literal and metaphorical." Ricoeur, 147. See also Paul, "Metaphor and Exegesis," 395.

nature. Stephen Wright shares three convictions about the nature of language. First, he points out that all humans "are *embedded* in language, yet have power to shape it," actively using it and creating new word associations.[50] Second, Wright says that "words do have meaningful reference beyond themselves to a 'real' world, but also shape our perception of it."[51] Words not only point a language user to a language system but also to the reality beyond it. Words and sentences evoke emotions, bring back memories, inspire new thoughts, and create pictures in people's minds. Wright's third conviction about language is that "*meaning is never final*, but *nonetheless words have effects*."[52]

The question of what effects words have has interested many philosophers and linguists. Attempting to answer this question, J. L. Austin distinguishes between three types of acts that can take place in an act of speaking. First, locutionary acts, which are acts of saying something or uttering a sentence. However, when a sentence is uttered, a second act is performed, namely, an illocutionary act, such as informing, asking a question, warning, or making a promise. Thus, the illocutionary act is what a person does in saying something or performing the locutionary act of making an utterance. Since words can have effects, illocutionary acts sometimes produce a third kind of act – effects that are called perlocutionary acts.[53] Perlocutionary acts are the consequences of locutionary and illocutionary acts – for example, somebody has been informed, comforted, warned, married, or received a promise. Austin distinguishes between the locutionary act, which "has *meaning*; the illocutionary act which has certain *force* in saying something; [and] the perlocutionary act, which is the *achieving* of certain *effects* by saying something."[54] Accordingly, words have both a performative capability and consequences.

Building on Austin's model, John Searle developed his theory of speech acts where, in defining metaphors, he both questions the common distinction

---

50. Wright, *Alive to the Word*, 40 (emphasis original).

51. Wright, 41–42.

52. Wright, 43 (emphasis original). Wright develops creative tension between two seemingly opposite, but complementary, convictions about the nature of meaning that explain the dynamics of language. He refers to Jacques Derrida, who believes in an endless deferral of meaning. See Derrida, *Writing and Difference* and *Of Grammatology*. He also notes that John R. Searle emphasizes that the effects of words on society can be seen in everyday life. See Searle, *Expression and Meaning*.

53. Austin, *How to Do Things*, 109.

54. Austin, 121 (emphasis original).

between literal meaning and metaphorical meaning and distinguishes between sentence meaning and the speaker's utterance meaning. Searle argues that "whenever we talk about metaphorical meaning of a word, expression, or sentence, we are talking about what a speaker might utter it to mean, in a way that departs from what the word, expression, or sentence actually means."[55] In his opinion, a literal utterance determines a set of truth conditions relative to a particular context. In this case, sentence meaning and speaker's utterance meaning are the same, and the truth conditions of an utterance are determined by the truth conditions of a sentence.[56] However, this is not the case when it comes to metaphorical utterances. Thus, Searle emphasizes, "The basic principle on which all metaphor works is that the utterance of an expression with its literal meaning and corresponding truth conditions can, in various ways that are specific to metaphor, call to mind another meaning and corresponding set of truth conditions."[57]

These observations are significant in interpreting biblical metaphors since many of these metaphors are not just locutionary acts but also illocutionary and perlocutionary. If someone says, "You have been washed from your sins," "You have been adopted to God's family," or "You are born again," these utterances are performative in nature and have consequences, such as transforming people's perception of themselves or changing their status or, possibly, their lifestyle. According to Austin and Searle, these words change reality. Thus, when people confess their sins, they are forgiven. When they become Christians, they are born again and become part of God's family. This fact changes the way they view themselves since they gain a new identity.

Austin and Searle emphasize the performative function of language with its extralinguistic dimension. Not only do speakers' utterances have extralinguistic effects but, in order to understand them, it is necessary to be aware of non-linguistic background assumptions shared by the speaker and the conditions of the utterance. Therefore, progress in metaphor study can be observed since scholars are no longer interested only in individual words or even sentences but also in the speaker's utterance meaning and the conditions of the utterance.

---

55. Searle, *Expression and Meaning*, 77.

56. Searle, 79, 81.

57. Searle, 85.

The chapters that follow will show that Cognitive Linguistics advances metaphor studies by placing metaphors in the context of human cognition, embodiment, perception, and cultural background. Cognitivists show how metaphors not only express ideas but also have the power to shape ideas. In addition, they have a performative function. This is seen, for example, in political discourse, where – as described by George Lakoff – they metaphors shape identities and values, and encourage actions such as participation in war.[58]

2.2 Understanding Basic Assumptions of Cognitive Linguistics and Conceptual Metaphor Theory

In discussing different approaches to metaphor theory, I analyzed issues such as the definition of metaphor, the meaning of metaphor, and similarity of elements creating metaphors. In this section, the same topics will be studied from the perspective of conceptual metaphor theory in order to show its unique perspective and contribution to studies of metaphor.

2.2.1 Definition of Conceptual Metaphors

Cognitive linguists present their own perspective on recognizing metaphors and distinguishing them from literal language. Lakoff and Turner define the idea of what is metaphorical by starting with the non-metaphorical and stating that a concept is non-metaphorical if it is "understood and structured in its own terms – without making use of structure imported from a completely different conceptual domain."[59] Therefore, the word "dog" is not metaphorical since it does not utilize any other concepts, but a "loyal dog" is a metaphorical expression since the dog is described in terms of human characteristics. For cognitive linguists, most of human thinking and language is metaphorical since explaining one concept in terms of another is a common feature of human communication. For instance, even simple expressions such as "to get on the bus" are metaphorical. In this expression, English speakers use the preposition "on," conceptualizing the bus as a moving platform or board,

---

58. Lakoff, *Moral Politics*.
59. Lakoff and Turner, *More than Cool Reason*, 57.

whereas Polish speakers would say "wsiąść do autobusu" (get into the bus), conceptualizing the bus as a container.

Hence, proponents of a cognitive approach to metaphors define conceptual metaphors as "understanding and experiencing one kind of thing in terms of another" or "conceptualizing one domain of experience in terms of another."[60] For example, people often talk about life in terms of journeys, theories are conceptualized in terms of buildings, and moral decline is described as a disease. The Psalmist utilizes the metaphor of life as a journey when he says, "Blessed is everyone who fears the Lord, who walks in His ways." (Ps 128:1). The apostle Paul talks about false teaching that spreads "like gangrene" (2 Tim 2:17). In each of these cases, one idea is understood or perceived in terms of another.

2.2.2 Similarity and Cross-Domain Correlations

One of the issues widely discussed in metaphor theory is the question of the kind of relationship between the elements creating the metaphor: Is this relationship based on similarity or dissimilarity, comparison or substitution, or maybe interaction between two elements? Cognitive Linguistics sheds new light on this issue and changes our perception of metaphors. Since metaphors are conceptual phenomena and are based on conceptualization of one domain in terms of another, it is not similarity between elements that is essential but cross-domain correlations that result in perceived similarity between domains. This similarity is based not on the meaning of the words making up the metaphors but is largely grounded in human embodiment and experience.

As Bonnie Howe stresses, "A significant part of our conceptual system is nonmetaphorical. In fact, metaphorical understanding appears to be grounded in nonmetaphorical understanding."[61] It is so because our conceptual system is experiential in nature and largely based on our bodily experiences. Kövecses defines conceptual metaphor theory as "a view of metaphor in which the metaphorical meaning construction is simply a matter of how our metaphors

---

60. Lakoff and Johnson, *Metaphors We Live By*, 5; Kövecses, *Where Metaphors Come From*, 2. As pointed out by Kövecses, some scholars, instead of speaking of understanding, prefer to use terms such as construing, conceiving, or conceptualizing. Kövecses, *Metaphor: A Practical Introduction*, 8. For a critical assessment of conceptual metaphor theory, see McGlone, "What Is the Explanatory Value?," 109–126.

61. Howe, *Because You Bear This Name*, 60.

arise from correlations in experience (for correlation metaphors) or from similarities between experiential domains (for resemblance metaphors)."[62] He provides examples for how an experience of a sudden feeling of increasing body heat can be the experiential basis for conceptualizing love, anger, sexual pleasure, physical effort, busyness, or psychological pressure.[63] We see this kind of conceptualization in Paul's warning to the Corinthians that "it is better to marry than to burn with passion." (1 Cor 7:9).

Resemblance metaphors are based on similarities between experiential domains, which means that, for example, a person may correlate an experience of a long and uncomfortable journey with going through a marriage crisis since both include the idea of moving, passing time, destinations, effort, and difficulties. As a result, the metaphor MARRIAGE IS A JOURNEY is formed. In this case, the similarities perceived are structural similarities between two domains, which means that while talking about two remote ideas or experiences, people see some patterns of resemblance between them in terms of their structure.

George Lakoff wrestled with the problem of why some metaphors in the form X is Y work and are understood, whereas others do not make sense to their listeners. He concluded that this was mostly due to the neural bindings of the human brain. When people conceptualize their experiences, this activates connections between different parts of their brains, and when the neurons that conceptualize a source domain fire, a group of target domain neurons also fire.

As a result, a metaphor is formed or comprehended, and we are able to see connections between two different ideas.[64] To sum up, it must be stressed that conceptual metaphors are not based on similarity of compared elements – such as tenor and vehicle – but on correlations in experience and similarities between experiential domains.

2.2.3 Meaning of Conceptual Metaphors

For centuries, scholars have debated whether metaphors can be reduced to literal propositional statements without losing their meaning. As shown

---

62. Kövecses, *Where Metaphors Come From*, 1.

63. Kövecses, 21.

64. Lakoff, "Neural Theory," 17–19. See Kövecses, *Where Metaphors Come From*, 22.

earlier, the most recent arguments seem to uphold the idea of irreducibility of metaphors. This issue of conveying the meaning of metaphors in propositional statements is crucial for biblical interpretation and preaching since it affects preachers' methodology and the form of their sermons. As stressed in the previous chapter, the preacher's task is communicating biblical metaphors and images. Preachers can even create new metaphors and images to convey the meaning of both metaphorical and non-metaphorical passages. However, the question remains: Is it possible to stay true to a metaphorical text and present it in the form of a non-metaphorical, propositional statement?

Traditional theories of metaphor propose that the meaning of metaphors emerges from substitution, comparison, or the interaction of elements creating the metaphor. Paul Ricoeur speaks of semantic innovation and existing tension between similarity and dissimilarity within the metaphor. Cognitive Linguistics offers a unique perspective on the issue of the meaning of metaphors and their reducibility to literal statements.[65]

According to conceptual metaphor theory, meaning does not emerge as a result of substitution of words, finding similarities between compared words that create the metaphor, or the interaction between these words It is not a matter of words, sentences, or even just language; rather, meaning resides in the sphere of thoughts and concepts and is the result of understanding one concept in terms of another. Nevertheless, these concepts do not exist in a vacuum. Human communication is largely based on a strategy of exchanging concepts, and conceptual metaphors are not the only example of the numerous means of communication that people utilize to interact with each other. Another factor that helps to understand metaphors and establish their

---

65. In their studies on meaning, Lakoff and Turner engage in a discussion with the Literal Meaning Theory, proving it false from a cognitive point of view. The Literal Meaning Theory can be summarized in two claims: the Autonomy Claim and the Objectivist Claim. The Autonomy Claim assumes that all conventional language is, by nature, semantically autonomous and, consequently, cannot be metaphorical. The Objectivist Claim is based on the presupposition that there is an objective reality that is autonomously structured in a way that does not depend on a human mind and human conceptual systems. Lakoff and Turner, *More than Cool Reason*, 117. For a more detailed summary of various spinoffs of the Literal Meaning Theory that are critiqued by Lakoff and Turner, see Lakoff and Turner, 120–127. As an alternative to the Literal Meaning Theory, Lakoff and Turner claim that many, but not all, conventional concepts are semantically autonomous, grounded in our bodily and social experience and neither independent from our minds non objectively given. They also believe that metaphorical expressions are based on non-metaphorical concepts. For instance, the metaphor "death is night" is based on a non-metaphorical conventional concept of night. Lakoff and Turner, 113–114.

meaning is their context, because they are usually used as a part of a larger discourse or even a communicative situation. Fauconnier argues that language "does not 'represent' meaning, it prompts for the construction of meaning in particular contexts with particular cultural models and cognitive resources."[66] Words evoke associations and memories of life experiences, and are access points to knowledge stored in our brains. John Sanders believes that "meaning construction is not autonomous (independent), because it is integrated with other forms of knowledge."[67] It is not mind-free and non-perspectival but, rather, dependent on our senses and bodily structure. Consequently, in order to establish the meaning of an utterance, listeners need to do more than just understand the meaning of words and grammatical structures. Sanders points out that these elements only "prompt for the construction of meaning, but meaning is not simply the sum of the parts of speech."[68]

Sanders also claims that "meaning is grounded in usage and experience" and is flexible and dynamic.[69] Changes in our environment, social situations, and culture find their expression in changes in language. Everyday terms such as "phone" keep evolving, affecting the ways we understand them. As an example of the construction of meaning, Sanders cites a few instances of the usage of the word "safe": "The child is safe," "The beach is safe," and "The shovel is safe." Even though the same word is used in all three sentences and all of them have the same grammatical form and syntax, the word "safe" has different meanings in each instance because, for instance, the child might not be safe in the same way the beach is safe or the shovel is safe.[70] Understanding these statements depends on their context, experience, and awareness that there are many possible ways of using the word "safe."

---

66. Fauconnier, "Cognitive Linguistics," 2.

67. Sanders, *Theology in the Flesh*, loc. 327 of 5234, Kindle.

68. Sanders, loc. 2084–2094. At this point, it needs to be stressed that even though cognitive linguists devote a lot of attention to analyzing speech utterances that take place in real time and space, their principles are also applicable to studying writings, even ancient ones. Kövecses, Lakoff, Turner, and others have shown how to apply Cognitive Linguistics to the analysis of various literary genres such poetry, narrative, political discourse, humour, and commercials.

69. Sanders, *Theology in the Flesh*, loc. 338, Kindle.

70. Sanders, loc. 226–227 of 5234.

2.2.4 Importance of Embodiment

One of the most important notions in conceptual metaphor theory is the idea of embodied minds. Earlier linguistics theories were only concerned with thoughts because the human mind was perceived as autonomous. Conceptual metaphor theory presents a more holistic view, where the human mind is seen as being a part of the human body that plays a crucial role in our perception and conceptualizing of the world around. It is because "the mind is not merely embodied, but embodied in such a way that our conceptual systems draw largely upon the commonalities of our bodies and of the environments we live in" and, as a result of our embodiment, "much of a person's conceptual system is either universal or widespread across languages and cultures."[71]

Mark Johnson goes even further. He does not talk about putting the mind back in the body but explains the idea of an embodied mind by talking about "putting the body back into the mind."[72] He argues that our bodily experiences and interactions with the world shape our minds, our thinking, and conceptual systems. For example, our perception of the world is largely dependent on our senses. We hear a certain range of sounds and see a certain range of colours. Some smells cannot be detected by humans, although other animals can detectable them. Unlike a jellyfish, we have a front and back, and so we talk about things being in front of us or behind us. Since we have faces, we talk about facing problems and having meetings face to face.

Numerous biblical metaphors and Christian practices reflect the idea of embodiment, such as the biblical metaphor that depicts forgiveness as being washed or cleansed. For example, "Be baptized, and wash away your sins" (Acts 22:16). This metaphorical expression is based on the conventional metaphor IMMORALITY IS IMPURITY or SIN IS IMPURITY and, consequently, the removal of sin is pictured in terms of washing even though it is impossible to wash our souls with water. Consequently, due to our embodiment, physical acts such as baptism become powerful and meaningful images of the internal transformation taking place. We use the metaphor SIN IS BURDEN, and so we talk about Christ taking our sins on himself and carrying them on the cross, which again reflects our own embodiment.

---

71. Lakoff and Johnson, *Philosophy in the Flesh*, 27.
72. Johnson, *Body in the Mind*, xxxvi.

Similarly, the Lord's Supper is a physical act that is grounded in embodiment. Even though we eat bread and drink wine, we believe that this action means much more. As Zoltán Kövecses explains, the idea of communion is based on the metaphor IDEAS ARE FOOD. Kövecses demonstrates that since THE BODY AND BLOOD OF CHRIST ARE THE BREAD AND THE WINE and GOD IS THE WORD, we conceptualize the Lord's Supper in terms of a metaphor: THE EMBODIMENT OF THE WORD (IDEAS) IS FOOD (BREAD AND WINE). Thus, he concludes that since "God is the Word and Jesus is the embodiment of God's Word, we symbolically partake in both Jesus and God in the form of the food during the Holy Communion."[73]

Given that there are numerous views on the Lord's Supper – including transubstantiation, consubstantiation, spiritual presence, and a symbolic approach – understanding the meaning of this event in terms of IDEAS ARE FOOD and THE EMBODIMENT OF THE WORD OF GOD IS OUR FOOD may not solve all controversies, but it could serve as a way of establishing common ground between various groups of Christians and as a starting point for further discussion.

Understanding the idea of embodiment is essential in rebutting the accusation that Cognitive Linguistics favours pure subjectivity in the ways in which it describes the world. As some critics say it really cannot define what is true or not or objectively describe reality, since everyone can see this reality differently. Surprisingly, the notion of embodiment actually "constrains the way we think" since, as stressed by John Sanders, people possessing "normal vision see the same ball, box, or a cat" and they "do not have different perceptions of my brown and black cat sitting on the mat."[74] This is the case because cognitivists insist that "there is truth as correspondence to reality, but it is truth according to our embodied sensory and cognitive capacities."[75] Thus, even though embodiment allows for some differences in perception or perspective depending on individuals, it also limits those differences.

Consequently, conceptual metaphor theory seems a particularly suitable instrument to analyze biblical metaphors that are a means of God's revelation. The idea of the embodied mind means that our conceptual system is

---

73. Kövecses, "Heart of the Matter," 99–100.
74. Sanders, *Theology in the Flesh*, loc. 1550 of 5234, Kindle.
75. Sanders, loc. 1618 of 5234.

shaped by our bodily make up and our senses. This concept is also essential for preaching since this eradicates traditional dichotomies between the mind and the body, and between the intellect and emotions, and allows preachers to perceive their listeners more holistically as psychophysical unities and preach to them accordingly without attempting to separately address their intellect and emotions. Moreover, in the process of communication, the idea of embodiment heightens preachers' awareness of the necessity of taking into consideration human bodies as a crucial factor in listeners' perception of the world and of the sermons themselves.

2.3 Chapter Summary

The purpose of this chapter was to show how Cognitive Linguistics and especially conceptual metaphor theory are productive in metaphor studies and how they advance our understanding of metaphors and language. Conceptual metaphor theory does not just rely on its findings in the area of linguistics but gives a holistic view of metaphors that is based on the newest research in psychology, sociology, neuroscience, and other sciences. This theory, while presenting the issue of metaphors, does not focus only on words, sentences, or even language but on conceptual structure and human cognition that is largely shaped by our embodiment. Metaphors are conceptual before they eventually become linguistic expressions.

As opposed to the traditional understanding, adherents of conceptual metaphor theory do not view metaphors as decorations of language but as permeating language, which is considered largely metaphorical. In defining the meaning of metaphors, adherents of conceptual metaphor theory stress that a metaphor emerges from understanding one concept in terms of another, and they emphasize that this understanding is grounded in our bodily experiences and cultural perceptions.

Traditional views of metaphors often tend to focus on individual metaphors and fail to identify general principles that explain how metaphors are related to each other. For instance, they do not explain the reason we use the single expression "to make our way" when talking about unrelated topics such as life, careers, relationships, sports, or education. Conceptual metaphor theory is based on the Generalization Commitment that seeks to recognize general principles governing language, and it also acknowledges the fact that, as human beings, we conceptualize many ideas in terms of a journey because one concept may be used to create numerous metaphorical expressions.[76]

Therefore, Cognitive Linguistics and conceptual metaphor theory are not merely additional tools to be used in studying metaphors and images or supplements to other, more traditional, approaches. On the contrary, utilizing Cognitive Linguistics requires a complete paradigm shift in relation to our understanding of language since language that includes metaphors works conceptually and is rooted in our bodily experience.

---

76. Howe, *Because You Bear This Name*, 98.

CHAPTER 3

New Ways of Seeing the Unseen: Understanding the Key Elements of Cognitive Linguistics and Applying Them to the Interpretation of Biblical Texts

In this chapter, I summarize the basic assumptions of Cognitive Linguistics and conceptual metaphor theory and then focus only on those elements that are essential for developing principles of interpretation of biblical texts and biblical metaphors. Thus, the purpose of this chapter is not only to present the key elements of Cognitive Linguistics but also to demonstrate – with biblical examples – how these can be productive in biblical interpretation.

I will begin my discussion with a general presentation of the model of the conceptual world and show how we, as humans, conceptualize reality in terms of concepts. Next, I will describe notions of categories, prototypes, and frames in the context of Cognitive Linguistics, showing how their application to biblical studies provides preachers with additional tools for textual analysis, organizes the whole process, and offers a better and more systematized way to understand the world of the original readers. Even though numerous scholars have undertaken the task of applying Cognitive Linguistics to biblical interpretation, the novelty of my approach lies in introducing the idea of operations of categories and prototypes that we can distinguish in the Bible.

In the final section, I will present major elements of metaphor structure that will help in understanding the methodology of analysis of biblical metaphors. This section will conclude with the notion of levels of metaphor that will help in developing a sermon structure, as demonstrated in chapter 5.

3.1 Model of the Conceptual World

Dirven and Radden express one of the key convictions of Cognitive Linguistics – that has been stated before – that language "resides, not in dictionaries, but in minds of the speakers of that language."[1] As I asserted in the previous chapter, meaning, which goes beyond encyclopedic definitions, is dynamic, actively constructed in the process of communication, and depends on our senses, embodied experiences, culture, and communicative situation. It is not a matter of single words or sentences but involves thoughts and concepts. Therefore, in order to comprehend the mechanisms of language, we must begin by paying attention to the human conceptual system and the way it finds expression in linguistic signs that we use. Thus, before analyzing the key concepts that serve as the building blocks of conceptual metaphor theory, it is prudent to begin with a closer look at a general model of the conceptual world and the interconnections between human conceptualizers and linguistic signs.[2]

Driven and Radden begin with the human conceptualizer who interacts with the world and, on the basis of these interactions, develops concepts and categories (Diagram 1). They define a concept as "a person's idea of what something in the world is like" and point out that "concepts can relate to single entities such as the concept I have of my mother or they can relate to a whole set of entities, such as the concept 'vegetable.'"[3] They observe that the concept of a vegetable is much broader than the concept of a mother and that it creates a category of different elements, such as cucumbers, potatoes, carrots, and so on. This notion of categorization will be described in more detail in the next section but, at this point, it must be stressed that categorization is

---

1. Dirven and Radden, "Cognitive Basis of Language," 13.

2. This model was offered by Dirven and Radden, "Cognitive Basis of Language," 14. But for the purpose of this book, I have combined the version suggested by Dirven and Radden with the one offered by van Wolde, "Wisdom, Who Can Find It?," 1.

3. Dirven and Radden, "Cognitive Basis of Language," 13–14.

an important element of our perception. It is our method of interacting with the world and understanding the complexity of our reality.

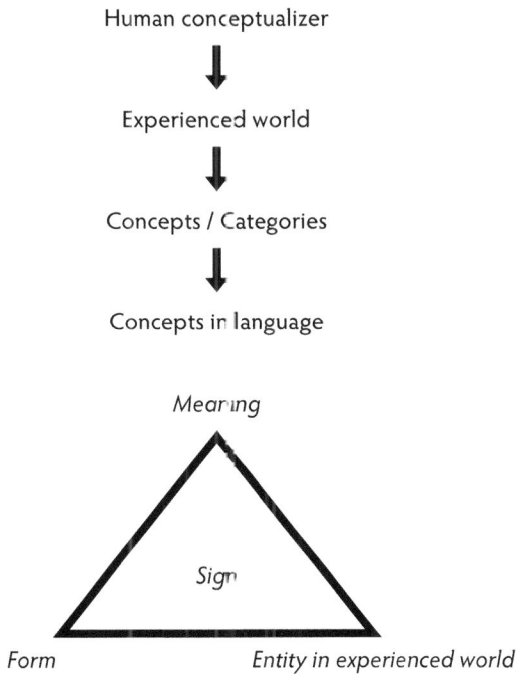

Human conceptualizer

↓

Experienced world

↓

Concepts / Categories

↓

Concepts in language

Meaning

Sign

Form   *Entity in experienced world*

Diagram 1. Model of the conceptual world

Thus, our perception of the world results in our developing concepts and conceptual categories that find expression in language; and these concepts and conceptual categories then become linguistic signs and linguistic categories. Every sign has a meaning that is identical with a concept in language, has its linguistic form, and "relates to some entity in our experienced world."[4]

This model shows that reality is not objectively given, but our linguistic expressions that describe reality are shaped by our perception and our individual ways of experiencing and conceptualizing the world.

---

4. Dirven and Radden, "Cognitive Basis of Language," 14.

3.2 Categories, Prototypes, and Frames

When applying Cognitive Linguistics to interpreting biblical texts, preachers encounter notions of categories, prototypes, and frames. Cognitivists argue that since categories, prototypes, and frames serve the purpose of organizing our knowledge of the world, they are helpful tools to analyze the biblical world. Therefore, I begin my discussion on utilizing Cognitive Linguistics in biblical studies with these notions.

3.2.1 Categories

In our everyday lives we may not be aware that categorization is an inevitable factor among every living organism since every creature, in order to survive, needs to be able to make distinctions such as food and not food, safe and not safe, enemy and not enemy.[5] In the case of humans, even the simplest decision, such as going shopping, includes numerous categorizations, such as the choice of a shop, product, and price. In a supermarket, we categorize fruits, vegetables, meat, dairy, beverages, kitchen supplies, products that are edible and inedible, healthy and unhealthy, tasty and disgusting, cheap and expensive.

As John Taylor notes, the human "ability to function in the physical and social world depends on elaborate categorizations of things, processes, persons, and social relations." The reason we categorize is "to reduce the complexity of the environment."[6] In order to survive and make daily decisions, we need to organize our world and put some entities in the same groups or categories. Eleanor Rosch explains this phenomenon by saying "that the task of category systems is to provide maximum information with the least cognitive effort." She also states that this is accomplished when "categories map the perceived world structure as closely as possible."[7]

Most of the time, our categorizing is done subconsciously and automatically. Without much thought or effort, we categorize entities and phenomena as "cars and animals," "smiles and frowns," "important phone calls and unimportant phone calls," "red and white," and so on. Lakoff and Johnson explain that this ability is rooted in our biological makeup and our brain structure. We are embodied neural beings, equipped with senses to gather

---

5. Taylor, "Categories and Concepts," 163.

6. Taylor, 163.

7. Rosch, "Principle of Categorization," 27–48.

information from the outside world. Thus, our perception is shaped by our senses and neural bindings, which can be seen, for example, in the way we see and distinguish colours – we see them even though they do not exist as physical entities.[8]

When addressing the whole issue of categorization, we need to understand how our brains identify different categories and determine what members or items to should be included in each of these categories. As Mark Johnson observes, since Aristotle, a classical category view has been prevalent and was based on identifying "necessary and sufficient conditions which specify the properties shared by all and only members of the category."[9] This view is based on several assumptions; for instance, categories have rigid boundaries, the human mind is disembodied and our bodies have no influence on the way we perceive the world, there is an objective reality and a correct way of interpreting it, and all people conceptualize the world in the same way.[10]

Over a period of time, however, various scholars have found this approach insufficient. Ludwig Wittgenstein points out that there are no rigid boundaries for the word "game" since there are no common necessary and sufficient features that exist equally in all games.[11] Therefore, he came up with notions of family resemblance, extendable boundaries, graded categories, and central and non-central members of a category. While observing that there is a shared resemblance among all members of a category, Wittgenstein notes that the boundaries are not always clear, as in the case of the category "old," which is graded. He also notes that some members of a given category display closer family resemblance than others and, in this respect, are more central.[12]

---

8. Lakoff and Johnson, *Philosophy in the Flesh*, 27.

9. Johnson, *Body in the Mind*, xi. For more on the traditional understanding of categories, see Croft and Cruse, *Cognitive Linguistics*, 76–77.

10. Lakoff, *Women, Fire, and Dangerous Things*, 9.

11. Wittgenstein, *Philosophical Investigations*, 66–71. Another example is the notion of "a bachelor," discussed in Taylor, "Categories and Concepts," 172, and Lakoff, *Women, Fire, and Dangerous Things*, 69–71.

12. Further research that broadened perspectives on the notion of categories was conducted by J. L. Austin, who focused on polysemy, Lofti Zadeh, who studied categories with fuzzy boundaries, Brent Berlin and Paul Kay, who conducted research on categories of colours, and Roger Brown, who focused on basic-level categories. For more information on the history of the development of categories, see Lakoff, *Women, Fire, and Dangerous Things*, 12–55.

3.2.2 Prototypes

Wittgenstein's new understanding of categories led to developing the prototype theory that was proposed by Eleanor Rosch. According to Rosch,
categories are not created on the basis of the shared necessary and sufficient
features of their members but are structured around good examples – that
is, a category's most typical members that are called prototypes.[13] It appears
that when categorizing, people view "certain members of a category as more
representative of the category than other members."[14] While all members of
a given category in some ways resemble the prototype, this resemblance may
vary and they do not need to have a set of common characteristics.

Consequently, as John Taylor explains, "prototype categories have an internal graded structure, with some members being more central, more typical,
than others."[15] The category boundaries can be fuzzy, as in the case of categories such as old, tall, or pretty, or they can be more rigid, as in categories such
as birds, furniture, or food. It is interesting to note that when people living in
the Western hemisphere are asked about a typical fruit, they usually name an
apple or pear, a typical bird is a sparrow or robin, and a hammer is the most
frequently mentioned prototype in the tool category, which indicates that
humans think in terms of categories that are built around prototypes.[16] On
the other hand, while building their categories around prototypical members, people are aware that there are some members of the category that are
non-prototypical – for example, a chicken or an ostrich are non-prototypical
members of the bird category.

Building on Brent Berlin's conclusions regarding basic-level categories and
animal and plant naming, Eleanor Rosch also observes that, in a taxonomic

---

13. Rosch, "Principle of Categorization," 27–48.

14. Lakoff, *Women, Fire, and Dangerous Things*, 41.

15. Taylor, "Categories and Concepts," 164.

16. Summarizing prototype theory, Barbara Lewandowska-Tomaszczyk, a Polish scholar,
says: "(a) Prototypical categories exhibit degrees of typicality; not every member is equally
representative for a category; (b) Prototypical categories are blurred at the edges; (c) Prototypical
categories cannot be defined by means of a single set of criteria (necessary and sufficient)
attributes; (d) Prototypical categories exhibit a family resemblance structure, or more generally,
their semantic structure takes the form of a radial set of clustered and overlapping readings."
Lewandowska-Tomaszczyk, "Polysemy, Prototypes, and Radial Categories," 145.

hierarchy, prototypes appear on the basic level, in the middle of the hierarchy as shown in the example.[17]

SUPERORDINATE	FURNITURE
BASIC LEVEL	CHAIR
SUBORDINATE	KITCHEN CHAIR

Diagram 2. Category levels

It seems that our knowledge of the world is organized mostly on the basic level and that elements appearing at this level take the least amount of time to identify and to create a single mental image, are most easily learned by children and second-language learners, are most neutral, and exhibit the most number of attributes of the remaining category members.[18]

Lakoff points out that some categories have a radial structure, which means that there is a central prototype and "conventionalized variations on it that cannot be predicated by general rules."[19] He gives the example of the category of a mother, with its numerous culturally conditioned subcategories, such as a stepmother, adoptive mother, foster mother, birth mother, biological mother, surrogate mother, unwed mother, and genetic mother.[20]

It appears that prototypes are also culturally conditioned. If somebody asked Polish people about typical food they eat for lunch, which is the main meal of the day, they would say potatoes. However, if the same question were asked of Chinese people, they would probably say rice. Moreover, even within one particular culture, we can distinguish several kinds of prototypes. Typical-case prototypes are used in situations where we do not have any specific contextual knowledge about a category member – for instance, we may say, "He is a typical husband." Ideal-case prototypes are expressions of our ability to evaluate different category members and compare them with others, as when we say, "He is an ideal husband." Social stereotypes express

---

17. Rosch, "Principle of Categorization," 7. For more detailed criteria about the distinction between subordinate-level, basic-level, and superordinate-level categories, see Croft and Cruse, *Cognitive Linguistics*, 83–87.

18. Lakoff, *Women, Fire, and Dangerous Things*, 47. For more about the identification of prototypical members, see Croft and Cruse, *Cognitive Linguistics*, 78.

19. Lakoff, 84.

20. Lakoff, 83.

established cultural trends and expectations, such as "A husband is a bread-winner." Salient exemplars are the best examples that come to mind when we think about a particular concept – for example, your friend John might be the salient exemplar of a good father or 9/11 may be a salient exemplar of terrorist attacks.[21]

Mark Johnson applies Cognitive Linguistics and the prototype theory to ethics and argues that our "basic moral concepts (e.g. person, duty, right, law, will) have prototype structure too."[22] This means that we make our moral judgements on how to behave in certain situations by referring to a prototypi-cal situation. Even though most of life's dilemmas may differ from prototypes, knowing prototypes is essential in making decisions about non-prototypical situations – since non-prototypical situations are analyzed and dealt with in the light of existing prototypes.

Thus, humans interact with the complexity of the world and organize their knowledge by categorization, and their categories are built around the best examples, which are called prototypes. As we will see in the following sections, awareness of existing prototype-structured categories influences both our exegesis and our preaching.

3.2.3 Categories in the Bible

I will now demonstrate how recognizing categories in biblical texts helps in their interpretation. In order to do so, and while reflecting on the applica-tion of the notion of a category to biblical studies, I identify below several processes that can be observed in biblical texts.

3.2.3.1 Category Creation

Category creation means introducing new categories that might previously have been unknown to the audience. When people who are unfamiliar with the Bible start reading it for the first time, they encounter a whole spectrum of new categories whose existence they might never have suspected. For in-stance, they learn about a category of actions, thoughts, and emotions that are called "sin," and they get acquainted with the categories of saved and

---

21. Lakoff and Johnson, *Philosophy in the Flesh*, 28.
22. Johnson, *Moral Imagination*, 9.

unsaved, holy and unholy, pure and impure, which did not function in their world view before.

In Genesis 1:1–31, we see God creating different categories by creating the earth, the light, the day, the seas, the land, plants, animals, and, eventually, human beings. In Genesis 2:16–17, God gives the first commandment telling Adam not to eat from the tree of the knowledge of good and evil, which resulted in creating categories of obedience, disobedience, and the consequence of disobedience, which is death. The prototype of obedience is listening to God and doing what he says, which, in this case, meant not eating from the tree of knowledge. The prototype of disobedience is not listening to or not doing what God says, which, in this account, is presented as eating the forbidden fruit. The key biblical prototype of the consequence of disobedience is separation from God that results in death.

3.2.3.2 Category Contrast/Comparison

Category contrast/comparison takes place when two different categories that function as opposites are contrasted or compared with each other. This phenomenon is illustrated in the conclusion of the Sermon of the Mount, where Jesus introduced a series of images that depict two different ways of living and express two general categories of those who are obedient and disobedient or faithful and unfaithful. Thus, he talked about two gates and two roads, two kinds of trees and two kinds of fruit, two builders and two foundations. In fact, Jesus was teaching about choosing one of two ways of life – entering through the narrow gate, listening to the right kind of people who bear fruit by practising what they teach, and building on the right foundation, which means listening to his word and translating it into action (Matt 7:13–29). Thus Jesus, after explaining the basic principles of his kingdom, used a series of metaphors to help his listeners understand that the most important life choice can be narrowed to just one decision about what they would do with the word of God that they have heard: Will they obey and follow him? Or will they decide to pursue their own ideas of life?

3.2.3.3 Category Transfer

Category transfer takes places when a member of one category moves to another one. When contrasting categories are presented in the Bible, this is often not for purely informative purposes but as a call to change categories and move from one to another. At other times, biblical authors present two contrasting categories to describe a process of transfer that has already taken place. In Ephesians, Paul, in talking about his own and his recipients' past, describes them as being "dead" in their sins (2:1) but points out that God "even when we were dead in our transgressions, made us alive together with Christ" (2:5). Thus, there is a transfer from the category of dead to the category of being alive. When speaking specifically about the past of his non-Jewish fellow believers, Paul uses several images: "separate from Christ," "strangers to the covenants of promise," and "far off" (2:12–13). But, because of Christ's sacrifice, those separate from Christ now have "access" to the Father (2:18), they are "no longer strangers and aliens" but "fellow citizens with the saints" (2:19), and those who "formerly were far off have been brought near by the blood of Christ" (2:12).

It is vital to notice these category transfers since they allow readers to comprehend the logic behind using various images. These category transfers also have fundamental theological implications – in this case, they show the consequences of our salvation.

3.2.3.4 Category Reversal

Category reversal takes place when the biblical authors challenge the traditional value system and accepted understanding of categories. In the Gospels, Jesus frequently reversed known categories, presenting a new perspective on value, importance, and humility.

In Matthew 19:13–20:28, Jesus used numerous images associated with the categories of being the first and the last, the privileged and the serving. This section begins with Jesus's encounter with children. The apostles perceived children as a nuisance, but Jesus said that "the kingdom of heaven belongs to such as these" (19:14). The next episode – about the young man with great wealth, and Jesus's disciples who had no status and reputation – concludes with the idea that the "first will be last and the last, first" (19:30), as in the parable of the workers in the vineyard (20:16). Finally, after Jesus, for the third time, announced his death, and the mother of the sons of Zebedee approached Jesus, asking that her sons be seated on his right and left hand in his kingdom, he said, "Whoever wishes to become great among you shall be your servant" (20:26). Throughout this section, Jesus reversed categories and challenged the common understanding of greatness. For the disciples, greatness was related to status, wealth, personal effort, and following the rules; for Jesus, greatness was about serving, and so the first were the last while the last would be first.

3.2.3.5 Category Development

Finally, there is category development, which means that a given category undergoes a process of transformation and, at some point, its meaning is redefined. Analysis of category development is especially important when tracing continuity and discontinuity of metaphors between the Old and New Testaments. In the Old Testament among the key categories used to depict God's expectations regarding his people's behaviour are the categories of clean and unclean. Joe Sprinkle explains these categories:

> In Old Testament times the ordinary state of most things was "cleanness," but a person or thing could contract ritual "uncleanness" (or "impurity") in a variety of ways: by skin diseases, discharges of bodily fluids, touching something dead (Num 5:2), or eating unclean foods (Lev 11; Deut 14).[23]

However, when analyzing continuity and discontinuity between the Testaments with regard to the categories clean and unclean, it appears that there is continuity in observing cleansing rituals by Jewish people in the time of Jesus. In contrast, there is discontinuity in terms of understanding of the notion of clean and unclean and the redefining of these categories by both Jesus and the apostles. Jesus himself was not afraid of contamination by contact with ritually unclean people. In the Gospels, he is described touching or being touched by lepers, the dead, and a woman suffering from bleeding (Matt 8:1–4; 9:18–26). In his disputes with the teachers of the law, Jesus condemned practising external purification laws and customs while failing to be transformed internally. Thus, in their teaching, Jesus and the apostles, employed the language of clean and unclean not in the context of rituals but in relation to moral behaviour (Matt 23:25–26; Mark 7:19; Luke 11:39–41; Rom 14:14; Heb 9:13–14; 1 John 1:7). In Leviticus 11, the Israelites are told to observe purity rituals in order to be holy as God is holy, but when Peter writes about being holy as God is holy, he stresses that holiness is a result of

---

23. Sprinkle, "Clean, Unclean."

Christ's sacrifice and is expressed in a clean life as seen in our daily choices (1 Pet 1:13–25). Therefore, when analyzing biblical categories, it is possible to trace the category development and movement from purity understood in ritual terms – as in the Old Testament – to its moral perception as presented by Jesus and the apostles.

3.2.4 Prototypes in the Bible

As stated earlier, all categories have prototypical members that are more characteristic of the given category than others. In exegesis that employs Cognitive Linguistics, recognizing and studying biblical prototypes is an important step because it prevents reading into the text any contemporary concepts or categories. Therefore, I have adopted and expanded a process of analyzing biblical prototypes creating a five-step process: (1) identifying prototypes; (2) examining differences between the prototypes of the original audience and our own prototypes; (3) recognizing interplays between typical, stereotypical, and ideal prototypes; (4) recognizing prototypical scenarios; and (5) understanding the role of prototypes in the moral teaching of the Bible.

3.2.4.1 Identifying Prototypes

The first challenge that Bible readers encounter when analyzing biblical texts from a conceptual metaphor theory perspective is the difficultly in identifying prototypes and deciding which members of a given category are more proto-typical than others. For instance, when studying the concept of the servant as a New Testament image of the people of God, it is essential to note that there are a few Greek words that are translated servant in our English versions.

One such word is the term δοῦλος (a slave or servant), which carries the idea of being "in bondage" and expressed "a relationship of dependence and the subordination of the δοῦλος to the κύριος."[24] However, δοῦλος is also a common word, used in a more general sense to denote a servant but, often, without connotations of slavery.[25] In contrast, διάκονος does not express the idea of subordination but "service on behalf of someone," and this term and its cognates are often used in the New Testament in the context of serving tables, helping by providing care, and service in general. When applied specifically

---

24. Balz and Schneider, "διακονεω," EDNT 1: 302.
25. Vine and Unger, "servant," in Vine's Complete Expository Dictionary, 562.

to Christian ministry, this term also denotes charitable service in the congregation and in church ministries.[26] There are other New Testament words describing various kinds of servants – for instance, παῖς (a child servant or an attendant), οἰκέτης (a house servant), and μίσθιος (a hired servant or paid worker).[27] While all these words belong to the general category of "servant," some of these words might be less prototypical than others.

3.2.4.2 Differences between the Prototypes of the Original Audience and Our Prototypes

The second step in analyzing biblical metaphors and images is to examine differences between the prototypes of the original audience and our own prototypes. A study of the biblical terms expressing the concept of a servant makes it clear that all these terms have their own culturally conditioned frames that provide an immediate context for their interpretation and that these frames vary radically from ours. When hearing the word "slave," a contemporary audience – not being aware of the structures of ancient society – may think about Afro-American chattel slaves working on cotton plantations. However, these more modern concepts of slavery differ greatly from the kind of slavery practised in Israelite society.[28] The same is true of children working as servants. In Western societies, child labour is illegal and considered unethical; but in ancient times, child labour was not seen as problematic.

Therefore, in the process of analyzing biblical metaphors and images, it is helpful to examine the prototypes of the original audience in order to avoid imposing our own prototypes on biblical texts. As readers of the Bible, we must bear in mind that all these different terms for servant functioned in secular language of the time long before they were used in the New Testament. Thus, preachers studying New Testament images and metaphors must trace how the common understanding of these words shaped their biblical meaning.[29] In other words, preachers should be able to see the connection between, for example, the common usage and understanding of δοῦλος and Paul's

---

26. Balz and Schneider, "διακονεω," EDNT 1:302–303.

27. Vine and Unger, "servant," in Vine's Complete Expository Dictionary, 562–563.

28. On a difference between an American chattel slave and δοῦλος see Howe, *Because You Bear This Name*, 63–64.

29. For more on the frames theory applied to interpretation of biblical texts, see Park, *Mark's Memory Resources*.

description of himself as a δοῦλος of Christ or the connection between διάκονος and a person serving tables as described in Acts 6:1–7.

3.2.4.3 Interplays between Typical, Stereotypical, and Ideal Prototypes

Another reason for examining prototypes is the fact that prototype theory provides preachers with an important distinction between typical-case prototypes, ideal-case prototypes, social stereotypes, and salient exemplars.[30] Thus, when analyzing biblical texts, preachers should look for interplays between what is typical, stereotypical, and ideal. In tracing the usage of the concept of δοῦλος in the New Testament, it sometimes appears to be used to depict typical members of this category – for example, when a centurion asks Jesus to heal his servant and expresses his faith in the power of Jesus's word by saying, "For I also am a man under authority, with soldiers under me; and I say to this one, 'Go!' and he goes, and to another, 'Come!' and he comes, and to my slave, 'Do this!' and he does it" (Matt 8:9). In a similar fashion, δοῦλοι is used in the parable of the tares and the wheat (Matt 13:24–30), where servants are depicted as those who work in the field and obey the landowner's orders. They are typical servants, doing the typical work of servants.

In Matthew 20:24–28, Jesus talked about an ideal-case prototype of a servant (δοῦλος) and proclaimed that "whoever wishes to become great among you shall be your servant." Jesus set new standards of greatness that are expressed in humility and voluntary service. He concluded his argument by stating that "the Son of Man did not come to be served, but to serve [διακονέω]" (Matt 20:28), which means that Jesus himself modelled this kind of attitude. In Philippians 2:7, Paul teaches more explicitly about Christ "taking the form of a bond-servant [δοῦλος]" and becoming not only our ideal-case prototype of a servant but also a salient exemplar of a servant. Thus, Paul does not hesitate to call Christians to "have this attitude in yourselves which was also in Christ Jesus" (Phil 2:5) and to embody in their lives the same qualities of a servant that Christ displayed in his incarnation and earthly ministry. Thus, this interplay between the typical and ideal in the New Testament is worth paying attention to since it is one of the key elements of the Bible's ethical teaching. Original readers of the New Testament had a clear understanding of

---

30. This was explained in more detail in section 3.2.2.

the roles and behaviour of typical and even stereotypical servants, but Christ called them to follow his own example and move from the typical to the ideal.

This teaching strategy is also evident in the Pauline household codes, where Paul writes that slaves are to be obedient to their masters "as to Christ," "as slaves of Christ," knowing that they "will receive back from the Lord" (Eph 6:5–7). Thus, they were not to act as typical slaves relating to typical masters but, rather, their moral behaviour was to be shaped by Christ who is not only the ideal-case prototype of a servant but also their ultimate master and the ideal-case prototype of the master whom we all serve. Therefore, while exploring prototypes of biblical images and metaphors, it is essential to pay attention to the interplay between the typical and the ideal, the possible reversals of roles, prototypes, and the social structures encoded in well-known conceptual frames.

3.2.4.4 Prototypical Scenarios

Finally, van Wolde, in her study of Job 28, stresses the importance of recognizing prototypical scenarios in a text. She defines a prototypical scenario as "the conventional procedure by which a continuum of experiences and events are expressed by a more or less fixed series of words."[31] These prototypical scenarios or repeated patterns can be recognized either by comparing various biblical texts relating to a particular situation or on the basis of historical research that describes how people behaved in given circumstances. For instance, in the parable about the workers in the vineyard, which was discussed earlier, it becomes clear that the element of surprise comes from the fact that the story differs radically from an expected prototypical scenario of rewarding workers (Matt 20:1–16). John's account of Jesus washing his disciples' feet (John 13:1–18) shocks readers because what took place differed from what was customarily expected. Thus, in order to grasp the element of surprise and the main conflict in the story, it might be prudent to study how the scenario described differs from a prototypical one.

3.2.4.5 Prototypes and the Moral Teaching of the Bible

Applying Cognitive Linguistics, especially prototype theory, to biblical interpretation changes the way we perceive moral reasoning and the ways we

---

31. van Wolde, "Wisdom, Who Can Find It?," 31.

make moral choices. As a result, it also changes our understanding of biblical teaching about morality and the ways we convey these ideas in our sermons.

Mark Johnson argues that "our moral understanding depends in large measure on various structures of imagination, such as images, image schemas, metaphors, narrative, and so forth."[32] In his opinion, this understanding "is based, not primarily on universal moral laws, but principally on metaphoric concepts."[33] In support of these ideas, he stresses that humans define their most basic moral concepts – such as freedom, rights, and forgiveness – metaphorically. For instance, when asked about justice and forgiveness, people do not quote a long list of rules but, rather, describe these notions using images, metaphors, or even narratives. The manner in which they conceptualize a particular situation and develop these metaphors is largely culturally conditioned.[34]

In applying the idea of prototypes to Christianity, Johnson argues that the Judeo-Christian tradition is an expression of so-called Moral Law Theory. In his opinion, since both Judaism and Christianity claim that humans are created by God, this means that God is their owner and the ultimate source of morality. Therefore, people are responsible before God for their moral choices, and they have to follow God-given rules and commandments.[35] Even though Johnson tries to give a fair account of the Judeo-Christian tradition, he seems to misrepresent the essence of the Christian faith by narrowing it down to following rules and principles. Except for making a few general comments, he does not give any in-depth account of the New Testament teaching on moral reasoning and fails to show clearly the change that occurs with the coming of Jesus.[36]

I, on the contrary, argue that Christianity is more prototype-based than rule-based. This can be seen in the fact that God made humans in his image and likeness and that, by so doing, he holds himself up as the ultimate prototype for all aspects of our existence. When reading the Old Testament laws, we may get the impression that the law is rule-based since it is expressed

---

32. Johnson, *Moral Imagination*, ix.

33. Johnson, 2.

34. Johnson, 2.

35. For more on Johnson's understanding of a Judeo-Christian tradition, see Johnson, 19–22.

36. Johnson, 20.

in the form of commandments that are apodictic and casuistic in nature; apodictic laws deal with general moral principles, whereas casuistic laws focus on specific life situations. However, a closer analysis of Old Testament laws shows that the ultimate purpose of the law was to reveal the character of God so that the people of Israel would strive to be holy as God was holy. Thus, even though the law was expressed in rules and regulations that shaped people's lives, it was about imitating the prototype so that people would grow into the likeness of God.

This ultimate purpose of the law became clearer with the coming of Jesus. In his Sermon on the Mount, Jesus taught that the essence of the Christian life is following the intent of the law rather than the letter of the law and showed the concepts and ideas underlying the law. He narrowed the whole discussion on morality to basic-level categories. Hence, when he discussed the commandment "You shall not kill," he taught on anger. When dealing with the topic of adultery, he focused on lust. When speaking about bearing false witness, he talked about honesty. When commenting on the idea of hating enemies, he stressed the idea of love. These are the basic concepts that Johnson would label prototypical.

When analyzing Jesus's teaching, it becomes apparent that he reinterpreted the law and explained its original intent. Jesus also introduced a new perspective on moral reasoning since he insisted that love is the ultimate fulfilment of the law (Matt 22:34–40; John 13:34–35; Rom 13:8–10; Gal 5:14). Thus, according to Jesus, love – rather than rules and regulations – is the main principle that must govern our moral reasoning, and so love becomes our prototype. This is precisely what Johnson argues for. He believes that there are some basic concepts, images, and metaphors that guide our moral choices. In his opinion, these concept are superior to rules and regulations because rules do not cover all possible life situations. However, these basic moral concepts allow us to evaluate how a given situation differs from a prototypical one and, in this respect, these concepts enable us to make decisions even in non-prototypical circumstances.[37]

As far as Christian doctrine is concerned, this idea of prototypical reasoning is even more explicit because love is not only the main virtue but is also embodied. When Christ called his disciples to love one another, he added, "as

---

37. Johnson, 9.

I have loved you" (John 13:34), and the apostle John states that "God is love" (1 John 4:8). Accordingly, love is not just some vague idea but is embodied and can be seen in its fullness in God incarnate – that is, in Christ who becomes our ultimate prototype of goodness and morality. Thus, it is not surprising that one of the main emphases of Jesus's teaching is the call to follow him, as the one who is the perfect image of God. The essence of a Christian life is not living by rules but following Christ and growing into the likeness of Christ since we are called to be conformed into the image of the Son (Rom 8:28).

3.2.5 Frames

As observed earlier, humans organize their knowledge in categories that are developed around best examples, which are called prototypes. However, another essential notion in Cognitive Linguistics is the idea of frames, as proposed by Fillmore, or Idealized Cognitive Models (ICMs), as described by Lakoff. Fillmore defines a frame as

> any system of concepts related in such a way that to understand any one of them you have to understand the whole structure in which it fits; when one of the things in such a structure is introduced into a text, or into a conversation all of the others are automatically made available.[38]

In characterizing his model, Croft and Cruse depict it as the semantics of understanding as opposed to a truth-conditional semantics.[39] Mark Johnson explains this idea further, noting that frames "are not objectively given *in* the situations they allow us to understand" but, instead, should be perceived as "idealized models and frameworks that grow out of our experience and that we bring to our understanding of situations".[40]

For example, when we hear the word "restaurant," this triggers opening the whole frame of concepts and basic-level categories related to a restaurant, such as food, order, waiter, building, paying the receipt, reservation, table, eating,

---

38. Fillmore, "Frame Semantics," 111.

39. Croft and Cruse, *Cognitive Linguistics*, 8. See also Lakoff, *Women, Fire, and Dangerous Things*, 68. Alan Cienki gives more insights on developments of Fillmore's and Lakoff's approaches and elaborates on major differences between them. Cienki, "Frames," 170–187.

40. Johnson, *Moral Imagination*, 9 (emphasis original). On frames and ICMs, see also Langacker, *Cognitive Grammar*, 46–47.

rest, fellowship, and so on. In contrast, words such as buying, paying, meat, bread, discounts, sections, washing powder, shop assistants, cashiers, and baskets derive their meaning in relation to a supermarket or a shop frame.[41] The same term may belong to different frames, and frames themselves might belong to larger frames. When a person says, "We open our presents in the morning," this statement opens a frame of a family Christmas tradition of opening presents on Christmas morning, even though neither a family nor Christmas is mentioned in the sentence. This is because, as Park stresses, "all knowledge is bunched into a frame in an ordered and predictable pattern, and retrieved as needed."[42] Therefore, frames are ways in which human minds comprehend, store, organize, and retrieve information about the world.

However, our perception of frames, as in the case of prototypes, is culturally conditioned. Fillmore gives the example of the term "weekend," understood as time off work beginning on Friday afternoon and ending on Sunday at midnight.[43] This term triggers the frame of a week. However, in order to understand this notion, it is necessary to have a concept of a seven-day week with two days off. If somebody had used the term "weekend" in Poland in time of communist rule, it would not have been understood since Polish people worked six days a week and had just Sundays off. The idea of a "weekend" would have been foreign to them. Even after a monthly "working Saturday" was introduced and the remaining Saturdays given off, the term "weekend" was not used. George Lakoff, to prove that a seven-day week is a culturally conditioned concept and does not exist objectively, gives the example of the Balinese calendrical system that has three different week structures – a five-day, six-day, and seven-day week.[44] Thus, the frame for a week has a very different content depending on the culture.

Therefore, it can be said that all our information about the world is structured in frames. Park claims that "Framed knowledge aids people to readily process what is happening in the real or story world by allowing them to make predictions as to what will take place and by allowing them to make

---

41. Fauconnier, "Mental Spaces," 152.
42. Park, *Mark's Memory Resources*, 23.
43. Fillmore, "Frame Semantics," 119–120.
44. Lakoff, *Women, Fire, and Dangerous Things*, 69.

inferences."[45] Thus, frames influence human behaviour and the way people act in social contexts. Every action – like answering the phone, doing shopping, going to a church or a restaurant – involves activating certain frames and acting upon prototypical knowledge that is stored in these frames. While this knowledge helps people survive in these social situations, it may sometimes result in complications. For example, when Western tourists decide to go to a market or a church in Africa, they soon discover that they need to learn new frames because their images of shopping or worship differs radically from those of the surrounding culture.

Applying the idea of frames to ethics and morality, Johnson points out that in the case of moral issues, different people might have different frames and, consequently, may make different choices in similar circumstances. As an example, he presents the diverse perspectives people may have on a fetus. For some, it is a fully human and valuable being with a personality, whereas others see it as just a part of a woman's body a living organism without a personality or a potential source of stem cells.[46] Different frames, filled with different concepts, result in different actions. Therefore, the frames that people have express their world view and influence their moral decisions.

3.2.6 Conclusion on Categories, Prototypes, and Frames

Cognitive Linguistics, and especially theories of categories, prototypes, and frames, may be usefully applied to interpreting biblical texts. Awareness of the existence of categories and category operations helps preachers to grasp the structure of the text and the development of concepts appearing in the text. Prototype and frame theories give preachers tools that help them to understand biblical concepts and how these concepts were perceived by their authors, while also pointing preachers to the cultural and historical setting of the text. While cautioning preachers against reading into biblical texts a contemporary understanding of biblical terms, these theories offer insights into ways of discovering the frames and prototypes behind biblical concepts.

Moreover, prototype theory conforms with the biblical vision of morality that is based on following Christ and growing into his likeness. It stresses that moral reasoning is not rule-based but prototype-based and, as such, is

---

45. Park, *Mark's Memory Resources*, 23.

46. Johnson, *Moral Imagination*, 9–10.

helpful in studying biblical texts that deal with moral issues. Prototype theory provides preachers with a method of looking beyond rules and principles and identifying prototypes of values, attitudes, and actions.

3.3 The Structure of Metaphor

This section focuses specifically on conceptual metaphor theory and the structure of metaphors. However, references to other theories such as blending theory will also be made to show interrelationships between these theories, their richness, and their contribution to biblical interpretation. Therefore, I will begin by presenting types of conceptual metaphors, then analyze various elements and principles of conceptual metaphor theory, and conclude with a discussion of levels of metaphor. The overall aim of this section is not only to present structural elements of metaphor but, as in the previous section, to show the usefulness of Cognitive Linguistics in biblical studies.

3.3.1 Types of Conceptual Metaphors

When studying biblical metaphors, it is helpful to begin by identifying general types of conceptual metaphors which we encounter in the Bible – for example, structural, ontological, and orientational metaphors. LIFE IS A JOURNEY is an example of a structural metaphor, where the structure of the concept of the journey provides understanding for the concept of life.[47] This metaphor is used frequently in the Bible. Jesus taught about entering through the narrow gate and following the narrow road (Matt 7:13–14); Paul describes the life of unbelievers as one where they follow "the course of this world" (Eph 2:2) and, in reflecting on his own life, says, "I have finished the course" (2 Tim 4:7). Other common structural metaphors in the Pauline Epistles include ARGUMENT IS WAR, especially when Paul uses diatribe in talking to his opponents, and ORGANIZATIONS ARE LIVING ORGANISMS, in depicting the church as the body of Christ.

Ontological metaphors are created when we conceive reality in terms of objects, substances, and containers. The metaphorical concept PEOPLE ARE CONTAINERS is behind metaphorical expressions such as being filled with the Holy Spirit, being filled with joy, love or fear, and receiving gifts of the Spirit.

---

47. Kövecses, *Metaphor: A Practical Introduction*, 37.

The Bible also uses metaphors that can be labelled orientational. According to Kövecses, "most metaphors that serve this function have to do with basic human spatial orientations, such as up-down, centre-periphery, and the like."[48] In the Bible, we find numerous references to being raised up with Christ and ascending and descending. Revelation 12 is a good example of orientational metaphors. The dragon is a sign appearing in the sky, and the boy is born on the earth. The dragon is up, but the boy comes down. The dragon is cast down from heaven, whereas the boy is taken up to heaven. So, there is a reverse movement – up and down. One symbolizes victory, the other defeat.

3.3.2 Image Schemas, Image Schema Metaphors, and Image Metaphors

Bearing in mind the division referred to above – to avoid confusion in terminology and to lay the foundation for developing the application of these concepts to preaching in chapter 5 – I now explain the distinction between image schemas, image-schema metaphors, and image metaphors.

3.3.2.1 Image Schemas

Cognitivists stress that one of the most basic cognitive capabilities of the human brain is an ability to generalize – this means that the brain, in the process of perception, focuses on the most essential aspects, ignoring irrelevant details and developing a simplified version of reality that is based on schematic structures.[49]

George Lakoff, pointing out that there is a relatively small number of image schemas – defines image schemes them as "relatively simple structures that constantly reoccur in our everyday bodily experience: CONTAINERS, PATHS, LINKS, FORCES, BALANCE, and in various orientations and relations: UP-DOWN, FRONT-BACK, PART-WHOLE, CENTER-PERIPHERY."[50] Croft and Cruse claim

---

48. Kövecses, *Metaphor: A Practical Introduction*, p. 40.

49. Langacker, *Foundations of Cognitive Grammar*, 132. See also Tuggy, "Schematicity," 82; Turner, *Origin of Ideas*, 265–258.

50. Lakoff, *Women, Fire, and Dangerous Things*, 267. Mark Johnson gives a fuller list of image schemas: "CONTAINER; BALANCE; COMPULSION; BLOCKAGE; COUNTERFORCE; RESTRAINT REMOVAL; ENABLEMENT; ATTRACTION; MASS- COUNT; PATH; LINK; CENTRE-PERIPHERY; CYCLE; NEAR-FAR; SCALE; PART-WHOLE; MERGING; SPLITTING; FULL-EMPTY; MATCHING; SUPERIMPOSITION; ITERATION; CONTACT; PROCESS; SURFACE; OBJECT; COLLECTION." Johnson, *Body in the Mind*, 126. See also Croft and Cruse, *Cognitive Linguistics*, 45. Len Talmy divides

that image schemas are "schematic versions of images."[51] For Todd Oakley, an image schema is "a condensed redescription of perceptual experience for the purpose of mapping spatial structure onto conceptual structure."[52] Beate Hampe enumerates four characteristics of image schemas: (1) directly meaningful ("experiential" or "embodied") preconceptual structures; (2) highly schematic structures; (3) continuous and analogue patterns; and (4) internally structured and consisting of very few parts but flexible.[53] This means that image schemas are basic mental structures that are grounded in a human experience, and the structure of our spatial bodily experience is expressed in the form of a conceptual structure. Therefore, image schemas are schematic and analogue patterns because they are based on correspondences between the physical structure and the conceptual structure. For instance, as humans, we have the experience of moving along a path, and this simple, schematic, and analogue image structure that we have in our minds is a skeleton that we use to develop metaphors such as LIFE IS A JOURNEY and metaphorical expressions like "This marriage is a bumpy road."[54]

Image schemas are often closely linked to prepositions and evoked by the use of prepositions. Lakoff and Turner note that "the spatial senses of

---

the image schemas enumerated above into three categories: topological, orientational, and force-dynamic, Leonard Talmy, 'How Language Structures Space', 225–282. See also Lakoff, "How the Body Shapes Thought," 59.

51. Croft and Cruse, *Cognitive Linguistics*, 44. For a more detailed discussion on image-schema, see Johnson, *Body in the Mind*, 23–40; Lakoff, *Women, Fire, and Dangerous Things*, 416–461; Dewell, "Over Again," 351–380; Gibbs and Colston, "Cognitive Psychological Reality," 347–378; Regier, "Model of the Human Capacity," 63–88; Regier, *Human Semantic Potential*; and Talmy, "How Language Structures Space," 225–282.

52. Oakley, "Image Schemas," 215.

53. Hampe, "Image Schemas in Cognitive Linguistics," 1–2. See also Oakley, "Image Schemas," 214–235. In defining image schemas, Zoltán Kövecses stresses that these are analogue patterns, and it is important to distinguish these from the notion of domains, which will be explained in the following sections. See Kövecses, "Levels of Metaphor," 3.

54. Johnson emphasizes that operations on image schemas – which people can perform in their minds – mirror physical spatial operations. He also describes several possible image schema transformations: (1) Path focus to end-point focus, which can be understood by considering the route of a moving object and imagining a place where it starts its journey and then a place where it ends the journey; (2) Multiplex to mass, which is a cluster of objects, and observers can imagine getting away from the cluster and getting closer so that they can see either a mass or are able to identify individual objects; (3) Trajectory, which involves focusing on the path of a moving object and following it in our imagination; and (4) Superimposition, which requires imagining a large sphere and a small cube, and then imagining an increase in the size of a cube so that the sphere can fit in it and vice versa. Johnson, *Body in the Mind*, 25–26.

prepositions tend to be defined in terms of image schemas (e.g. in, out, to, from, along, and so on)."[55] Prepositions trigger image schemas because they describe spatial relations, both physical and abstract. Someone may say, "Mary is in the house" or "Mary is in love." In both cases, a preposition – "in" – triggers the image schemas of a CONTAINER and IN-OUT. In the first case, a house is conceptualized as a container; but in the second instance, the abstract emotion of love is also perceived in terms of a container. Being in love is also an actualization of the conceptual metaphor STATES ARE LOCATIONS, which is based on the idea that we conceptualize emotional states in terms of locations.

If the preposition "in" is used metaphorically and evokes an image schema of a container, it suggests that something is inside an enclosed space. It may suggest belonging or being a part of something bigger, identifying with something, being in a particular state or emotion, being controlled by something or someone, but also being protected from external influences. Being "in" has some logical consequences. If A is in B, this means that whatever happens to be in A is also in B. Moreover, the logical consequence of the idea of being "in" is the possibility of being "out."[56]

Lakoff and Turner conduct more in-depth analysis of the usage of the preposition "out." They explain that "the basic meaning of 'out' is being exterior to a bounded space which is regarded having an interior."[57] Therefore, if we think of a house as bounded space, it is possible to go out of the house. In a similar fashion, if a country is a bounded region, somebody might be out of a country. The preposition "out" can also describe abstract concepts such as passing out – which may mean losing consciousness – being out of control in the sense of misbehaving, or being snuffed out or taken out as a depiction of death. If STATES ARE LOCATIONS, being present, being conscious, behaving within accepted limits, or being alive mean staying within some abstract boundaries, whereas being out means crossing these boundaries.[58]

---

55. Lakoff and Turner, *More than Cool Reason*, 99.
56. Howe, *Because You Bear This Name*, 238.
57. Lakoff and Turner, *More than Cool Reason*, 97.
58. Lakoff and Turner, 97.

3.3.2.2 Image Schema Metaphors

Explaining the idea of image-schema metaphors, Zoltán Kövecses points out that while most metaphors can be understood on the basis of knowledge of the concepts that form them, this is not the only way metaphors come into existence. Conversely, he distinguishes another kind of metaphor – namely, image-schema metaphors – and explains that in the case of these metaphors, "it is not conceptual elements of knowledge (like traveller, destination, and obstacles in the case of journey) that get mapped from a source to a target, but conceptual elements of image-schemas."[59] As examples of image-schema metaphors, he gives a number of expressions with the preposition "out" – such as pass out, zone out, space out, tune out, veg out, conk out, snuff out, out of order, and to be out of something. These expressions are used in metaphorical expressions such as "I am out of money," which are image-schema metaphors.[60] It is essential to stress that image-schema metaphors, just like conceptual metaphors, are based on mapping elements from the source domain to the target domain, but they are not as rich in content as conceptual metaphors since they do not map concepts but only very simple and schematic image structures.

3.3.2.3 Image Metaphors

To avoid confusion in terminology, I must clarify the distinction between image-schema metaphors and image metaphors. As mentioned earlier, image-schema metaphors are developed on the basis of very schematic mental image structures called image schemas. Image metaphors are also called one-shot image metaphors because they do not map a rich structure of one domain into another, but, rather, "the mapping is of the one-shot kind generated by two images brought into correspondence by the superimposition of one image onto the other."[61] Instead of conceptual domains, there are two images that get mapped one into the other. A classic example of an image metaphor is the sentence, "My wife ... whose waist is an hourglass."[62] In this case, an image of an hourglass is superimposed or mapped onto an image of the wife's

---

59. Kövecses, *Metaphor: A Practical Introduction*, 42.
60. Kövecses, 43.
61. Kövecses, 44.
62. Lakoff and Turner, *More than Cool Reason*, 90.

figure because of correspondences in shape. And although the words creating the metaphor do not suggest which part of the hourglass corresponds to the wife's waist, this gap in listeners' minds is filled by common knowledge of both these images. Lakoff and Turner stress that because "the proliferation of images limits image mappings to highly specific cases," these metaphors are called one-shot image metaphors.[63]

3.3.2.4 Image Schemas and Image Schema Metaphors in the Bible

It is not surprising that image schemas and image-schema metaphors are present in numerous biblical texts. Consequently, while studying these passages, it is wise to pay attention to the simplest schematic structures such as containers, LINKS, PATHS, IN-OUT, PERIPHERY-CENTER, UP-DOWN, and PART-WHOLE and take notice of prepositions that help to identify image schemas evoked by these structures.

Bonnie Howe presents five different examples of New Testament usage of "in" (ἐν): (1) as a reference to a spatial location, such as "in the wilderness" (Matt 3:1); (2) as a reference to a physical or emotional state, such as "in torment" (Luke 16:23); (3) as a reference to an abstract state, such as Paul's depiction of the difference between earthly bodies that are perishable and heavenly bodies that are imperishable, where he writes that the body that is sown in a perishable state (ἐν φθορᾷ) will be raised in an imperishable state (ἐν ἀφθαρσίᾳ) (1 Cor 15:42); (4) as a reference to "a (theoretical) social association, or even a theological distinction" such as in being "in the Father" (John 10:38);[64] and (5) as a depiction of a cause or reason as in a structure (ἐν τῷ λόγῳ) meaning "because of" (Acts 7:29).[65]

A common New Testament image used to depict the Christian life is found in the expression "in Christ" (ἐν Χριστῷ). In Romans 8:1–2, Paul uses this expression twice: "Therefore there is now no condemnation for those who are *in Christ* Jesus. For the law of the Spirit of life *in Christ* Jesus has set you free from the law of sin and of death" (emphasis added). The preposition "in" evokes the IN-OUT image schema of a CONTAINER. Paul uses an image of being in Christ in the sense of being in a bounded container to depict a state of belonging to Christ and being under Christ's control and influence.

---

63. Lakoff and Turner, 91.

64. Howe, *Because You Bear This Name*, 236.

65. Howe, 236.

He contrasts the state of death and condemnation with the state of no condemnation that is only possible in Christ. Christians also experience the law of the Spirit of life, which is available in Christ who sets them free from another kind of law – namely, the law of sin and death. So, the state of being in Christ, in this passage, is a state of being free from condemnation and from the law of sin and death.

3.3.3 Source and Target Domains

As stated earlier, conceptual metaphors can be defined as perceiving one conceptual domain in terms of another domain. A source domain is the domain we are most familiar with, which we utilize to understand a target domain, which, by definition, is less familiar.[66] For instance, when people talk about dealing with new ideas, they use numerous metaphors related to eating, such as THINKING IS EATING, IDEAS ARE FOOD, COMMUNICATING IS FEEDING, ACCEPTING IS SWALLOWING, and UNDERSTANDING IS DIGESTING.[67] These metaphors are used in metaphorical expressions like "Your words are hard to swallow," "I am still digesting what you have said," "Your lecture was a real feast," "He feeds them with the word of God every Sunday," and "Your letter made me sick."

It is sometimes assumed that a source domain has to be physical or concrete, whereas a target domain needs to be abstract. Even though this is frequently the case, the metaphor THE ATOM IS A SOLAR SYSTEM is an example of two physical domains where the only difference is that one is more known and accessible.[68] Therefore, the key is "conceptualizing a relatively *less intersubjectively accessible* domain or frame in terms of a *more intersubjectively accessible* domain or frame".[69]

Hence, Kövecses defines the domain as "any coherent organization of experience."[70] He also points out that "unlike image schemas, domains are not analogue, imagistic patterns of experience but propositional in nature in

---

66. Kövecses, *Where Metaphors Come From*, 2. See also Kövecses, *Metaphor: A Practical Introduction*, 4. This understanding of metaphor originated from Lakoff and Johnson, *Metaphors We Live By*, 5.

67. Lakoff, "How the Body Shapes Thought," 64.

68. Sweetser and DesCamp, "Motivating Biblical Metaphors," 10.

69. Sweetser and DesCamp, 10 (emphasis original).

70. Kövecses, *Metaphor: A Practical Introduction*, 4.

a highly schematic fashion."[71] This means that domains convey more information than image schemas because they are developed around concepts or mental experiences. Thus, Alan Cienki claims that the idea of "domain covers a range of types of cognitive entities, from mental experiences, to representational spaces, concepts, or conceptual complexes."[72] Following Langacker, Cienki also differentiates between basic and abstract domains, where a basic domain "cannot be reduced to any other domains," but the abstract domain is complex and presupposes the existence of other domains. For instance, to understand the idea of an elbow, one has to understand the idea of an arm, which, because of its complexity, is an abstract domain.[73]

Thus, it needs to be said that domains are organizations of experience that are propositional in nature since they are built around concepts and can differ depending on the level of complexity. The notion of domains is fundamental in defining conceptual metaphors that are based on perceiving one domain in terms of another.

3.3.4 Metaphorical Mappings and Entailments

Conceptual metaphor theory is based on the idea of systematicity of metaphorical concepts, which means that while people understand one domain in terms of another, as in the case of arguing being conceptualized as having a battle, they "form a systematic way of thinking about the battling aspects of arguing."[74] These metaphorical concepts, which appear in various metaphorical expressions, structure human perception and actions. Thus, metaphorical mappings are an essential element of metaphorical systematicity and are understood as a set of correspondences between source and target domains in such a way that elements of one domain are paired with elements of the other.

Gentner and Bowdle explain structure-mapping theory by stating that "analogical mapping is a process of establishing a *structural alignment* between two represented situations and then projecting inferences."[75] George Lakoff argues that "mappings should not be thought of as processes, or as algorithms that mechanically take source domain inputs and produce target

---

71. Kövecses, "Levels of Metaphor," 3.

72. Cienki, "Frames," 182.

73. Cienki, 182.

74. Lakoff and Turner, *Metaphors We Live By*, 7.

75. Gentner and Bowdle, "Metaphors and Structure-Mapping," 109 (emphasis original).

domain outputs," but each mapping is to be considered "a fixed pattern of ontological correspondences across domains that may, or may not, be applied to a source domain knowledge structure: or a source domain lexical item."[76]

In his neural theory of metaphor, George Lakoff provides a neurological basis for the existence of metaphorical mappings. Following research conducted independently by Johnson and Narayanan, he concludes that

> in situations where the source and target domains are both active simultaneously, the two areas of the brain for the source and target domains will both be active. Via the Hebbian principle that Neurons that fire together wire together, neural mapping circuits linking the two domains will be learned.[77]

Lakoff argues that mappings result from forming connections between areas of the brain for the source and target domains. Mappings come into existence when these areas of the brain get activated and neural bindings are formed.

Olaf Jäkel applies the cognitive theory of metaphor to religious texts and studies how the metaphor LIFE IS A JOURNEY is used in the Bible. In his essay, he identifies a whole set of mappings based on different biblical texts. Below there are a few of Jäkel's examples of metaphorical mappings:

Travelling		Life
Choosing path	→	Moral choices
Paths	→	God's commandments or immoral life
Traveller	→	The righteous or the wicked
Good way	→	God's way, following the commandments, Christ
Guide	→	God
Observer	→	God
Deviating	→	Sin
Returning	→	Repentance
Destination	→	Eternal life

Diagram 3. Mappings in LIFE IS A JOURNEY metaphor[78]

---

76. Lakoff, "Contemporary Theory of Metaphor," 211.

77. Lakoff, "Neural Theory," 26 (emphasis original).

78. Jäkel, "Hypotheses Revisited, 25–37. For a similar analysis of mappings in the metaphor LIFE IS A JOURNEY in Jeremiah 17:5–8, see Robinette, "Looking Beyond the Tree," 27.

Zoltán Kövecses provides his analysis of Matthew 25:31–45, where he identifies the main metaphor JESUS IS THE KING and the following mappings:

Source		Target
The king	→	Jesus
The king separates his subjects	→	Jesus separates people
The king judges his disobedient	→	Jesus judges people sinners
The king punishes disobedient	→	Jesus punishes sinners
by torturing and killing them	→	by eternal punishment
The king gives inheritance	→	Jesus gives eternal life
The inherited kingdom	→	heaven

Diagram 4. Mappings in Matthew 25:31–45[79]

Thus, source and target domains are interconnected by a set of systematic correspondences called mappings. This is not to say that readers, while interpreting extended metaphors in a narrative form such as parables, have to impose some meaning on every single element or allegorize each element of a given parable but only that these mappings that are highlighted in a text are legitimate. As I will explain later, the selection of mappings is not a purely subjective process because metaphors appear in communicative contexts and are a part of the wider discourse and, therefore, these contexts combined with the communicative intentions of the writer narrow the possible range of mappings.

However, before discussing the topic of hiding and highlighting, it is necessary to introduce one more term that is closely related to the notion of mappings, namely, the concept of metaphorical entailments. Zoltán Kövecses defines metaphorical entailments as "rich additional knowledge about a source mapped onto a target" as distinct from the typical metaphorical mappings described above.[80]

This means that in a communication process, apart from mappings that structure a relationship between domains, speakers have extensive background knowledge about the source domain – based on their general knowledge and everyday experiences – and this knowledge can be activated in

---

79. Adapted from: Kövecses, "Biblical Story Retold," 345–349.
80. Kövecses, *Metaphor: A Practical Introduction*, 122.

the process of communication. People can use metaphors such as LIFE IS A JOURNEY, ARGUMENT IS WAR, and THEORIES ARE BUILDINGS by conceptualizing various abstract concepts because they have concrete knowledge of journeys, wars, and buildings. One of the questions that should be asked in the process of interpreting metaphors is about the authors' exposure to the source and their knowledge about it.

3.3.5 Hiding and Highlighting

The idea of hiding and highlighting serves the purpose of capturing the interconnections between the source and the target that. These interconnections can, at times, be surprising and even shocking. Some critics of conceptual metaphor theory claim that this theory is based on similarities between the domains and mechanically set correspondences. However, partiality of mappings – explained as hiding and highlighting of metaphorical mappings – allows showing both similarity and dissimilarity. Highlighting refers to "the selective mappings of source domain features onto target domains," whereas "suppression of other features" is called hiding.[81] This means that some aspects of a metaphor are brought into focus, whereas others remain hidden because they do not contribute to conveying information that the speaker wants to communicate.

Even a brief analysis of the examples presented above shows that, in a given metaphor, not all potential elements of the source domain are utilized in the target domain. Calling Jesus – who was a son of a simple carpenter – the king was striking and unexpected because Jesus did not fit the typical image of a king. Moreover, in depicting Jesus as the king, the apostle Matthew does not mention a crown, a royal court, wars, battles, and many other elements that might have come to mind when people thought about different rulers because these elements were not important or relevant in conveying Matthew's context-specific concept of the king. This is an instance of the partial nature of metaphorical mappings, where only parts of the source domain are mapped in the target domain. Matthew focuses only on those aspects of Jesus's kingship that are relevant to his narrative – namely, being just, rewarding good and punishing evil, and the king's eternal reign. This vision of Jesus as the king clashed with people's typical experiences of kings

---

81. Knowles and Moon, *Introducing Metaphor*, 43.

because most of these earthly rulers were evil tyrants who did not care about justice or about the well-being of their subjects. Thus, Matthew teaches and shocks his readers with his vision of Jesus as the king both by what he says about it and what he does not say.

3.3.6 Principle of Unidirectionality

Another important feature of metaphorical mappings is the principle of unidirectionality, which states that the relation between the source and target is irreversible and that the direction of mappings is always from the source to the target.[82] Thus, while the metaphor LOVE IS WAR is utilized in a number of metaphorical expressions such as "He is fighting for his marriage," "She is just one of his many conquests," and "He pursued her and won her heart," it cannot be substituted with the metaphor WAR IS LOVE.[83] These metaphors have completely different meanings, demonstrating that metaphorical mappings are unidirectional.

This principle is seen at work in the fact that we conceptualize births as arrivals and deaths as departures but do not talk, for instance, about flight arrivals as births or departures as deaths. This principle is also seen in numerous New Testament metaphors. For instance, "Jesus is the king" cannot be changed to "the king is Jesus" without changing its meaning. We may conceptualize Jesus as the king, but this does not mean that we conceptualize kings as Jesus.

3.3.7 Invariance Principle and Inference Structures

George Lakoff defines the invariance principle by saying that "metaphorical mappings preserve the cognitive topology (that is, the image-schema structure) of the source domain, in a way consistent with the inherent structure of the target domain."[84] This means that there are constraints on metaphorical mappings and a schematic structure of the source domain is mapped onto the target domain. Therefore, source domain structures such as containers get mapped to the target as containers, paths as paths, exteriors as exteriors, but never as interiors. Thus, when Paul says, "Now may the God of hope fill

---

82. Jäkel, "Hypotheses Revisited," 21–22.

83. Lakoff and Turner, *Metaphors We Live By*, 49.

84. Lakoff, "Contemporary Theory of Metaphor," 214.

you with all joy and peace" (Rom 15:13), he evokes a containers schema of the source domain and the same image schema is mapped onto the target domain where believers are conceptualized as containers. Therefore, there is structural consistency between the source and target domains.

Joseph Grady goes even further and claims that this "systematic projection of elements from one conceptual domain onto elements of another involves not merely the objects and properties characteristic of the domain (e.g. buildings, sturdiness vs. flimsiness, etc.) but also the relations, events, and scenarios that characterize the domain."[85] His observation captures and defines another element of conceptual metaphor theory – namely, inference structures.

By conceptualizing one domain in terms of another, people do not merely compare two phenomena but borrow whole structures from one domain to explain the other. Joseph Grady gives the example of a person who "blows off steam" and points out that the whole point of this expression is to show that a person's intensity of anger has decreased.[86] When human beings talk about abstract concepts – such as love, morality, forgiveness, or time – they borrow the structures of more concrete concepts and project them onto these more abstract ones, which results in speaking of love as play, morality as accounting, and forgiveness as cancelling debts.

Depression is often conceptualized as a container. For instance, people may say, "He has fallen into a deep depression" because they understand that the deeper the object lies in a container, the more difficult it is to take it out. In a similar fashion, the deeper a person is in depression, the more complicated it is to get out of depression and recover.[87] It appears that the source domain structures shape and influence our perception and our way of speaking on the subject. In a similar fashion, Paul's words on being filled with joy and peace exemplify not only the invariance principle – where the structure of the source is reflected in the target domain – but also projecting inference structures. The more liquid there is in a container, the fuller it is. In a similar fashion, the more Christians are filled with joy and peace, the more these qualities are visible in their lives.

---

85. Grady, "Metaphor," 191.
86. Grady, 191.
87. Rohrer, "Embodiment and Experientialism," 36.

Lakoff, explaining metaphorical inferences from the standpoint of his neural theory, points out that metaphorical inference takes place when "a metaphorical mapping is activated in a neural circuit, there is an inference in the source domain of the mapping, and a consequence of the source domain inference is mapped to the target domain, activating a meaningful node."[88] By showing this, he aims to prove that the earlier theoretical work on conceptual metaphor theory has strong support in neurological sciences and is reflected in the ways the human brain operates.

3.3.8 Primary Metaphors

Primary metaphors can be defined as "cross-domain mappings, from a *source domain* (the sensorimotor domain) to a *target domain* (the domain of subjective experience), preserving inference and sometimes preserving lexical representation."[89] In other words, primary metaphors "consist of correlations of a subjective experience with a physical experience."[90] The combination of these two elements – namely, sensorimotor experience and subjective experience – are important components of primary metaphor theory. Sensorimotor experience means a physical experience that is shaped by our senses and based on our embodiment, while subjective experience is a state or emotion that we feel and try to describe. For instance, as Kövecses explains, "HAPPY IS UP is best viewed as a primary metaphor, where being happy is a subjective experience and being physically up is a physical one that is repeatedly associated with it."[91] Lakoff and Johnson provide a list of primary metaphors that includes the following metaphors: AFFECTION IS WARMTH, IMPORTANT IS BIG, INTIMACY IS CLOSENESS, BAD IS STINKY, DIFFICULTIES ARE BURDENS, and PURPOSES ARE DESTINATIONS.[92]

George Lakoff and Mark Johnson revisited previous proposals of primary metaphor theory and, building on their predecessors' findings, developed the integrated theory of primary metaphor.[93] This theory takes into consideration Christopher Johnson's theory of conflation in learning, Grady's theory of

---

88. Lakoff, "Neural Theory," 29.

89. Lakoff and Johnson, *Philosophy in the Flesh*, 53 (emphasis original).

90. Kövecses, *Where Metaphors Come From*, 5.

91. Kövecses, 5–6.

92. Lakoff and Johnson, *Philosophy in the Flesh*, 54–57.

93. Lakoff and Johnson, *Philosophy in the Flesh*, 50.

primary metaphor, Narayanan's neural theory of metaphor, and Fauconnier and Turner's theory of conceptual blending.[94]

In his theory of conflation in learning, Christopher Johnson conducted a study on the process of metaphor acquisition in children and how they learn using the metaphor KNOWING IS SEEING. He observed that children initially use the word "see" in a literal sense: "Let's see what is in the box." In the early stages, source and target domains are conflated in children; but since most of their knowing comes from seeing, they quickly learn to use "see" in a metaphorical sense: "Let's see what sound it makes," "See, it is hot," or "I see what you mean."[95] Lakoff and Johnson conclude that "early conflations in everyday experience should lead to the automatic formation of hundreds of primary metaphors that pair subjective experience and judgment with sensorimotor experience."[96]

Joseph Grady, building on Lakoff and Johnson's theory of conceptual metaphor and Johnson's theory of conflation, formulated his own theory of primary metaphors. Grady observes that there is "a set of pervasive conceptual metaphors which seem to reveal with special directness the deep relationships between word usage, conceptual structure, and the way we experience the world."[97] He maintains that complex metaphors are "elaborations of conceptualizations which are, at bottom, primary metaphors."[98] He also believes that primary metaphors are universal because "humans everywhere share the basic patterns of perception and experience that are reflected in primary metaphor."[99] Therefore, it is not surprising that similar primary metaphors appear in various languages and cultures. Grady gives as an example of such a broad cross-linguistics distribution metaphorical expressions that are

---

94. Grady, "Foundation of Meaning"; Narayanan, "Karma,"; Fauconnier and Turner, *Way We Think*.

95. Lakoff and Johnson, *Philosophy in the Flesh*, 52–53

96. Lakoff and Johnson, 53.

97. Grady, "Metaphor," 192.

98. Grady, 193.

99. Grady, 194. Ning Yu conducted a study on primary metaphors and their dependence on body and culture, arguing that "while the body is a potentially universal source for emerging metaphors, culture functions as a filter that selects aspects of sensorimotor experience and connects them with subjective experiences and judgments for metaphorical mappings." Yu, "Metaphor from Body and Culture," 247.

conceptualizations of "important" as "large." When people say, "It is a big day!" they mean that is a very important day.[100]

Narayanan and, later, Lakoff and Johnson – while working on their neural theory of language – describe primary metaphors as "neural connections learned by coactivation" and point out that "whenever a domain of subjective experience or judgment is coactivated regularly with a sensorimotor domain, permanent neural connections are established via synaptic weight changes."[101]

Fauconnier and Turner's theory of conceptual blending – which also plays a vital role in Lakoff and Johnson's integrated theory of primary metaphor – will be presented in more depth in the next section.

The New Testament is filled with examples of primary metaphors. In the Gospel of Mark, the primary metaphor KNOWING IS SEEING underlies Jesus's conversation with his disciples, and its force is better appreciated when its context is taken into consideration. Mark 8:1–21 describes Jesus feeding 4,000 people and then turning down the Pharisees' demand of to give them a sign that would confirm his messianic status. As Jesus crossed over to the other side of the sea with his disciples, he exhorted them to "beware of the leaven of the Pharisees" (Mark 8:15), but they were worrying about not taking any bread with them. Noticing their preoccupation, he said, "Do you not yet see or understand? Do you have a hardened heart? Having eyes, do you not see? And having ears, do you not hear?" (8:17–18). He asked a similar question in verse 21: "Do you not yet understand?" Here again, Jesus was talking about understanding in terms of hearing and seeing, and his words are emphasized by the fact that this whole account is bracketed by two miracle stories. In the first story, Jesus opened the ears of a deaf man by saying "Ephphatha," which means "Be opened" (Mark 7:31–37). In the second story, he opened the eyes of a blind man, but did so in stages (8:22–26). Jesus opens ears and eyes, but here were his disciples who had ears and eyes but did not really hear and see – they did not understand.

From a hermeneutical point of view, a study of primary metaphors is essential since these metaphors are largely universal and cross-cultural. As Bonnie Howe argues, "the existence of these universals helps explain how

---

100. Grady, "Metaphor," 194.

101. Lakoff and Johnson, *Philosophy in the Flesh*, 60. See also Lakoff, "Neural Theory," 26–27.

understanding and translation can work across cultural differences and temporal distances as significant as the ones that loom between modern readers and the writers and first readers of the New Testament."[102] Furthermore, identifying primary metaphors is an essential step in analyzing and understanding complex metaphors. From a homiletical perspective, recognizing image schemas and primary metaphors is a vital stage in developing complex new metaphors that are based on these image schemas and primary metaphors.

3.3.9 Mental Spaces and Blendings

The concepts of mental spaces and blending theory give rise to another approach within an area of Cognitive Linguistics that seeks to describe and explain the phenomenon of metaphors and the way they function. Fauconnier defines mental spaces as "very partial assemblies constructed as we think and talk, for purposes of local understanding and action" and adds that "they contain elements and are structured by frames and cognitive models."[103] Lakoff, explaining this notion from a neurolinguistic perspective, states that a mental space "is a mental simulation characterizing an understanding of a situation, real or imagined."[104] Several elements in these definitions are worth emphasizing. Similar to frames and domains, mental spaces serve the purpose of organizing our knowledge. They are mental simulations or constructs that come into existence as we think or talk. The notion of mental spaces is more specific than domains and frames since mental spaces carry more information, as will be shown in the next section. Furthermore, mental spaces "are not equivalent to domains, but, rather, they depend on them: spaces represent particular scenarios which are structured by given domains."[105] Thus, mental spaces represent ideas and are made of numerous sources including different conceptual domains.[106]

The most important element of this theory is the fact that when we come up with new ideas, they are the result of a blending of mental spaces. When discussing the issue of human creativity, Mark Turner boldly states that "the

102. Howe, *Because You Bear This Name*, 84.

103. Fauconnier, "Mental Spaces," 351

104. Lakoff, "Neural Theory," 30.

105. For a more detailed discussion on differences between conceptual metaphor theory and blending theory, see Grady, Oakley, and Coulson, "Blending and Metaphor," 101–124.

106. Fauconnier, "Mental Spaces," 352

human spark comes from our advanced ability to blend ideas to make new ideas" and claims that "blending is the origin of ideas."[107] He believes that our ability to blend ideas is an intrinsic cognitive feature of human beings and cites the example of the discovery of a thirty-two-thousand-year-old figurine of a lionman that was found in Germany in 1939.[108] Even though lions and men differ greatly, at some point, somebody blended these two concepts and came up with the idea of a lionman. Turner stresses, "*Lions* and *man* are not merely held in mind at the same time; they are also used to create a new, blended concept, a *lionman*, which is neither a lion nor a man, exactly".[109] This process of creating new ideas can also be seen in children's games, where a child may run around shouting "I am a tiger," blending together the idea of a child with the idea of a tiger and, by doing so, creating a new concept.[110]

Mark Turner describes this process of emerging new concepts. He points out that mental spaces create integration networks and a prototypical integration network typically consists of four elements: two input spaces, a generic space, and a blended space.[111] A prototypical integration network can be presented in the form of a diagram.

In this diagram, there are two input spaces that represent different ideas that are put together. In the case of a lionman, it will be the ideas of a lion and a man. As in conceptual metaphor theory, there are partial cross-space mappings that "connect counterparts in the input mental spaces."[112] Then, there is a generic space and, as Fauconnier and Turner explain, "a generic mental space maps onto each of the inputs and contains what the inputs have in common."[113] Coulson elaborates on this by saying that it "represents abstract properties that apply to structure in all the spaces."[114]

---

107. Turner, *Origin of Ideas*, 15. iBooks.

108. Turner, 34.

109. Turner, 35 (emphasis original).

110. Turner, 35–36.

111. Coulson, *Semantic Leaps*, 118.

112. Fauconnier and Turner, *Way We Think*, 41.

113. Fauconnier and Turner, 41.

114. Coulson, *Semantic Leaps*, 118.

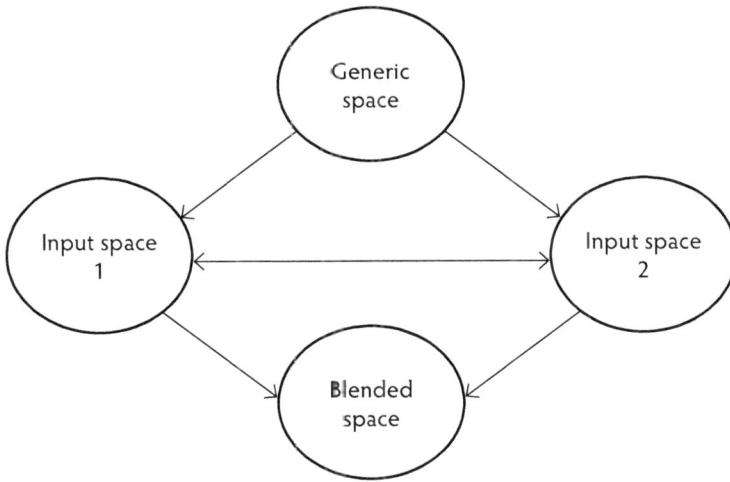

Diagram 5. Mental spaces

Finally, there is the fourth space, called a blended space. As Mark Turner explains the blend is "not an abstraction, or an analogy, or anything else already named and recognized in common sense."[115] However, he stresses that "a blend is a new mental space that contains some elements from different mental spaces in a mental web but that develops new meaning of its own that is not drawn from those spaces."[116] This blended space is a space where new meaning emerges.

3.3.9.1 Conceptual Metaphors and Blendings

Even though blending theory is not seen as competing with but, rather, complementing conceptual metaphor theory, there are some significant differences between these two theories.[117] As stated earlier, mental spaces are not equivalents of domains. Grady, Oakley, and Coulson point out that blending theory differs from conceptual metaphor theory because it is based on four or more mental spaces instead of two domains as basic organizational units.

---

115. Turner, *Origin of Ideas*, 23.

116. Turner, 23.

117. For more details on how conceptual metaphor theory and blending theory are complementary, see Fauconnier and Lakoff, "On Metaphor and Blending," 393–399.

[118] Some cognitivists emphasize that even though both theories can be used to describe metaphors and explain how they function, in some cases, blending theory produces better results when it comes to explaining the meaning of metaphors.

Grady, Oakley, and Coulson give the example of the metaphor "this surgeon is a butcher," which means that the surgeon is incompetent. They point out that while conceptual metaphor theory, with its source and target domains, can be used to describe how this metaphor functions, it does not explain how the idea of incompetence appears since it is not a part of a source domain and, consequently, cannot be projected to a target domain. Being a butcher does not mean lack of competence, but butchers use a less precise technique for cutting meat than surgeons do when performing surgeries.[119] This new concept of incompetence emerges as a result of the conceptual blending of several mental spaces. Kövecses explains it by saying that in this case there are two input spaces: surgery and butchery. There is also the generic space of a person who uses a sharp tool to cut either meat or the body, and this generic space has a structure that is shared by both input spaces.

Finally, there is a blended space that utilizes some of the structures of both input spaces, such as a butcher using the means of butchery to cut meat and a surgeon using the means of surgery to bring healing. Kövecses explains that "in the blend there is a surgeon in the role of a butcher who uses a tool and the means of butchery for the purpose of healing a patient"[120] and concludes that "a surgeon cannot do a good job in trying to heal a human patient by using the means of butchery."[121] Any surgeon who did so would be considered incompetent. Thus, by blending two mental spaces of a surgeon and a butcher, a new blended space appears and new meaning emerges – namely, a surgeon who acts like a butcher.

3.3.9.2 Blendings in the Bible

Blending theory is also very relevant in biblical interpretation. Bonnie Howe, analyzing the biblical metaphor of the devil who, as our adversary, "prowls

---

118. For a more detailed discussion on differences between conceptual metaphor theory and blending theory see Grady, Oakley, and Coulson, "Blending and Metaphor," 101–124.

119. Grady, Oakley, and Coulson.

120. Kövecses, *Metaphor in Culture*, 268.

121. Kövecses, 268–269.

around like a roaring lion" (1 Pet 5:8), says that in order to understand this metaphor, it is necessary to take into consideration more domains than just a source and a target domain. She proposes that the following domains must be considered in analyzing this metaphorical statement: the Interpersonal Conflict Domain (an opponent, an adversary); the Legal Domain (an accuser, a slanderer); the Supernatural Beings and the Powers Domain (the devil as an evil supernatural being); and the Animal Domain (a roaring lion, which prowls).[122]

In order to understand how this model functions, it is helpful to analyze the biblical metaphor of Christians as the temple (ὁ ναός) of the Holy Spirit or God. The word ὁ ναός appears forty-five times in the New Testament, usually referring to the temple in Jerusalem but sometimes referring to pagan temples or to the body of Christ. This word is used four times to depict believers (1 Cor 3:16–17; 6:18–20; 2 Cor 6:16; Eph 2:19–21.[123] In 1 Corinthians 3:16–17, Paul says that God's temple is holy, that whoever destroys it will be destroyed, and that the church, as God's temple, is holy and protected by God; as God's temple, it is also the dwelling of the Holy Spirit. In 1 Corinthians 6:18–20, Paul writes that the bodies of believers are God's temple since they are indwelled by the Holy Spirit. Thus, since, as Christians, our bodies do not belong to us, we should not indulge in immorality but worship God in our bodies. In 2 Corinthians 6:16, a whole discussion about Christians being the temple of God is placed in the ethical context of unhealthy relationships with a pagan culture. Again, Paul depicts the temple as a place of God's dwelling and, in a similar fashion, the Christian community as a place where God dwells since it is a community that belongs to God. Finally, in Ephesians 2:19–21, Paul describes the Christian community as being made up of both Jews and Gentiles who, as one temple, "built on the foundation of the apostles and prophets," with Christ himself as its "corner stone." One more time, this temple is depicted as holy and as a dwelling of God himself.

Even a brief analysis of these texts indicates that they all have a blend of two ideas – namely, a Christian community and the temple of God. A closer look at the Pauline depiction of the temple reveals common features, such as a holy place, belonging to God, and being God's dwelling. Even though

---

122. Howe, *Because You Bear This Name*, 84–87.
123. Balz, EDNT 2:457.

it is possible to harmonize all these passages and analyze the metaphor of a Christian community as the temple of God, from a biblical preaching perspective, it is much more relevant and useful to focus on one particular metaphor as presented in a single text and interpret it in its context, and this is my intention as well.

In considering the blending process as it occurs in Ephesians 2:19–21, we can identify two input spaces – namely, the input space of the temple of God and the input space of a Christian community that is made up of both Jews and Gentiles. In fact, Paul's understanding of Christian community is a result of yet another blending – that of various nationalities forming one church. Returning to the metaphor of the church as the temple, the input space of the temple of God has several features of the temple – a building, having a foundation, being built, holy, a physical sign of God's presence (God's dwelling).[124] On the other hand, the input space of a Christian community has the following characteristics: being established by Christ, founded on the teaching of the prophets and apostles, growing, being made up of different people, and belonging to God.

A generic space presents the common properties of both input spaces – for example, being established on a common foundation, the idea of growth, being made of different parts, and the idea of ownership. Thus, in the generic space, there are generalized elements that are common to both input spaces, and these are the elements the hearer or reader brings to the metaphor.

In a blended space, new ideas emerge – for example, a community of believers as the temple of God. It appears that the church as God's temple is built on a foundation of the apostles and prophets, with Christ is its cornerstone. This temple is made of many different people, including Jews and Gentiles, who have been made one in Christ. This temple is being built by God, and it is growing because it is made up of people who are being built together. The church is holy since it is a dwelling place of God.

Thus, the blended space differs from the generic space in that the common elements – which are very general when they appear in the generic space – become more specific and form a new blend that combines the ideas of the temple and the church. As a result, the reader starts perceiving the church as the temple of God. What is important in the blended space is that there are

---

124. Balz, EDNT:457.

elements that do not appear in the input space of the church. For instance, we do not typically think about a Christian community as a dwelling. This new idea emerges as concepts of temple and church are blended together.

In summary, despite some differences, conceptual metaphor theory and conceptual blending theory are complementary and are based on the same theoretical framework. Behind both these theories is the presupposition that two different concepts, when put together, lead to the emergence of a new concept. Moreover, since both theories enrich our understanding of the mental processes underlying the creation of metaphors, they are effective tools for interpreting biblical texts.

3.3.10 Levels of Metaphor

When studying Cognitive Linguistics, some terms may seem confusing and overlapping – for example, image schema, domains, frames, and mental spaces. This is partly because these terms belong to different theories but still describe different phenomena that might be difficult to differentiate and relate to each other. Therefore, Zoltán Kövecses undertakes the task of explaining the interrelationships between these notions on the basis of levels of schematicity and specificity and explains his "multi-level view of conceptual metaphor."[125] He claims that these four conceptual structures – namely, image schemas, domains, frames, and mental spaces – belong to four different levels of schematicity, as shown in the diagram below.

Most schematic	image schema	Least specific
	domain	
	frame	
Least schematic	mental space	Most specific

Diagram 6. Levels of schematicity[126]

This diagram shows the interrelationship between image schemas, domains, frames, and mental spaces. As evident in the diagram, image schemas are the most schematic – as pictured by the upward arrow – and the least

---

125. Kövecses, "Levels of Metaphor," 1.
126. Adapted from: Kövecses, 2.

specific, as pictured by the downward arrow. Domains and frames are more specific but less schematic than image schemas, whereas mental spaces are the least schematic and the most specific.

In trying to capture differences between various levels of schematicity, it is helpful to see differences between image schemas, domains, frames, and mental spaces. Image schemas, as analogue patterns, are the most general conceptual structures and are the basis for the development of more complex structures, such as domains, frames, and mental spaces.

Domains, as opposed to image schemas, are not "analogue, imagistic patterns of experience but propositional in nature in a highly schematic fashion."[127] They belong to a different level of schematicity because they consist of more parts than image schemas and carry more information.

Frames, on the other hand, "elaborate particular aspects of a domain matrix; that is, particular higher level concepts within a domain."[128] Following Karen Sullivan, Kövecses argues that "frames involve more conceptually specific information than domains." [129]

Finally, there are mental spaces that are defined as "highly specific structures occurring in online processing in particular communicative situations."[130] This notion of online processing refers to structures coming into existence during the time of speaking or writing in a particular communicative situation. Kövecses points out that mental spaces "borrow their structure from frames, but the generic structures from frames are further elaborated by specific information from context."[131] While distinguishing mental spaces from other conceptual structures, he emphasizes the fact that they are used for purposes of local understanding as "online representations of our understanding of experience in working memory, whereas frames and domains are conventionalized knowledge structures in long-term memory."[132]

In summary, I believe that Kövecses has shown, convincingly, that the conceptual structures described above belong to different levels of schematicity.

---

127. Kövecses, 3.

128. Kövecses, 4.

129. Kövecses, 4. For a further discussion on frames and domains, see Sullivan, *Frames and Constructions.*

130. Kövecses, 6.

131. Kövecses, 4.

132. Kövecses, 4.

According to Kövecses, image schemas differ from other conceptual structures in that they are analogue patterns, whereas mental spaces are online representations that come into existence during the time of speaking.

These levels of schematicity can be seen when examining the metaphor of the church as the body of Christ. This particular metaphor is an elaboration of several different image schemas such as VERTICALITY, UP-DOWN, CONTAINER, OBJECT, and PARTS-WHOLE. These image schemas can be seen in the fact that Christ, who is the highest authority over the church, is the head of the church; since the head is the highest part of the body, it evokes the image of VERTICALITY and UP-DOWN. The church is made of many people, who are presented as body parts, which is an example of a PARTS-WHOLE image schema.

Speaking of domains, the church as the body of Christ is an actualization of a general metaphor – ORGANIZATIONS ARE LIVING ORGANISMS – and, in this particular case, consists of two domains: the source domain of a human body and the target domain of a church. Metaphorical mappings highlight key aspects of this metaphor, such as the importance of the head, existence of different parts, various levels of importance of the parts, and mutual cooperation.

The source domain of the body evokes frames such as anatomy, health and disease, proper and improper functioning, hierarchy, hygiene and taking care of the body, and the function of different parts.

Finally, following Kövecses's model, there are mental spaces that can result in blendings, such as a church as being unhealthy, a headless church that denies Christ's authority, or a church that is missing a leg and an arm after a severe conflict and division. Thus, while examining this particular metaphor of the church as the body of Christ on different levels of schematicity, there is a clear progression of conceptual structures from the most schematic to the most specific in terms of carried information.

3.4 Chapter Summary

The aim of this chapter was to present those elements of Cognitive Linguistics, especially conceptual metaphor theory, that are most applicable to the analysis of biblical texts. In order to show how these theories are productive when applied to biblical interpretation, I provided examples of their usefulness in biblical exegesis.

I am convinced that Cognitive Linguistics is productive in biblical exegesis because it advances our understanding of human cognition by considering the newest findings in linguistics, sociology, psychology, neuroscience, and other fields of knowledge. Cognitive Linguistics attempts to explain human perception of the world by emphasizing the fact that human minds are embodied and that this factor shapes our whole conceptual system. Human beings perceive the world in terms of categories, frames, and prototypes that serve the purpose of organizing and reducing the complexity of their environment. Consequently, human language is largely metaphorical and conceptual metaphors are ubiquitous since they permeate the majority of human verbal communication.

Even though various insights presented in this chapter can be gained using more traditional approaches to hermeneutics, Cognitive Linguistics enhances our methodology of biblical studies, giving us a helpful language to conduct biblical analysis and express its findings. For instance, the notions of categories, prototypes, and frames are useful in recognizing the key concepts in the text, but they also provide the preacher with a systematized approach to conducting an analysis of the understanding of these concepts in their original setting. The notion of prototypes changes the preacher's approach to biblical ethics, stressing the fact that it is not based on rules but on prototypical models. Consequently, this enhances our reading and understanding of the text since, instead of perceiving its message in terms of rules, we start identifying mental models.

Various elements of conceptual metaphor theory, as discussed in this chapter, help preachers to interpret biblical metaphors and images in a much more holistic fashion, seeing them not only as linguistic decorations but as conceptual phenomena.

As opposed to the traditional understanding, which sees metaphors as embellishments – which must be removed in the process of interpretation in order to discover the underlying concepts – metaphors are viewed as vehicles for conveying concepts.

Finally, Kövecses's model of levels of metaphor is enlightening in its presentation of the various theories belonging to the broad family of Cognitive Linguistics as being interconnected and interdependent. This approach is important and is also reflected in the final chapter, which deals with sermon structure on both the micro and macro level.

CHAPTER 4

Sharpening the Vision: Applying Cognitive Linguistics to Hermeneutics

The previous chapter presented numerous examples of the application of Cognitive Linguistics to biblical interpretation. In this chapter, I expound on correlations between Cognitive Linguistics and biblical hermeneutics, and also elucidate the general hermeneutical principles governing the interpretation of biblical metaphors and images. The aim of this chapter is to apply Cognitive Linguistics to biblical interpretation in order to make sense of biblical images and to be able to convey these images in preaching. While I will engage with a number of hermeneutical issues that need to be taken into consideration when it comes to interpreting and preaching biblical metaphors, I am well aware that each of these issues could well be a topic for a separate book. Therefore, I do not intend to present an exhaustive treatment of these hermeneutical issues nor to develop a comprehensive theory of biblical interpretation. Instead, I want to build on the theological assumptions and the theories of metaphors presented in the previous chapters in order to show how they influence preachers' interpretation of biblical metaphors.

Thus, in the first part of this chapter, I will discuss the question of the relationship between the authors, the texts, and the readers, showing that Cognitive Linguistics sheds a new light on some old dilemmas associated with this subject and questioning the idea of stressing the importance of only one element of communication over the others.

While presenting the Cognitive Linguistic perspective on issues of the author, the text, and the reader, I will also take into consideration the notions of cultural universality and variation and show how these concepts allow us to see cultural distance and closeness between the reality as presented in the text and our own reality. In this section, I will also discuss the problem of identifying in the text timeless truths that are not culture-bound. Even though I appreciate the idea of cultural variations and understand the limitations of individual human perceptions, I will argue with John Sanders' view on the impossibility of identifying timeless truths in the text.

In the second part of this chapter, I will show the importance of perceiving and analyzing metaphors as part of discourse, exposing how a discourse analysis that utilizes the apparatus of Cognitive Linguistics affects our interpretation of biblical metaphors and images. In this section, the importance of a contextual study of metaphors will be emphasized.

This chapter will conclude with a presentation of a summary of a hermeneutical methodology that could be applied to sermon preparation. Although there are several studies on how Cognitive Linguistics can be applied to hermeneutics, there is a gap in literature with regard to resources that address the issue of Cognitive Linguistics in hermeneutics in the context of homiletics and sermon preparation. Therefore, this short section is an important step towards developing a preaching methodology that utilizes Cognitive Linguistics.

4.1 Cognitive Linguistics on the Author, the Text, and the Reader

In any discussion on hermeneutics, the challenge of defining a relationship between the author, the text, and its readers is inevitable. These three elements are foundational in every hermeneutical system and are indispensable in communication. Any communication act can only take place because there is a communicator who wants to communicate some kind of a message, a message that is being communicated, and a recipient of this message. Thus, in the process of studying biblical texts, interpreters can discern three kinds of meaning: the meaning intended by the author, which is called the authorial intention; the semantic and grammatical meaning of a text, which is labelled the textual meaning; and, finally, the meaning that is the result of the reader's understanding and interaction with a text, which is called the perceived meaning.[1] Hence, generally speaking, there are three approaches to interpreting biblical texts. The first approach is focused on the author, and can be called author-centred, author-oriented or authorial intention. The second is focused on the text itself, and can be called text-oriented or text centred approach. Finally, there are approaches focused on the reader, which can be called reader-oriented, reader-centred or reception theory.

Although a detailed analysis of the approaches listed above goes beyond the scope of this book, it is necessary to summarize these approaches briefly in order to be able to look at them from a Cognitive Linguistics perspective and develop a new proposal.

4.1.1 The Author-Centred Approach

The author-centred approach is based on the assumption that in order to interpret the text correctly, readers have to understand the author's intentions because "what the author intended is both *accessible* by means of the text, and is also *controlling* in interpretation".[2] Friedrich Schleiermacher, who is considered the father of modern hermeneutics, was one of the pioneers of the authorial intention approach. His method is based on both grammatical analysis of the text and reconstructing a psychological picture of the author and the author's perception of the text. Schleiermacher believes that when reading the text, the reader – in order to comprehend the author's intentions and personality – consciously or unconsciously uses a divinatory method and "transforms oneself into the other person and tries to understand the individual element directly."[3]

One of the prominent adherents of this approach is E. D. Hirsch, who, instead of psychologizing the author, proposes identifying the author's intentions as communicated in the text by means of shareable linguistic conventions. Hirsch believes that "verbal meaning is whatever someone has willed to convey by a particular sequence of linguistics signs and which can be

---

1. Klein, Blomberg, and Hubbard, *Introduction to Biblical Interpretation*, 169.

2. Paul, "Value of Paul Ricoeur's Hermeneutic," 151 (emphasis original).

3. Schleiermacher, *Schleiermacher: Hermeneutics and Criticism*, 92. A similar notion was later developed by Wilhelm Dilthey, who claimed that our understanding of the author on the basis of the text must surpass the author's own self-understanding. See Dilthey, "Hermeneutics and the Study of History," 232.

conveyed (shared) by means of these linguistics signs."[4] Therefore, it is reasonable to assume that the text means what its author meant and that this meaning can be understood in the process of studying the text.

According to Klein, Blomberg, and Hubbard, the author-centred textual meaning is "that which the words and grammatical structures of that text disclose about the probable intention of its author/editor and probable understanding of that text by its intended readers."[5] Several other proponents of this approach follow similar lines of reasoning and, instead of talking about authorial intentions, prefer using terms such as "communicative intentions" or "embodied intentions."[6]

Over the years, concerns have been raised regarding the authorial intention approach. Some scholars – following the footsteps of Wimsatt and Beardsley, who created the term "intentional fallacy" – believe that authorial intentions cannot be accessed by readers and are actually redundant because texts are autonomous sources of meaning.[7] Since readers do not have direct access to the authors' minds and cannot ask them for clarification, some scholars view this approach as highly subjective, especially in an analysis of ancient writings where the distance between the author and the reader is much greater than in live speech or even contemporary writings.

In the exegesis of biblical texts, it is sometimes difficult to identify the author at all, as with the Epistle to the Hebrews, or there may be more than one author, or the work may include later editors. It is possible that the authors said something they did not mean or said something in a way that was unclear. Some texts, especially prophetic ones, may have several different fulfilments or might have been used in contexts that were far removed from the original one.

4.1.2 The Text-Centred Approach

Some scholars suggest that instead of focusing on what authors might or might not have wanted to say, it seems more prudent to emphasize the autonomy

---

4. Hirsch, *Validity in Interpretation*, 31.

5. Klein, Blomberg, and Hubbard, *Introduction to Biblical Interpretation*, 185.

6. For communicative intentions, see Brown, *Scripture as Communication*, 70. For embodied intentions, see Sternberg, *Poetics of Biblical Narrative*, 9.

7. Wimsatt and Beardsley, "Intentional Fallacy," 1–13.

of a text and search for textual meaning instead of authorial intentions.[8] In his essay with the telling title "The Death of the Author," Roland Barthes insists that the text is a closed and self-governing entity and, as such, should be studied on its own terms, independently of its author.[9]

Paul Ricoeur provides further arguments against the idea of authorial intention and in favour of the autonomy of the text. He insists that there is a distinction between spoken and written communication and argues for distanciation between the author and the text that takes place once an utterance is written down. Moreover, he argues that meaning is never final, which is especially true in the case of metaphorical language that results in a "surplus of meaning" that goes beyond the original author's meaning.[10] Thus, the textual meaning can be established on the basis of an analysis of the text that is perceived as a complete whole; and its parts are studied in relation to the whole and the whole in relation to its parts.[11]

Michael Gorman, while rejecting the notion of discovering authorial intention as the ultimate goal of exegetical endeavours, claims that a "more modest and appropriate primary goal would be to achieve a credible and coherent understanding of the text on its own terms and in its own context."[12]

4.1.3 The Reader-Response Approach

According to proponents of the reader-response approach, the meaning of the text is neither established by its author nor determined by an analysis of the text but is produced by the reader on the basis of the reader's interaction with the text. Martin Heidegger provides the philosophical foundations for the development of this theory. He claims that when reading the text, readers bring to it their individual presuppositions that shape their understanding of its meaning. Some of these presuppositions might change in the process of

---

8. Among early adherents of this approach are John C. Ransom, Rene Wellek, and Monroe C. Beardsley. For a more detailed depiction of the text-oriented approach or the New Criticism, see Thiselton, *Hermeneutics*, 24–29.

9. Barthes, "Death of the Author," 125–130.

10. Ricoeur, *Interpretation Theory*, 75.

11. This approach prompted the application of literary theory to biblical studies, which can be seen in the works of Barr, *Semantics of Biblical Language*; Alter, *Art of Biblical Narrative*; Prickett, *Words and The Word*; and Paul, "Value of Paul Ricoeur's Hermeneutic," 154.

12. Gorman, *Elements of Biblical Exegesis*, 10.

reading, which results in the emergence of new presuppositions. Thus, the establishing meaning of the text is a result of the reader's interaction with it.[13]

Hans-Georg Gadamer pictures the idea of understanding a text as the fusion of two horizons – the horizon of the text and the horizon of the reader. In his view, meaning emerges in this process of dissolving the boundaries between the reader and the text so that "a person reading a text is himself part of the meaning he apprehends."[14]

Wolfgang Iser and Hans Robert Jauss represent a more moderate perspective on the role of the reader and place more significance on the text, while Norman Holland – who talks about "a transaction between the reader and the text" – and Stanley Fish – who stresses the authoritative role of the community interpreting the text – are more radical in their understanding of the active role of the reader in the creation of meaning.[15]

Anthony Thiselton summarizes this approach by saying that reader-response theory is based on the assumption that "a reader or a community of readers 'completes' the meaning of a text" because "the reader is not a passive spectator but actively contributes something to the meaning."[16]

Even though it is unquestionable that readers read texts through the lenses of their own experiences, personalities, and backgrounds, numerous scholars point out the weaknesses of the reader-centred approach. Mirosław Marczak argues that

> if we regard the reader as the ultimate determinant for the meaning of the text, this sets the meaning in an ever-changing flux, since the same reader on the second or third reading may alter his or her understanding of the meaning.[17]

Stephen Wright, even though he does not "hold to any naïve view of the accessibility or necessary relevance of an author's intention," stresses that "to

---

13. Brown, *Scripture as Communication*, 66.

14. Gadamer, *Truth and Method*, 340.

15. Marczak, "Significance of Peak," 37. See also Iser, *Act of Reading*; Jauss, *Toward an Aesthetic of Reception*; Fish, *Doing What Comes Naturally*; and Clines, *Bible and the Modern World*.

16. Thiselton, *Hermeneutics*, 306. For more on the reader-oriented approach, see Thiselton, 306–314.

17. Marczak, "Significance of Peak," 44.

focus only on the response-side is to miss *what the receiver is responding to*".[18] For this reason, he finds "the concept of authorial intention indispensable and important," while, at the same time, not minimizing the significance of the fact that some texts may convey more than their authors intended.[19] Consequently, he stresses that "to attend to the intention behind texts – whether, in the present context, they be texts of Scripture or texts of Scriptural interpretation – is to imply attentiveness to 'non-intended revelation' as well."[20]

Sean Burke provides a thoughtful critique of the idea of the death of the author and the emerging reader-centred approach. He points out that these critics of the author's role express their ideas in writing, becoming authors themselves, and notes:

> A vast body of secondary literature has grown up around their work, one which generally has sought not to contest or deconstruct what they say, but rather has re-enacted precisely the predominance of source over supplement, master over disciple, primary over secondary.[21]

Thus, even though some scholars advocate the death of the author and the primacy of the reader, these scholars have their own readers and followers who want to understand their ideas correctly and make great efforts to faithfully convey these ideas.

However, the greatest weakness of the reader-centred approach is divorcing the reader and the text not only from the context of communication – understood as an exchange of concepts between two parties – but even from the larger theological context of God's revelation, which also presupposes intentionality in God's communication with humans.

Consequently, it is not surprising that an increasing number of voices within biblical scholarship are calling for developing new and more mediated positions that would take into consideration the influence of the author, the text, and the reader in establishing the meaning. Jeannine Brown, who perceives Scripture as communication, is one of the proponents of this mediated approach. She defines meaning as "the complex pattern of what an author

---

18. Wright, "Voice of Jesus," 21–22 (emphasis original).

19. Wright, 22.

20. Wright, 21.

21. Burke, *Death and Return*, 160.

intends to communicate with his or her audience for purposes of engagement, which is inscribed in the text and conveyed through use of both sharable language parameters and background-contextual assumptions."[22] For Brown, the communicative intention that should be identified in the process of studying a text is "what an author actually does communicate by intention in a text."[23]

Kevin Vanhoozer rejects the idea that "meaning and reference are indeterminate, as well as the related idea that the author is 'dead' or irrelevant to the process of interpretation" and, at the same time, disagrees with the notion that "readers are free to manufacture or to manipulate textual meaning."[24] Instead, Vanhoozer claims that "the paradigm for a Christian view of communication is the triune God in a communicative action," which presupposes the existence of the sender and the receiver and understanding communication as an intentional action that aims at conveying communicative and informative intentions.[25] In his approach, a communicative action taken by the author assumes that the author's communicative intention can be determined in the text by the active reader. Accordingly, he defines meaning as "the result of communicative action of what an author has done in tending to certain words at a particular time in a specific manner."[26]

4.1.4 Implied Authors and Implied Readers

Considering that one of the main criticisms of the author-centred approach is the fact that authorial intentions are inaccessible since we cannot ask authors any questions for clarification, adherents of literary theory introduced the concept of the implied author and the implied reader. While it is true that readers do not have access to actual authors, they do have access to the writings where these authors present their ideas. Therefore, Jeannine Brown defines the notion of the implied author as "the textually constructed author who communicates with and seeks to persuade the implied reader." Identifying the implied author does not require psychologizing or speculating about the motives of the actual author since the implied author "can be

---

22. Brown, *Scripture as Communication*, 48.
23. Brown, 22.
24. Vanhoozer, *First Theology*, 164.
25. Vanhoozer, 168–169. See also Vanhoozer, *Is There a Meaning*, 201–280.
26. Vanhoozer, *First Theology*, 173.

discerned wholly from the text itself; the construct is implied in the text."[27] This textual construct is especially helpful because we, as the readers, do not have insight into the thoughts, motives, and intentions of the actual authors. In the case of some texts, the actual author is unknown or there is more than one author since these texts had several editors. However the concept of the inspiration of the biblical text means that we can understand the implied authors writing as conveying God's revelation.

Since we also do not have direct access to the actual readers, we try to identify the implied readers who are "textually constructed" and "presupposed by narrative or text."[28] Accordingly, the purpose of constructing the implied reader in the text is not only to envision the addressees of the authorial communicative intention – who were capable of understanding the text – but also to envision their responses to the text. This notion of the implied reader is especially applicable to biblical texts because these texts are meant to evoke both cognitive responses – expressed in deeper understanding and transformed thinking – and non-cognitive responses, which are seen in transformed behaviour.[29]

In analyzing biblical texts by employing the categories of the implied author and the implied reader, preachers attempt to envision the author's intentions and possible ways that readers may receive the text. However, I must point out that this process does not give them certainty about their conclusions.

Even though, by applying the tools provided by Cognitive Linguistics, preachers may be able to imagine the impact the author intended a particular metaphor to have or how that metaphor was received by readers, they cannot claim that they were able to establish the original meaning of the text. There is a difference between recovering the role of the author by stressing that the author matters in communication and claiming to have established the final meaning of the text. Thus, while an act of interpretation requires that we use our imagination, our predictions regarding the meaning of a text should be reinforced by clues found in the text itself. Imagination seems to be indispensable in entering the world of the implied author, the text, and

---

27. Brown, *Scripture as Communication*, 41.

28. Brown, 40. See also Eco, *Role of the Reader*, 7.

29. Brown, 40–41.

the implied reader, and it can be enhanced by utilizing the tools of Cognitive Linguistics – as will be shown below and in the next chapter.

4.1.5 Relationship between Authors, Texts, and Readers from a Cognitive Linguistics Perspective

The issue of meaning and the complex relationship between the author, the text, and the reader can also be addressed from the perspective of Cognitive Linguistics applied in the context of God's revelation, which is the means of God's communication. As we study the Bible, our goal is to discover what the authors wanted to communicate about God in their texts; however, considering the perspective of God's revelation and inspiration, we believe that it is actually God who communicates through the text and its human authors.

From the perspective of Cognitive Linguistics, and especially conceptual metaphor theory, communication, writing, reading, and interpretation are regarded as encounters of the minds of those involved in a communication process. John Sanders states that meaning "develops when minds encounter one another using shared conceptual structures that arise out of our embodiment experiences with our environment and from cultural frames."[30] Hence Cognitive Linguistics offers a new perspective on the issue of the author, the text, and the reader as presented above. Cognitivists do not focus separately on the authors, the texts, and the readers since all these elements belong to a single process of communication and are necessary for understanding human conceptualization. Thus, cognitivists are not interested in psychologizing the author's or reader's intentions but, rather, in discovering how thinking takes place and how both authors and readers conceptualize the world and individual pieces of information on the basis of their ways of using language. Hence, even though we do not have access to the actual authors, we can analyze the ways of conceptualization of the textually constructed implied authors. Moreover, Cognitive Linguistics allows us to overcome some of the distance between the actual authors and the implied authors since both share the same conceptual system that is largely shaped by their embodiment, which affects their thinking and construction of meaning.

Thus, in order to understand the close relationship between the implied authors, the texts, and the implied and contemporary readers, it is worth

---

30. Sanders, *Theology in the Flesh*, loc. 2063 of 5234, Kindle.

remembering that conceptual metaphors are based on conveying concepts. As stated earlier, conceptual metaphors can be defined as understanding one concept in terms of another to create a new concept. This definition presupposes that the authors, when employing metaphorical expressions in their discourses, do so intentionally in order to convey certain ideas. Consequently, the quest for identifying the concepts underlying conceptual metaphors is not only justifiable but also indispensable. When analyzing metaphorical texts, preachers should identify and analyze the concepts that were employed in order to create a metaphorical expression and understand what kind of new, blended concepts emerged as a result of this process.

Therefore, Cognitive Linguistics gives essential tools for thinking about and interpreting the Bible. In debates on biblical interpretation, various biblical scholars distinguish between the world of the text, the world of the author, and the world of the reader as if these were separate realms, often stressing the importance of one of these elements over the others. Cognitive Linguistics allows us to bring these separate worlds back together and place them in a unified process of communication. It helps to resolve the debate about the role of the implied author, the text, and the broadly understood readers in the process of interpretation. Instead of stressing the importance of only one element, it forces the interpreter to analyze the text holistically by taking into consideration the implied author, the text, and the implied and contemporary readers since the process of communication is always based on an encounter of minds in which all these elements play a part.

All writers bring their own concepts and perception of reality into their works, which are products of their conceptualization shaped by their experiences, frames, and embodiment; and all readers read texts through the lenses of their own perception, which are shaped in a similar fashion. Therefore, the text is the meeting point between the implied author and the implied and contemporary readers. It reveals the implied author's communicative intentions and challenges the perceptions and assumptions of the reader. Cognitive Linguistics gives us tools and categories to analyze the factors shaping these perceptions of the implied authors and the implied and contemporary readers, helping us to better understand the implied author, the text, and ourselves as we engage in the communication process.

4.1.5.1 Universality and Variation in Biblical Interpretation

When studying conceptual metaphors, it is necessary to consider both their universality and variation. Kövecses argues that universality of metaphors is based on our embodiment, whereas variation arises from differences in context.[31] In his opinion, "both universal embodiment and nonuniversal context affect the way people conceptualize the world in real communicative/ discourse situations."[32] This fact has important implications for our perception of the author, the text, and the reader.

Considering the fact that our perception of reality, our conceptual system, and the ways we use metaphors are rooted in our embodiment and primary bodily experiences, authors and readers, even though separated by centuries of history, share the same bodily structure and some universal conceptual frameworks that arise from their physical makeup.

Some cognitivists argue for the existence of panhuman truths, which are understood as "species-specific concepts shared by all normally functioning humans."[33] These panhuman truths include common image schemas such as UP-DOWN, FRONT-BACK, and NEAR-FAR. Justin Barrett talks about "expectation sets" that are universal and which include notions such as the passage of time, time being irreversible, causes preceding effects, the laws of nature being constant, an object having just one location, and solid objects being unable to easily pass through other solid objects.[34] As pointed out earlier, humans in all cultures organize their knowledge in categories. From a theological perspective, both authors and readers share the same human nature that results from being created in the image of God, but they also share the same fallen condition that results from sin. Thus, universality of the human conceptual system actually shortens the distance between the author and the reader.

On the other hand, variation and non-universality of particular concepts might be seen as an obstacle in grasping the implied author's communicative intention. However, from the perspective of Cognitive Linguistics, this is not a reason to ignore the implied authors in the process of interpretation but,

---

31. Kövecses, *Where Metaphors Come From*, 14

32. Kövecses, 51.

33. Sanders, *Theology in the Flesh*, loc. 1668 of 5234, Kindle.

34. Barrett also discusses our common expectations regarding animacy, mentality, and biology. Barrett, *Cognitive Science*, 61–68.

rather, could be a prompt to analyze their context, their language, and the ways they express their concepts in the text.

Zoltán Kövecses believes that variation in metaphors can be categorized as cross-cultural and within-culture variations. As an example of cross-cultural variations, Kövecses points to two factors – namely, congruence and alternative metaphorical conceptualizations – that result in the creation of metaphors that are unique to a given culture.[35] To illustrate congruence, Kövecses gives as an example the metaphor THE ANGRY PERSON IS A PRESSURIZED CONTAINER, which is a common metaphor existing in many cultures. However, he shows that this metaphor does not specify the kind of a substance that fills the container, the kind of container, or ways in which the pressure rises. Thus, despite congruence in the fact that this metaphor appears in many cultures, different cultures find their own ways to specify these elements. Japanese locate anger in the belly, whereas Zulus conceptualize the heart as a container for anger. Speaking of alternative metaphorical conceptualizations, Kövecses talks about the concept of happiness, which is captured in Chinese by a metaphor that does not exist in English – namely, HAPPINESS IS THE FLOWERS IN THE HEART, which is a completely different conceptualization.

Cross-cultural variations are also evident in the different ways of describing reality in egocentric and allocentric cultures. In egocentric cultures, the observer – who is the main point of reference – might say that a pen is to the right of a laptop; in allocentric cultures, people would use cardinal directions and say that the pen is to the southwest of the laptop. Consequently, applying Cognitive Linguistics to biblical studies requires an analysis of the cultural and historical context of both the authors and the texts that are the expressions of their conceptualizations.

Another example of cultural variation lies in the perception of certain emotions that are often culture-specific.[36] In Western culture, for instance, the biblical concept of God being jealous opens a frame of desiring to have something possessed by somebody else or fearing that somebody might steal the love of a person we love. Thus, jealousy is perceived as a negative emotion.

---

35. Kövecses, "Universality and Variation," 55–58. For a more extensive treatment of universality and variation in the use of metaphor, see Kövecses, *Metaphor in Culture*, 195–229.

36. For an extensive study on the subject of conceptualization of emotions, see Wierzbicka, "Everyday Conceptions of Emotion," 17–47.

In the Bible, however, this same emotion triggers a different frame because "jealousy is prompted by a perceived wrong when someone possesses something they should not."[37]

As far as within-cultural variations are concerned, Kövecses demonstrates how they can be seen in the following dimensions: social (including age, gender, social class, and education), regional, ethnic, stylistic, subcultural, diachronic, and individual. Kövecses draws his conclusions on the basis of his observations of how members of a given group use language and which metaphors they prefer.[38]

Conversely, while studying the text and its various contexts, readers have an opportunity to discover the universality and variation, closeness and distance, similarity and dissimilarity between the cultural context presented in the text and their own context. Some biblical concepts and metaphorical expressions are universal due to human embodiment and common cognitive systems; however, some concepts and expressions require further analysis due to cultural variations. In chapter 3, I provided examples of concepts such as a slave, a king, or a father – as used in the expressions "God is the king" or "God is the father" – that may be understood differently in various cultures. In order to determine differences in understanding of these concepts between biblical times and the present, it is necessary to study how the Bible itself presents these concepts.

To sum up, the notion of universality is a helpful concept in the analysis of the biblical text since it enables preachers to see connections between the biblical world and our world that are based on our embodiment, panhuman truths, and universal experiences. There are many primary metaphors, such as GOOD IS UP or AFFECTION IS WARMTH that are probably culturally universal because they are grounded in our embodiment. Kövecses argues that primary metaphors tend to be universal, while complex metaphors usually capture cultural differences.[39] Even metaphorical expressions that differ between cultures often refer to universal concepts and experiences such as happiness or anger.

---

37. Sanders, *Theology in the Flesh*, loc. 4098 of 5234, Kindle.
38. Kövecses, "Universality and Variation," 57–60.
39. Kövecses, 11–13.

Variation, on the other hand, allows us to appreciate the richness of biblical texts since we encounter numerous cultures, influences, and perspectives in the Bible. While immersing ourselves in understanding the concepts that are expressed differently due to cultural differences, we are also prompted to reflect on our own ways of conceptualizing such concepts.

Thus, the notions of universality and variation are helpful because they allow us to recognize the tension between the closeness and the distance between the preacher and the text. In order to identify similarity and variation, readers can can look into the cultural background which forms the context of the text. Even though knowledge of the cultural background might help in understanding the ancient perception of certain ideas, the primary source of knowledge about universality and variation is the text itself, an analysis of expressions that are used in the text, and how these expressions convey concepts. Moreover, the analysis of universality and variation can be an important step towards identifying the timeless truth of the text.

4.1.5.2 Timeless Truth of the Text

Another aspect of the debate about the author, the text, and the reader concerns the possibility of defining timeless truths or ideas that are behind biblical texts. Since, we are dealing with both universality and variation in human conceptualization – which depends on a time and a culture – is it justifiable to talk about the timeless meaning or timeless principle of the text?

John Sanders argues strongly against this notion of identifying timeless and culture-free principles behind biblical texts. He strongly criticizes this approach, saying that since readers are shaped by their own cultures, there is no culture-free perspective. He points out that even those who believe in identifying timeless truths in the text do not agree with each other on interpretations of major texts. He also sees a danger in the principlizing approach since this is an attempt to translate all biblical genres into propositional statements. In addition, he shows how different Christian communities, depending on a place, time, and culture, may read the same texts differently and over time even change their interpretations, adopting some teachings and rejecting others.[40]

---

40. Sanders, *Theology in the Flesh*, loc. 2110–2280 of 5234, Kindle.

For instance, Mark Allan Powell, after reading the parable of the prodigal son to Christians from the United States, Russia, and Tanzania, asked them why the younger son was hungry. The vast majority of Americans – who were living in a culture that tends to stress individual responsibility – said that it was due to his extravagant lifestyle. The Russians said it was because of the famine – and it is possible that their values and perspective had been shaped by their recent experiences of famine during World War II. And the Tanzanians, growing up in a very communal culture, believed that the son was hungry because nobody shared their food with him.[41]

Consequently, some scholars argue that finding the timeless and culture-free meaning is impossible. In order to prove this point, Sanders cites a few texts in which Paul instructs women to dress modestly (1 Tim 2:9). Sanders points out that while for Paul, immodest clothing was expensive clothes, in modern Western societies, this would refer to clothing that was inappropriate because it was sexually provocative. Quoting the commandment about children honouring their parents, Sanders states that in ancient times this commandment would also have included marrying a person of their parents' choice, which would be unthinkable for contemporary Western Christians.[42]

However, these two examples prove exactly the opposite of what Sanders intended. In the case of the word "modestly" (αἰδώς), even though cultural understanding of what modesty entails might differ, the context clarifies Paul's intentions because he explains that it means not adorning oneself with "braided hair and gold or pearls or costly garments." Thus, a preacher explaining the word "modestly" as only not dressing in sexually provocative ways would miss the point of this text, which exhorts women to take more pride in their character qualities than in their outward appearance. Taking pride in fashionable clothes and expensive jewellery continues to be an issue in our Western culture and people need to understand this.

On the other hand, there are different ways of trying to attract people's attention by outward appearance, and this might include wearing sexually suggestive clothes. So, after explaining the problem Paul had to deal with in respect of women in Ephesus, and then defining the timeless truth in these verses – namely, that Christians should pay more attention to the beauty of

---

41. Powell, *What Do They Hear?*, 11–27.

42. Sanders, *Theology in the Flesh*, loc. 3722 of 5234, Kindle.

their characters rather than to the beauty of their appearance – it is possible
to show some other applications of this truth that are more culture-specific.
This truth is applicable in every culture, even though the practicalities of the
application may vary. Speaking of honouring parents, it is true that in different times and cultures honour was expressed differently, but the general
principle that children should show respect to their parents holds true for all
times and is challenging and demands humility in every culture.

In my opinion, Sanders confuses timeless principles of the text – which
can be identified if we understand the meaning of the text – with culturally
conditioned and specific applications of the text that may vary depending
on time and place. Even though it might be possible to identify the timeless
truth of the text, this does not mean that the text must always be applied in
the same way and that we will never debate between better and worse, more
faithful and less faithful applications of the text.

Since the authorial or communicative intentions presented in the text
may go beyond what its human writers intended and may not be clear to us
due to cultural distance – because as humans we do not perceive the world
from a culture-free and body-free perspective – preachers should be aware
of the perils of the "intentional fallacy" (described in section 4.1.1. above).
However, the fact that revelation comes from a timeless God, whose character
does not change, makes it possible to identify the timeless truth about God
and his character as depicted in the biblical text. The text – which is inspired
by God and is part of his revelation – ultimately expresses the intentions of
its divine author.

4.2 Metaphors as a Part of Discourse

Determining the author's communicative intention plays a vital role in the
analysis of metaphors because without recognizing the underlying intentions behind a given statement, readers may have problems with interpreting
metaphors and even with recognizing them. If someone says that "John is a
butcher" or "Mary is a witch," this might be a simple description of their oc-
cupations, but it might also be a metaphorical depiction of their characters.
In isolation, these statements are ambiguous because they allow for the possibility of both interpretations, leaving readers bewildered regarding their true
meaning. In the Epistle to Philemon, the apostle Paul calls Onesimus his son.

Does this mean that these men were related by blood or is this a metaphor? This question might be impossible to answer if interpreters were not aware of the context of Paul's words and other relevant biblical texts.

One of the problems with the interpretation of metaphors is the fact that they are sometimes perceived in isolation. But when interpreting metaphors, we should take into consideration their larger literary context and the genre in which they are situated. While studying metaphors in their immediate literary context, we must also attempt to see how they function in the wider context of the Bible and whether they have the same meaning in different passages or whether these meanings differ or even change over time. Such changes may become apparent as preachers examine continuity and discontinuity between the Testaments or explore the Old Testament sources of New Testament images. Consequently, for the purpose of preaching, we need to investigate metaphors as a part of a discourse.

Paul Ricoeur defines discourse utilizing Saussure's terminology of *langue* and *parole*, where *langue* is "the code – or the set of codes – on the basis of which a particular speaker produces a *parole* of a particular message".[43] Starting with this Saussurean distinction, Ricoeur argues that discourse should be understood as the event of language, as opposed to language as an abstract system.[44] For Bonnie Howe, the term discourse refers to "naturally occurring connected speech and written texts, and 'discourse analysis' refers mainly to linguistic analysis of speech and written texts."[45] William Varner claims that discourse analysis "deals with grammatical and semantic functions as they affect meaning above the level of the sentence."[46] Mirosław Marczak summarizes three key tenets of a discourse analysis as follows: "(1) The interpreter/translator takes seriously the roles of the author, the audience, and the text in the communicative event. (2) The language is examined at a linguistic level broader than a sentence. (3) The discourse is analyzed in its social context."[47] Thus, in order to interpret metaphors correctly, it is necessary to apply the principles of discourse analysis.

---

43. Ricoeur, *Interpretation Theory*, 3.

44. Ricoeur, 9. For more on Ricoeur's view of discourse, read Chapter 1 of his book.

45. Howe, *Because You Bear This Name*, 168.

46. Varner, "Discourse Analysis," 211.

47. Marczak, *Significance of Peak*," 22–23.

Kövecses and other scholars claim that "a major function of the metaphors
we find in discourse is to provide coherence to discourse," and this coherence
can be intertextual or intratextual, which means that "metaphors can either
make several different texts coherent with each other or lend coherence to a
single piece of discourse."[48] Having said that, it is essential to point out that
metaphors and discourse are mutually complementary and indispensable
in that discovering coherence metaphors often allows for recognition of the
main idea of the discourse, but discourse as such provides the context for
the interpretation of metaphors, helping to identify them and to establish
their meaning.

Ian Paul makes a similar observation on metaphors and narrative, stressing that they appear to be "mutually inclusive." He states that metaphors are
an important component of narrative, which, in a sense, can be considered
"the extension of the metaphoric process across the larger texts."[49] However,
he also asserts that "the end result of narrative is also metaphoric, in that,
along with models in scientific discourse, and utopias in political discourse,
the narrative representation effectuate[s] a metaphorization of the real, a
creation of new meaning."[50]

Considering the fact that metaphors and discourse are closely intertwined,
it is time to establish some principles of interpreting metaphors in the context
of discourse. In order to do so, I will adopt and modify the methodology
presented by Kövecses. Among several contextual factors enumerated by
Kövecses that influence the creation of metaphors in various communicative situations, there are five which refer directly to the idea of the discourse:
(1) knowledge about the main elements of the discourse; (2) surrounding
discourse; (3) previous discourses on the same topic; (4) dominant forms of
discourse and intertextuality; and (5) the ideology underlying discourse.[51]
Even though Kövecses discusses factors that impact the formation of metaphors, I believe that these same factors should be taken into account when
studying metaphors in context. Thus, I am going to reverse Kövecses's methodology – instead of applying his observations to the formation of metaphors,

---

48. Kövecses, *Metaphor: A Practical Introduction*, 285.

49. Paul, "Value of Paul Ricoeur's Hermeneutic," 61.

50. Paul, 61.

51. Kövecses, *Where Metaphors Come From*, 53–57.

I utilize them for the purpose of a contextual analysis of existing metaphors in the discourse.

First, since metaphors are "specific to a particular discourse situation," it is important to begin by studying the key components of a discourse, namely, the speaker, the topic or theme of discourse, and the hearer or addressee.[52] Therefore, in the case of biblical metaphors and discourse, readers have to gather contextual information on biblical writers, their audiences, their relationships, and also on authorial communicative intentions as expressed in their texts. At this point, historical and literary analysis of the discourse is indispensable.

Second, it is crucial to become familiar with the surrounding discourse. Since metaphors provide coherence to discourse, readers should analyze the immediate context to find metaphorical repetitions, allusions, and repetitive image schema.

Next, readers have to take into consideration previous discourses that dealt with the same subject and their intertextual correlations. In the case of biblical texts, intratextuality and intertextuality intertwine since there is one complete canon of Scripture, which is made up of numerous books. Consequently, while studying biblical metaphors, there is a need not only to pay attention to instances of usage of the same metaphor in different passages in one book of the Bible but also to note its occurrences in other books of the Bible, including possible Old Testament sources of a given New Testament metaphor and textual allusions.

Fourth, the interpreter should become familiar with existing dominant forms of discourse. Conceptual metaphor theory does not exist in a vacuum; so, in order to use this theory effectively, readers have to be aware of principles of interpretation of different genres and literary forms of the Bible. For example, parables can be considered extended metaphors; however, in interpreting parables, preachers must respect the nature and interpretative limits of this genre by not allegorizing parables or trying to force meaning on every single narrative element of a given parable.

Finally, Kövecses talks about awareness of the ideology underlying a discourse, which must also be taken into account in interpreting a text.[53] In

---

52. Kövecses, 53.

53. Kövecses, 54–57.

respect of biblical metaphors, rather than speaking of ideology, it is more precise and appropriate to use the term biblical theology. Metaphors are to be interpreted not only in their immediate literary context, or even in the wider canonical context, but also in the context of biblical theology that presents God's vast plan for redemption of the world. This theology is based on the assumption that God chose to reveal himself and that he did so through the act of creation, especially through the creation of humans in his image, through Scripture, which is filled with images and is largely metaphorical in nature, and through the incarnation of Christ, who is the perfect image of God. Moreover, this revelation becomes personal in the Holy Spirit, who enlightens us, helping us to understand God's revelation, and conforms us into the image of Christ. Therefore, when we study metaphors, we do so in the context of the whole discourse and perceive these metaphors as elements uniting the discourse.

4.3 Summary of Methodology of Biblical Metaphor Analysis

In this part of the chapter, I present a summary of the methodology of biblical metaphor analysis that was described in this and the previous chapter. I am aware that many preachers may find the whole process of interpretation of metaphors from a Cognitive Linguistics' perspective challenging. However, the difficulty with utilizing this theory is not greater than with other theories, and understanding its basics is a prerequisite for its application. Analogically to use of traditional approaches to exegesis, the degree of application of this approach to a sermon preparation will depend on the preacher's level of expertise. Depending on their knowledge, skills, and experience, some preachers conduct extensive exegesis, whereas others are able to carry out only a very basic analysis of the text. Similarly, with regard to applying Cognitive Linguistics to biblical interpretation, preachers may find this confusing at the beginning but, with time and practice, the process becomes more natural.

Thus, in order to make the whole process of interpreting biblical metaphors using tools of Cognitive Linguistics more accessible for preachers, I have summarized it in a few steps that form a workable pattern they may follow and apply in sermon preparation. These five steps do not cover the whole exegetical process that is required in sermon preparation, nor are they meant to replace traditional exegesis; rather, their aim is to supplement exegesis with a clear methodology for interpreting metaphors and images that is based on the findings of Cognitive Linguistics. Utilizing this theory in hermeneutics changes our understanding of the dynamics of biblical interpretation by stressing the cognitive aspect of language and communication. It also gives tools, not only for the analysis of metaphors but also for analyzing prototypes, frames, and mental spaces. This methodology includes the five steps described below.

First, preachers should study metaphors as a part of a particular discourse and other discourses where they also appear, taking into consideration the elements of the discourse and its structure. During this process, it must be borne in mind that while metaphors often give unity to a discourse, discourse provides the context necessary for understanding metaphors.

Second, preachers must identify the key categories and prototypes that appear in a given text and recognize the processes that these categories undergo – for instance, category creation, contrast/comparison, transfer, reversal, and development. Since categories are developed around the most prototypical members of a given category, it is important to identify these members and understand them in a way that is as close as possible to their perception by the implied author and the implied audience. When studying prototypes, it is also helpful to pay attention to ways in which these prototypes appear in a text and the interplay between the typical, the stereotypical, and the ideal. Preachers should be able to recognize if a text pictures a typical prototypical member of a given category or the ideal one. The same applies to noticing prototypical scenarios in a given passage – for example, the scenario of meeting a future wife by the well in the Old Testament narratives – and understanding how portrayed scenarios differ from prototypical ones (Gen 24:1–67; 29:1–12; Exod 2:16–22).

Third, preachers should recognize the most basic phenomena – such as primary metaphors and image schemas – existing in a text. This is important because it may give clues about the internal structure of a text that might be based either on primary metaphors – for example, more is up – or elementary orientations, such as up and down, periphery and centre, a container, or a path.

Fourth, preachers must isolate conceptual metaphors and identify their source and target domains. In doing so, they will need to observe existing mappings and pay attention to elements of the source that are hidden or highlighted in the target. During this process, it is also relevant to ask questions about the implied author's knowledge of and personal exposure to the source domain.

This leads to the fifth step, which is analyzing domains. Preachers will find it helpful to identify the main conceptual frames that were shared by the implied author and the implied audience and to distinguish these frames from our contemporary ones. At this stage, the preacher must take into consideration issues such as cultural universality and variation, and the question of the timeless meaning of the text.

This methodology of biblical interpretation that utilizes Cognitive Linguistics allows us to study the text in a more holistic way since it does not only focus on the text from a linguistics perspective but also considers the fact that metaphors are conceptual phenomena and that the process of communication is an encounter of minds that includes the implied author, the text, and the implied and contemporary readers.

Moreover, this methodology of interpretation is a necessary step towards utilizing Cognitive Linguistics in homiletics, which aims to convey the meaning of the biblical text and address the whole human person by speaking to listeners' embodied minds, emotions, and imagination.

4.4 Chapter Summary

In this chapter, I have shown how Cognitive Linguistics can be applied to biblical interpretation and how it offers a new perspective on issues such as the importance of the author, the text, and the readers, as well as the principles of interpretation of metaphors in the context of the whole discourse. Since cognitive linguists perceive communication as an encounter of minds, they do not stress just one element of the communication process – such as the implied author, the text, or the implied and contemporary readers – but view this whole process in a unified fashion, as a single process, thereby underscoring the importance of all these elements. Moreover, as shown in the previous chapter, Cognitive Linguistics provides preachers with categories and methods of analysis of frames, prototypes, ways of conceptualizing both authors and readers, and an apparatus for interpretation of the text.

The notions of universality and variation are also helpful in interpreting the text because they allow the preacher to recognize the tension between cultural and experiential closeness and distance between the text and the reader. Universality helps preachers to see concepts and experiences that are common to the text and to their listeners. Variation can help them to appreciate the various cultural voices within the Bible itself and to perceive the distance between the world of the Bible and our world. Moreover, understanding universality and variation are among the factors that contribute to identifying the timeless truth of the text. Even though this notion is controversial among cognitivists, I am convinced that this idea of recognizing the timeless truth of a text is justified because the Bible, as the written record of God's revelation, contains panhuman truths and concepts that are considered universal.

I also discussed the fact that metaphors do not exist in a vacuum but that discourse analysis plays a vital role in their interpretation because the whole discourse affects understanding of metaphors, while metaphors often give unity to the discourse.

I concluded this chapter with a summary of a methodology for interpreting biblical metaphors, which is a starting point for preachers in their analysis of metaphors in the Bible.

CHAPTER 5

Showing the Unseen: Cognitive Linguistics and Preaching Metaphors and Images

Karl Barth believes that theology "as a church discipline ought in all its branches to be nothing other than sermon preparation in the broadest sense."[1]

Therefore, in this chapter, previous theological and hermeneutical discussions on ways of utilizing Cognitive Linguistics for preaching will be applied to homiletics and sermon preparation. The aim of this chapter is to give homiletical justification for using Cognitive Linguistics and to demonstrate how this theory is productive in sermon preparation by giving preachers a systematized approach to analyzing the world and images of the listeners, developing prototype-based application, conveying biblical images and metaphors in sermons, and developing a sermon structure.

This chapter consists of two major parts, the first of which is devoted to the issue of connecting the world of the Bible and the world of the listeners. In order to accomplish this task, I show the importance of imagination in preaching. Moreover, I demonstrate how preachers can analyze the world of the listeners – by using notions of universality, variation, and prototypes – in order to develop a prototype-based application.

In the second part of this chapter, I focus on the methodology for preaching biblical images and creating new images to convey the meaning of biblical texts. This section ends with a proposal for developing a sermon structure

---

1. Barth, *Homiletics*, 17.

that is based on Kövecses's levels of schematicity. I show how his notion can be applied to developing a sermon structure in general and sermon images in particular.

5.1 Preaching and Imagination: Connecting the World of the Bible and the World of the Listeners

From a homiletical perspective, it is difficult to disagree with Karl Barth's provocative statement that "a man without imagination is more an invalid than the one who lacks a leg."[2] Therefore, in this section, I will present the Cognitive Linguistics perspective on the topic of imagination, showing how this theory, in comparison to other approaches, greatly enriches our understanding of imagination and how imagination is an indispensable tool for preachers to understand the world of their listeners.

In this section, I will discuss how the notions of universality and variation – which were introduced in the previous chapter in the context of studying the text – can also be applied to gain a better understanding of our listeners.

Finally, I will depict a methodology for developing a prototype-based application that utilizes metaphors and narratives. This approach to application is based on the prototype theory described in chapter 3 and builds on the assumption that biblical morality is not rule-based but prototype-based.

5.1.1 Importance of Imagination in Preaching

If it is true that "God is a poet and speaks to the world in metaphors, symbols and parables," as Paul Avis claims, then preaching that echoes God's own speaking needs to recover its poetic dimension.[3] Thus, Walter Brueggemann argues that "the event of preaching is an event of transformed imagination."[4] It starts with imaginative listening to the word of God – which reveals the nature of God and his plan for humanity – and ends with equally imaginative listening to the listeners in order to communicate God's revelation effectively. According to Walter Burghardt, preaching "can be described as an appeal to

---

2. Barth, *Doctrine of Creation*, 91.

3. Avis, *God and the Creative Imagination*, 3.

4. Brueggemann, *Finally Comes the Poet*, 109.

the imagination of the hearers through the images of scripture."[5] He says that this can be accomplished when preachers are aware of their task in this process, which is "to meditate and facilitate that encounter by engaging his or her own imagination, which becomes the link between the scripture and congregation."[6]

The term "imagination" is closely related to the notion of images since it comes from the Latin word *imaginatio* and its root is *imago*, meaning "image."[7] For Trygve David Johnson, "imagination is an intentional act of the mind that is the genesis of creativity, novelty, and originality" and, in his understanding, "ties all perception, memory, emotional and rational thinking together."[8] Green suggests that imagination "re-presents what is absent; it makes present through images what is inaccessible to direct experience."[9] His definition is particularly applicable to preaching because it requires preachers to become immersed in the reality of ancient texts, then relate them to the listeners' lives, and, finally, help listeners to relate to the invisible God and live in this world as if they could see him.

Stephen Wright, explaining his approach to the biblical interpretation of history – which he calls "figural interpretation" – emphasizes that an imaginative engagement is necessary if preachers want to "juxtapose a passage from Scripture with an aspect of history, past or present."[10] Thus, he claims that imagination enables preachers to accomplish three goals, namely, "to penetrate beneath the surface of text and event, to perceive connections and to discern the way in which the juxtaposition can be made most meaningfully for one's hearers or readers."[11] Thus, an imaginative approach to Scripture is necessary at every stage of sermon preparation, which includes textual analysis, noticing connections between the listeners and the text, and formulating its application.

However, this understanding of the role of imagination in preaching is relatively novel since, for a long time in history, imagination was viewed

---

5. Burghardt, *Preaching*, 149.
6. Burghardt, 149.
7. Bruce, "Vital Importance," 37.
8. Johnson, "Preacher as Artist," 16.
9. Green, *Imagining God*, 62.
10. Wright, "Inhabiting the Story," 514.
11. Wright, 514.

with suspicion as belonging to the realm of fantasy or art and, therefore, not useful in science, theology, and preaching. A detailed analysis of the history of various approaches to imagination extends beyond the scope of this study and can be found elsewhere.[12] Nonetheless, for the purpose of this study, I discuss, in the following sections, the most characteristic views on imagination in preaching, and I will show that taking into account the contribution of Cognitive Linguistics to our understanding of imagination is foundational for developing new approaches to audience analysis and developing new application strategies.[13]

5.1.1.1 Views on the Role of Imagination

In this section, I briefly discuss the perspectives of a few scholars – representing various branches of Protestantism – who have contributed to studies on the role of imagination in preaching.[14]

Walter Brueggemann develops his idea of poetic imagination and preaching as reimagining. He asserts that "prophetic preaching, ancient or contemporary is a contest of competing imaginations – a contest between old Torah imagination that features YHWH as character and agent and the dominant imagination that predictably assimilates God into its powerful socio-political claims."[15] Brueggemann claims that imagination is poetic and that preaching employing imagination is to be perceived as reimagining because it aims at reshaping our vision of God, the world, and ourselves.[16]

John Stott values imagination as a tool in communicating the dominant thought of a text, but he also stresses the superiority of the text over

---

12. Avis, *God and the Creative Imagination*, 14–29; Green, *Imagining God*, 9–27; Bruce, "Vital Importance," 37–47; Johnson, "Preacher as Artist," 12–18; Green, *Theology, Hermeneutics, and Imagination*; Jensen, *Envisioning the Word*; and Troeger, *Imagining a Sermon*, 141–166.

13. For more on the importance of the imagination, see Elliott, *Creative Styles of Preaching*; Brueggemann, *Hopeful Imagination*; Fischer, *Inner Rainbow*; Green, *Theology, Hermeneutics, and Imagination*; Avis, *God and the Creative Imagination*; Wilson-Kastner, *Imagery for Preaching*; and Tracy, *Analogical Imagination*.

14. Walter Brueggemann (United Church of Christ), John Stott (the Church of England), Fred Craddock (Christian Church – Disciples of Christ), Barbara Brown Taylor (The Episcopal Church), Thomas Troeger (the Presbyterian Church and the Episcopal Church), Richard Eslinger (the United Methodist Church), and Paul Scott Wilson (the United Church of Canada).

15. Brueggemann, *Practice of Prophetic Imagination*, 27. For an overview of the different roles of imagination in preaching, see Elliott, *Creative Styles of Preaching*; Bruce, "Vital Importance," 48–86.

16. Brueggemann, *Cadences of Home*, 24.

imagination and sermon illustrations. For Stott, imagination must serve the ultimate purpose of expounding the text. He also sees a place for imagination in developing a sermon application as a skill that enables preachers to tie the message of the Bible with lives of listeners.[17]

Fred B. Craddock, stressing the role of imagination in entering the world of listeners, talks about empathetic imagination, which is "the capacity to achieve a large measure of understanding of another person without having that person's experiences."[18] According to Craddock, empathetic imagination, as practised by preachers, offers listeners both an understanding and a distance from their problems since people who are trapped in a difficult situation need a sense of being understood but also need to gain a new perspective on their situation that can often be offered by someone on the outside.[19]

Barbara Brown Taylor defines imagination as a risk. She suggests that to improve preaching, preachers need to be willing to take risks to experience life, try new exegetical approaches, tell new stories that do not sound religious, and play with untried sermon structures. From her perspective, imagination is visiting unfamiliar places in life, in ministry, and also in preaching. In order to preach well, one has to put aside well-used sermon strategies and experiment with new ones.[20]

Thomas Troeger talks about imagination as attentiveness that leads to imaginative theology. He is convinced that the primary principle for using and developing our imagination is the principle of being "attentive to what is."[21] By saying this, he opposes common views that present imagination as "fickle and fanciful, dealing more with dreams and visions than with actuality"[22] and points out that it is enough to look at works of art to be able to see that these artists "have drawn the raw material of their creativity from close observation."[23]

---

17. Stott, *I Believe in Preaching*, 252.

18. Craddock, *Preaching*, 95.

19. Craddock, *Preaching*, 96.

20. Taylor, Preaching Life, 48.

21. Troeger, *Imagining a Sermon*, 15. For more on using images in sermons, see Troeger, *Creating Fresh Images*.

22. Troeger, *Imagining a Sermon*, 15.

23. Troeger, 15.

This art of attentiveness to what is results in developing imaginative theology that "employs the visionary and integrative capacities of the mind to create theological understanding."[24] Troeger claims that this kind of theology "uses the powers of observation to become receptive to the Holy Spirit, who works upon our consciousness through patterns of association and juxtaposition."[25] Hence, preachers are the ones who make the observations and show their significance, but the Holy Spirit is the one who gives the new understanding.

Richard Eslinger develops the concept of narrative imagination, explores the notion of imagination as an image-making ability of the human mind, and introduces a categorization of various imagination types. He describes imagination as "seeing as," which he calls a perceptual model. This kind of imagination is at work as we perceive the world around us, seeing things as they are, memorizing them, recalling them, and creating mental images of the real world in our minds. The second type of imagination is "imagine that," which is at work when somebody imagines a state of affairs that is impossible in our world. The third type is "imagine how," which is about imagining consequences of this impossible state of affairs and how it could affect our life.[26]

Paul Scott Wilson, presenting a holistic understanding of imagination, states that imagination of the heart "reconciles heart and head, body and mind, in discerning God's purpose."[27] It aims at speaking to the whole person. Wilson explains how imagination works "as the bringing together of two ideas that might not otherwise be connected and developing the creative energy they generate."[28] He compares imaginative thinking to igniting a spark between two poles of a generator. "The spark of imagination happens when two ideas that seem to have no apparent connection (standing 'poles apart,' we might say) are brought together."[29] For Wilson, the power of imagination is a function of language that is about bringing together two opposites.[30] Wilson offers a few examples of these opposites that may generate creative tension:

---

24. Troeger, 15.
25. Troeger, 26.
26. Eslinger, *Narrative Imagination*, 57–69.
27. Wilson, *Imagination of the Heart*, 18.
28. Wilson, 32.
29. Wilson, 34.
30. Wilson, 34–36.

the biblical text and our situation, the Law and the Gospel, judgement and grace, the story and the doctrine, and, finally, the pastor and the prophet.

Even this brief presentation of various understandings of imagination in preaching shows that although numerous scholars agree that imagination is a vital factor in preaching, they still differ in their perception of its role and the way it functions. As Bruce observes, there is a lack of a "detailed theology of imagination, neither do we see a framework which holds together the complex field of meaning embraced by the term in a coherent and cognate way."[31] Various homileticians emphasize different aspects of imagination – for instance, the ability to see differently or create a transformed vision of reality (Brueggemann, Troeger, Eslinger, Wilson), helping to convey the main idea of a text (Stott), entering the world of the listeners (Craddock), and trying new approaches (Taylor). Bruce attempts to offer such a framework, pointing out different functions of imagination, such as sensory, intuitive, affective, and intellectual. She also discusses this notion of imagination within a wider theological context.[32]

5.1.1.2 Cognitive Linguistics Perspective on Imagination

Even though Cognitive Linguistics does not have a fully developed theory of imagination, cognitivists address its various aspects, and cognitive theory offers a helpful framework to address the notion of imagination in a much more systematic way. What is especially helpful in the cognitivist perspective is the fact that it provides terminology to describe imagination and explains the various cognitive processes involved in imagination. It appears that our imagination is based on the same processes that we employ in our conceptualization of the world. Thus, it is dependent on our embodiment and cultural experiences, and it utilizes cognitive structures such as image schemas, frames, and conceptual blendings.

Cognitivist Mark Johnson states that imagination is "the capacity for novelty" and "the capacity to organize mental representations (especially precepts, images, and image schemas) into meaningful coherent units."[33] Following the same line of reasoning, Mark Turner argues that the process of conceptual

---

31. Bruce, "Vital Importance," 86.
32. Bruce, 87–130.
33. Johnson, *Body in the Mind*, 140.

blending is the basis for all human creativity, including generating new ideas and imagination. Turner demonstrates how humans are able to imagine themselves in different situations, in other times and places. This is how people dream about the future, both its possible and desired versions, and not only dream about but also plan their future. Parents use blending when they warn their children about future consequences of their actions. They help children to blend their present behaviour with its possible results so that children can see themselves in the future. Without having an actual conversation, we can engage in reflecting on and debating various ideas and points of view by predicting what others might say This same process is applied when we empathize with other people despite not having experienced their trauma and not having access to their minds. In the process we bring "to the blend not only much of what we perceive of the other person, but also something from our own knowledge of ourselves: the possession of a mind lying behind behaviour."[34] To put it metaphorically, through blending, we can put ourselves in another person's shoes.

Thus, from a Cognitive Linguistics perspective, blending is a mechanism beyond empathetic imagination as described by Craddock because it does not only state that we can empathize with others but actually describes how this is done at a cognitive level. Blending can also be used to describe what Paul Scott Wilson meant by imagination's "poles" – namely, putting together two ideas that are distant to generate new meaning. However, blending theory explains, in much greater detail, how new ideas emerge. Blending can be used to portray Brueggemann's "poetic imagination" – with its aim of reimagining reality – and Eslinger's imagination as "seeing as," "imagine that," and "imagine how." In a similar way to Thomas Troeger, who understands imagination as attentiveness to what is and using the "raw material of life" to create something new, Kövecses, Lakoff, and Turner also argue that imagination employed in poetic creativity is based on the use and reworking of conventional metaphors.[35]

Thus, Cognitive Linguistics provides a coherent explanation and unified perspective on various understandings of imagination showing their common features. Moreover, Cognitive Linguistics provides a strong theoretical

---

34. Turner, *Origin of Ideas*, 62.
35. Kövecses, *Metaphor: A Practical Introduction*, 49.

foundation – that is based on linguistics, psychology, neuroscience, and other branches of knowledge – to explain the mechanisms behind the human imagination. While different understandings of imagination in preaching focus on what imagination can accomplish, they neglect to describe how the human mind works so that we are able to imagine what processes are involved in the act of imagination.

In conclusion, I must mention the notion of moral imagination developed by Mark Johnson, which assumes that our moral reasoning is imaginative in nature.[36] Consequently, he argues that "the way we frame and categorize a given situation will determine how we reason about it, and how we frame it will depend on which conventional metaphors we are using."[37] Johnson then gives some practical examples of employing moral imagination, such as empathetic imagination, imaginative moral reasoning, imaginative envisionment of possibilities for acting, and the application of moral imagination to aesthetic dimensions of experience.[38]

This notion of moral imagination is important in understanding the world of our listeners and developing new imaginative strategies of sermon application that utilize a Cognitive Linguistics' perspective.

5.1.2 Entering Listeners' Galleries of the Mind

Macneile Dixon maintains that the human mind "is not, as philosophers would have you think, a debating hall, but a picture gallery."[39] Fred Craddock explains that these "galleries of the mind are filled with images that have been hung there casually or deliberately by parents, writers, artists, teachers, speakers, and combinations of many forces" and points out that "images are replaced not by concepts, but by other images."[40] Hence, the desired change happens when these old images that have been hung in the galleries of listeners' minds are replaced with new images that reflect biblical ideas. Transformed thinking leads to transformed living, transformed imagination

---

36. Johnson, *Moral Imagination*, 2.
37. Johnson, 2.
38. Johnson, 199–209.
39. Quoted in Stott, *Between Two Worlds*, 238.
40. Craddock, *As One without Authority*, 64.

finds its expression in transformed action, and preaching plays an essential role in this whole process.

In this part of the chapter, I discuss the process of entering listeners' "galleries of the mind" from a Cognitive Linguistics perspective. In order to hang new images in the galleries of their minds, preachers must first use their imagination to understand their listeners' way of thinking. Thus, in the following sections, the issue of universality and variation of our audience will be applied to preaching. As stated in the previous chapter, notions of universality and variation are vital in an analysis of the text, and analogical principles can be employed in understanding the world of the listeners because preachers and their listeners share some general panhuman truths that are universal and perceive the world from the perspective of their embodiment, culture, and experience. They also differ in terms of culture, race, age, education, social status, and many other factors.

Therefore, in order to apply the notions of universality and variation to preaching, I will employ Mark Johnson's theory of moral imagination that includes several elements such as the prototype structure of concepts, framing of situations, metaphors, and narratives.[41]

5.1.2.1 Universality and Variation among the Listeners

In the previous chapter, I described how the concept of the universality and variation of metaphors is a helpful tool to understand the cultural context and conceptualize the world as presented in the biblical texts. I pointed out that when we recognize the universality of certain concepts and metaphors, we can see connections with the authors and readers of the biblical texts. This connection is based on the common fact of embodiment, common human experiences, common panhuman truths and concepts, and common metaphorical expressions of these concepts.

As we study variations, we notice that, even in the Bible, different cultures are presented, each of which have their own unique world view, language, and metaphorical expressions. Moreover, as contemporary readers we encounter a number of variations between our perception and metaphorical expressions that we use that are culturally conditioned and those that we find in the Bible.

---

41. Johnson, *Moral Imagination*, 189–198.

The same dynamics occur when preachers try to understand their listeners and their world. They recognize universality of concepts and experiences that are rooted in the fact that we are humans who share the same kind of embodiment and cultural similarities. As people, we need food and water, we crave to be loved and happy, we fear pain and death, but we also commonly talk about life in terms of journeys, we conceptualize good as healthy, and so on.

On the other hand, preachers also recognize variations. For missionaries, who preach to people from different cultures, these variations are much more visible. However, even variations appearing within one culture – such as gender, social status, education, or age – can become obstacles in communication.

I am aware that in order to study universality and variation, it is possible to conduct extensive cultural research. But since Cognitive Linguistics focuses mostly on ways people conceptualize reality as expressed in language, my research will be limited, for the most part, to an analysis of linguistic expressions that listeners use.

In order to accomplish this goal of understanding our listeners' concepts, I adopt Mark Johnson's theory of moral imagination and, based on this theory, propose new implications and methods of application. As stated in chapter 3, Mark Johnson believes that even though rules and laws might play some role in everyday life or social interaction, moral reasoning is not based on rules but is imaginative and metaphorical in nature and, as such, is based on prototypes. Johnson claims that the purpose of his theory of moral imagination is not to give straight answers about which behaviours are to be considered good or evil; instead, he is convinced that a theory of morality "should be a theory of moral understanding" that gives "insight into the nature of human understanding" and offers ways to "increase our own moral understanding."[42]

Consequently, Johnson enumerates basic elements of our moral reasoning – namely, the prototype structure of concepts, framing of situations, metaphor, and narrative. These elements are helpful in entering the world of the listeners and analyzing their values and moral reasoning. These imaginative elements of moral reasoning that help to enter the reality of the listeners are analogical to those elements of exegesis that allow us to enter the textual reality of the author and readers. In the process of a contextual analysis of the situation of the author and readers, we have to understand their categories

---

42. Johnson, 188.

and prototypes, their frames of reasoning, and the images and metaphors they use and see these in the context of a discourse. In this process, they are the speakers and we are the hearers. In communicating to a contemporary audience, however, we are the speakers and they are the hearers, but the methodology for understanding their world remains the same.

Mark Johnson, in explaining his theory, merely lists and explains the four elements of moral imagination. However, I am convinced that these elements actually form a process in which our prototypes are the basis for developing our perception or framing of situations. The ways we frame situations are expressed in the metaphors and narratives we use to talk about these situations. These frames are also the foundation for creating our life narratives, in which we live out our prototypes. In the sections that follow, I describe how this process functions and show how prototypes, frames, metaphors, and narratives are productive in understanding the world of the listeners.

5.1.2.2 The Listeners' Prototype Structure of Concepts

As explained in chapter 3, moral concepts have a prototype structure. It can be argued that people define their moral categories using prototypes that are most representative of a given category. Eve Sweetser gives the example of a prototype structure of the concept of a lie. Except for clear situations where someone makes a false statement in order to deceive or harm, there are numerous non-prototypical members of the category of lying, such as fibs, white lies, social lies, tall tales, jokes, honest mistakes, oversimplifications, exaggerations, understatements, and overstatements. Sweetser argues that having a clear understanding of what a lie is allows humans to evaluate other non-prototypical situations and decide if what took place was a lie or a joke or maybe an honest mistake.[43]

Mark Johnson demonstrates how prototypes "represent experimentally basic types of situations," such as children developing the idea of justice by learning from the fair distribution of cookies.[44] However, he points out that prototypes are also "malleable and flexible," which means that as children grow, they start perceiving more nuances and non-prototypical situations where

---

43. Sweetser, "Definition of Lie," 43–66. On the prototypical nature of lying, see also Johnson, *Moral Imagination*, 91–98.

44. Johnson, *Moral Imagination*, 190.

the simple model of a fair cookie distribution will not suffice.[45] According to cognitive linguists, this is how people conduct their moral reasoning and make moral choices.

Therefore, in order to understand the world of the listeners, we have to learn about their prototypes. Thus, preachers need to grasp the prototypes of the key life concepts of their listeners – for example, happiness, family, honesty, love, forgiveness, success, and work. If moral reasoning is prototypical, the danger is that we may use the same words but understand these words differently, which may result in miscommunication.

The issue of prototypes is even more important than communication problems because prototypes actually influence human choices, attitudes, and behaviour. If love is perceived as just a romantic feeling or an emotional reaction that may come and go, rather than as a choice and commitment, this could have serious consequences for the way a married couple will approach their relational crisis. If happiness is understood in terms of wealth and health, this concept may not suffice in times of crisis and sickness and, what is worse, may produce self-centred and egoistic individuals. Therefore, in order to change the mental images of their listeners, preachers must first understand their prototypes. Especially in the case of very diverse audiences, this understanding should take into consideration both universality and variation of prototypes.

Consequently, in order to address a diverse audience, preachers should recognize the dominant prototypes in a given social setting. For instance, a perception of roles in marriage in a small, conservative, rural community will be very different to the perceptions prevalent in a big city. Even though both groups may consist of people who have different views and opinions on a given subject, it is possible to observe some general trends and prototypes that are more dominant. These dominant trends can be starting points for a discussion with listeners' prototypes.

Second, preachers should recognize the diversity of prototypes and metaphors among their listeners and, by respectfully naming just a few of them, show their awareness of how people tend to conceptualize a given idea. Even without enumerating all possible prototypes and metaphors, by giving just a few examples, preachers can show that they understand the world of their

---

45. Johnson, 191.

listeners, which helps to build a connection with their audience. For instance, when talking about marriage, the preacher may acknowledge a variety of prototypes in the audience by saying:

> For some of you, marriage might be a relic from the past about which we no longer need to bother. For some, it might be a mistake that you do not want to make again. Others may perceive it as a burden. You might think about your marriage as a bloody battlefield from which you wish you could flee. We might have different experiences and different convictions, but we share one thing in common . . .[46]

The third step preachers need to follow is to question some of these prototypes and metaphors by showing their insufficiency, which should lead to replacing them with biblical prototypes and metaphors. This third step will be presented more fully in later sections of this chapter.

5.1.2.3 The Listeners' Framing of Situations

Understanding prototypes is insufficient to understand listeners because these prototypes do not exist in a vacuum but are the basis for developing typical ways of framing of situations, which is another step in audience analysis. In this step, preachers move beyond recognizing their listeners' values and focus on how listeners conceptualize various ethical situations. For instance, one father, upon hearing that his son had spent a night with his girlfriend, may be saddened that his son had sinned and behaved immorally. Another father, however, may view the same situation simply as his son becoming a man and learning about life and intimacy; from his perspective, experimenting is viewed as an essential part of maturing. For some people, telling little lies is just a part of life, necessary to make life run smoothly, whereas for others, it is a sign of dishonesty.

Framing of situations affects the ways in which people deal with traumatic life situations, such as when a loved one dies. For the atheist, this is the end of the deceased person's existence, and the only way that person may "exist" is in the memory of those left behind. In this situation, friends and family

---

46. This sermonic sample – and a few others that appear in this chapter without any reference – have been created specifically for this study.

are the only source of comfort. For a person suffering with terminal illness, death may appear as deliverance from pain. For Christians, death is never the end since they believe that it is the beginning of an eternity with God. Death is not only deliverance from pain but also deliverance to the fullness of life, and those who are left behind may experience comfort both from other people and from God. This illustrates how one life event might be framed in very different ways.

Changing framings may turn out to be revelatory and transformative, as in a case of a man whose friends keep telling him that he has a drinking problem, while he keeps insisting that he just likes drinking and is able to control it; until, one day, he finally admits that he is an alcoholic. Thus, preachers not only have to understand the moral prototypes of their listeners but must also be aware how listeners frame situations.

5.1.2.4 The Listeners' Metaphors

Typical ways of framing of situations find their expressions in the listeners' metaphors that they use to talk about these situations. As emphasized earlier, people express moral concepts metaphorically. Mark Scott boldly states that metaphors "help us to know what *people* are". He points out that "humankind is made in God's image" and that this means that, in numerous cases, "we can properly only speak about ourselves in metaphor."[47] Thus, one way to understand listeners' prototypes and ways of framing of situations is by paying attention to their language and, especially, to the metaphors they use.

Different people use various metaphors to describe marriage – for instance, a burden, a grave of love, a battlefield, a garden to be cared for, an adventure, travelling together, a reflection of Christ's relationship with his church, or a commitment. Depending on people's values, prototypes, and framings of their own marriage relationship, they will choose different metaphors to describe it. Thus, Mark Johnson believes that it is possible to determine those basic metaphors that are foundational to our moral reasoning and their structure. He believes that knowing "our metaphorically structured moral understanding is thus crucial for our self-understanding." He is also convinced that analysis of our moral reasoning "is one of the central ways

---

47. Jones and Scott, *Letting the Text Win*, loc. 2934 of 4226, Kindle (emphasis original).

to come to know what our values are, what they presuppose, and what they entail for our actions."[48]

5.1.2.5 The Listeners' Narratives

The final element of our moral reasoning is to realize that listeners' prototypes, framings, and metaphors develop into their life narratives. Johnson builds his theory on the assumption that our lives "have a narrative structure" and that narratives are one of the most important means of learning about life. It is through narratives "that we come closest to observing and participating in the reality of life as it is actually experienced and lived."[49] However, people not only learn from stories but are also influenced by the prevalent cultural narrative, on the basis of which they then develop their personal narratives.

Timothy Keller emphasizes the importance of understanding the listeners' narratives and presents several cultural narratives that characterize what he calls "late modernity." Keller talks about the "technology narrative," which assumes that all humanity's problems can be solved by technological advancement; the "historical narrative," which says that history naturally progresses towards a better future and is preoccupied with the newest since the newest must be the best; the "freedom narrative," which presupposes that all people can live and act the way they choose without any external hindrances; the "morality" or "justice narrative," which assumes that it is important to pursue justice in the world but also that humans are the ones who define what is moral and just; and the "identity narrative," which is built on the belief that human identity does not come from the outside – from God or social roles – but is rooted in our dreams and desires, and that our ultimate goal is to be "ourselves." [50]

Consequently, Johnson claims that in order to understand our moral reasoning, "we must recognize the narrative dimension of our lives, which includes the narratives we inherit from our culture and that particular instantiations of those narratives that we are construing in our own lives."[51]

---

48. Johnson, *Moral Imagination*, 193.

49. Johnson, 196.

50. Keller, *Preaching*, 129–133.

51. Johnson, *Moral Imagination*, 198.

Thus, our prototypes and typical ways of framing of situations influence the choice of metaphors and narratives we use to talk about our lives, which in turn find their expression in the way in which we shape our life narratives by living our lives. Depending on their moral values and their perception of moral dilemmas, our listeners make various moral choices that can be seen in the ways they function in their lives.

5.1.2.6 Recognizing Listeners' Prototypes and Framings of Situations

As I reflected on Johnson's elements of moral imagination, I realized that not only did these elements form a process but that understanding this process has implications for identifying the listeners' prototypes and typical ways of framing situations. As presented in the diagram below, prototypes and framings of situations are listeners' mental structures that are inaccessible to preachers.

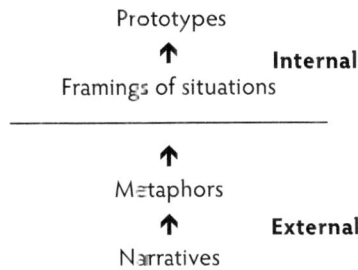

Prototypes

↑   **Internal**

Framings of situations

———————————————

↑

Metaphors

↑   **External**

Narratives

Diagram 7. Identifying the listeners' prototypes and framings

As preachers, we do not have any access to listeners' minds to discover their values and how they perceive various life events. However, we can listen to their metaphors and narratives, and we can watch their life narratives as expressed in their daily actions and choices. Since metaphors and narratives are external expressions of internal prototypes and framings, they are accessible for preachers as a starting point for understanding their listeners. Therefore, in order to understand the images in the listeners' galleries of the mind, preachers have to begin with the other end of the whole process and move backwards. In order to recognize their listeners' prototypes and framings, they can benefit from listening to their metaphors, linguistics images, and the narratives they use to describe their beliefs and perception of life. They also can watch their listeners' lives to see how their individual choices form the larger narratives of their lives.

As preachers, we might not know the prototypes and framings of the situations of the two fathers whose sons slept with their girlfriends. However, in a pastoral situation, we might listen to their metaphors and narratives. One father might say that his son is a young warrior, who conquers and wins, expands his territory, and is maturing and becoming stronger. This father might relate this story with pride. Moreover, the father's own life story of two failed marriages might give further insights into his framing of this particular situation that reveals his actual prototypes. The other father might use completely different language, saying that his son had strayed from the right path, polluted his young life, and engaged in an unhealthy relationship. He would tell this story with sadness because it does not adhere to his personal values and his narrative of a life of integrity and faithfulness to one woman. The language and stories of the two fathers would give a preacher insight into their values and their perceptions of moral choices.

The same strategy is helpful not only in pastoral situations, where the preachers try to identify prototypes of individuals, but also in preaching situations, where preachers try to understand the prototypes and frames of their audience by studying their metaphors and narratives. As preachers, we do not have any access to the internal values and perceptions of our listeners, but we have access to their external shared linguistic expressions and their stories – both those that are told and those that are lived.

In the previous chapter, I referred to Kövecses's methodology when discussing the analysis of biblical metaphors as part of a discourse. This methodology is also helpful in studying the narratives or discourses of listeners. Kövecses points to several principles that are relevant for understanding metaphors in context: recognize that metaphors are "specific to a particular discourse situation"; be familiar with the surrounding discourse; take into consideration previous discourses that dealt with the same subject and their intertextual correlations; become familiar with existing dominant forms of discourse; understand ideology underlying a discourse. In his theory, he also adds elements related to the situation of the participants of the discourse, such as physical environment, social and cultural situation, history of a particular group, and, finally, their interests and concerns.[52] These principles are also applicable to the analysis of listeners' metaphors, life narratives, and discourses – either cultural or personal – that they participate in.

As an example of familiarity with surrounding discourse and discourses that deal with the same subject, Kövecses cites a speech in which Tony Blair said that, as a politician, he used to move forward and back, depending on what was easier, but then, deciding to do not what was easy but what was right, he announced, "I can only go one way. I've not got a reverse gear."[53] A BBC commentator decided to enter Blair's discourse and said, on the evening news, "But when you're on the edge of a cliff it is good to have a reverse gear."[54]

Analogously, when preachers stand before their listeners and begin addressing issues that are vital for their congregations, they immediately enter the ongoing discourse that takes place in other sermons, Bible studies, prayers, individual conversations, and conversations in the media or in politics, and so on. In Autumn 2016, a heated debate about whether or not refugees should be allowed to come and live in Poland swept across the whole country. During that time, I had to preach a sermon based on 1 Peter 1:1–12, about our Christian identity. I could have titled this sermon in various ways – for example, "Who are You?," "True You," or "Your New Identity" – but, considering the surrounding cultural discourse and many discourses on the same subject in the media and at home, I decided to use images taken from the text itself and chose the title "A Citizen or a Refugee?" ("Obywatel czy Uchodźca?"),[55] which was a way of showing that we belong to both categories. Even though the sermon was not about the attitudes we should have towards refugees, it entered the wider discourse and listeners started seeing implications for how understanding their own identity in Christ should be reflected in the way they view their possessions and the people around them. By recognizing prevailing cultural narratives regarding refugees as expressed in language that included metaphors, I was able to address underlying typical framings of the problem of refugees that were based on certain prototypes.

---

52. Kövecses, *Where Metaphors Come From*, 53–59.

53. Kövecses, 54.

54. Kövecses, 55.

55. Szumorek, "Obywatel czy Uchodźca?"

As examples of familiarity with dominant forms of listeners' discourse on a cultural level, consider the title "Logged Out" – for a sermon series devoted to spiritual disciplines and time alone with God – or the title "No App" – for a sermon series about character qualities that must be developed, as opposed to simply being "downloaded." In these times of the Internet, modern technology, smartphones, downloads, and being constantly connected to others, technological terminology becomes one of the dominant forms of contemporary discourse and, more and more frequently, is being used in a metaphorical sense to describe various aspects of life.

The whole notion of understanding the world of the listeners is not new in homiletics and has been addressed by numerous authors. For instance, John Stott talks about "double listening" to the voice of the Bible and the voice of the world.[56] David Schlafer encourages preachers to listen to different voices – namely, the voices in Scripture, in their congregation, in the liturgy, and within the preacher.[57] Timothy Keller urges preachers to listen to their listeners so that they will be able to express and address their listeners' "doubts and objections with appreciation and respect, in a coherent form, showing that they have listened long and hard to them."[58] To enter the world of listeners, Fred Craddock suggests that preachers practise empathetic imagination by writing "What's It Like to Be?" at the top of a sheet of paper and then choosing "one concrete facet of human experience," such as "facing surgery," "living alone," or "suddenly wealthy."[59] When Haddon Robinson prepared a sermon, he would imagine that there were various people standing around his desk – including a committed believer, a friend who is a cynic, a businessperson, and a bored teenager – and ask himself, "*What does this have to say to them?*"[60] Frank Pollard would go into an empty church and sit in different seats, praying about the people who usually sit there and thinking about how they might listen to his sermon and what it could say to them.[61]

---

56. Stott, *Contemporary Christian*, 24–29.

57. Schlafer, *Surviving the Sermon*, 34–57.

58. Keller, *Preaching*, 110.

59. Craddock, *Preaching*, 97.

60. Robinson, "Heresy of Application," 306–311 (emphasis original). On imagination and pastoring, see Wiersbe, *Preaching and Teaching*, 30.

61. Pollard, "Preparing the Preacher," 135. Richard Pratt devotes a whole chapter titled "From People to People" to the subject of applying an ancient text to a modern audience. Pratt, *He Gave Us Stories*, 383–402. On methods of audience analysis, see Allen, *Hearing the Sermon*;

Even though traditional homiletical textbooks offer various approaches to audience analysis and understanding the listeners, Cognitive Linguistics gives preachers a new theoretical tool that can be used to effectively express homiletical theory with new precision and give new insights regarding ways of understanding listeners in a much more methodologically systematized fashion. As a pragmatic approach, it confirms many of the methods proposed by traditional homiletics but also advances their application by clarifying the process of identifying listeners' prototypes and providing preachers with a holistic view of their listeners.

5.1.3 Developing Prototype-Based Application

Understanding listeners' prototypes is an important step towards developing effective sermon applications that can take the form of prototype-based application. Thus, while being respectful to and aware of other approaches to Christian ethics, I suggest that Christian morality and ethics are not built primarily on rules but on prototypes – for example, the image of God, the character of God, love, and Jesus Christ as our ultimate prototype. Thus, in this section, I will demonstrate how to develop prototype-based application. This process is, in many ways, analogical to the methodology of recognizing listeners' prototypes. Considering the fact that listeners' prototypes and frames are cognitive structures that are internal and not accessible to preachers, the best way to change these prototypes and frames, according to this theory, is by using external linguistic forms such as metaphors and narratives because prototypes are often expressed in the form of such metaphors and narratives.

Therefore, in order to present my methodology for developing prototype-based application, I will first define the foundational assumptions, which include establishing among the listeners the theocentric and Christocentric perspective on life that is a prerequisite for accomplishing the goal of shaping new prototypes, framings of situations, and acquiring an ability to make moral choices in non-prototypical situations. I will then show how metaphors and narratives play an important role in helping the audience to embrace new prototypes that will influence the ways in which they frame their life situations.

"Listening to Listeners," 69–84; and "Turn Towards the Listener," 165–194; see also Allen, Mulligan, and Turner-Sharazz, *Believing in Preaching*.

The idea of developing ethics based on paradigms, focal images, exemplars, or prototypes is not new or limited just to Cognitive Linguistics.
Garrett Green regards "the imagination as the paradigmatic faculty, the ability of human beings to recognize in accessible exemplars the constitutive
organizing patterns of other, less accessible and more complex objects of
cognition."[62] Green illustrates his approach by referring to the role of the
creeds that express the essence of Christian beliefs, affirming that Christ
"was conceived . . . born . . . suffered . . . crucified . . . descended . . . rose . . .
ascended . . . sitteth . . . will come again."[63] He demonstrates that for centuries
Christians have viewed their lives and all history through the lenses of these
statements and the narrative presented in the creeds. Thus, "employing the
concept of paradigmatic imagination," it can be said that "Christians have
imagined the world according to the paradigm exemplified in the creed".[64]

Richard Hays perceives ethical reasoning as metaphor-making, which is an
act of "placing our community's life imaginatively within the world articulated
by the texts."[65] For Hays, to develop New Testament ethics is to "formulate
imaginative analogies between stories told in the text and the story lived out
by our community in a very different historical setting."[66] Thus, even though
Hays does not employ Cognitive Linguistics with its notion of prototypes,
he utilizes some elements of the theory. Instead of talking about prototypes,
he identifies three focal images – the Community, the Cross, and the New
Creation – which become the reference points for ethical decision-making.[67]
Thus, every moral judgement is made in a relation to these focal images. The
key difference between his approach and Cognitive Linguistics is that Hays's
focal images are a given and their number is limited, whereas the number of
prototypes is not limited in Cognitive Linguistics, where they are the basic
elements for developing new categories.

Adherents of virtue ethics propose the notion of exemplars. Aristotle understood exemplars as persons whose virtuous lives could be characterized

---

62. Green, *Imagining God*, 66.

63. Green, 67.

64. Green, 67 (emphasis original).

65. Hays, *Moral Vision*, 299.

66. Hays, 298.

67. Bonnie Howe gives a critical analysis of Hays's approach from the perspective of
conceptual metaphor theory. Howe, *Because You Bear This Name*, 127–146.

in terms of eudaimonia – namely, "happiness" or "the good life." Gregory Peterson and others explore the importance of exemplary members for a community that seeks to imitate them and the correlation between the cognition and emotions.[68] This notion of exemplars also appears in the works of Linda Zagzebski, who stresses that exemplars motivate others to imitate their moral behaviour but also points out that it is more desirable to imitate exemplars' motives rather than mimicking their specific actions. Except for exemplars such as God or Christ, nobody embodies all the qualities that should be imitated, and so we need various exemplars to learn various virtues.[69] Stanley Hauerwas understands exemplarity in the Christian life in the context of narrative. He emphasizes the importance not merely of imitation of an exemplar but imitation coupled with reflection on the exemplar's life that results in adopting the exemplar's values to our own situation and leading a similar kind of life.[70] James William McClendon Jr. also stresses the prominence of a narrative and story as a context for moral reasoning and believes that in order to live a good Christian life, we have to get acquainted with stories of those who finished well and who exemplify this good life in its various aspects.[71]

In comparing prototype theory with the exemplar approach, it is worth noticing that the former is broader since prototypes may include not just people who are prototypical members of a given category but also prototypical concepts such as love, hatred, honesty, peace, war, and lies.

5.1.3.1 Foundation: Theocentric and Christocentric Perspective

Considering the fact that humans owe their existence and moral nature to God who created them in his image, I begin the whole discussion on developing prototype-based application with the picture of God that our listeners have in their minds. Paul Froese and Christopher Bader studied what people believe about God and his involvement in the world and identified four major views of God among Americans: (1) Authoritative God – engaged and judgemental; (2) Benevolent God – engaged and non-judgemental; (3) Critical

---

68. Peterson et al., "Rationality of Ultimate Concern," 139–161.

69. Zagzebski, "Moral Authority of Exemplars," 117–129. See also Zagzebski, *Virtues of the Mind*; Zagzebski, *Divine Motivation Theory*; Zagzebski, "Exemplarist Virtue Theory," 41–57.

70. Hauerwas, "Character, Narrative, and Growth," 221–254.

71. McClendon, *Ethics: Systematic Theology*, 111.

God – disengaged and judgemental; and (4) Distant God – disengaged and non-judgemental.[72] These different views of God can be summarized in two categories – a Strict God and a Caring God – and find their expression in moral choices their adherents make. For instance, some Christians who believe in Strict God see HIV/AIDS as God's punishment for widespread immorality, whereas many who lean towards the idea of Caring God describe him as being compassionate to those who suffer, desiring to ease their struggle.

Developing balanced prototype-based applications begins with helping listeners to acquire a biblically grounded picture of God because the way people perceive God will shape their vision of themselves and their lives. Thus, it might be prudent for preachers to start by re-examining their own understanding of God and his nature. When studying the Bible or preparing their sermons, they need to remember the theocentric approach to the biblical text, which assumes that God is the main character of the Bible. Consequently, one of the key questions to ask about a biblical text is this: What does this text say about God and his character?

Considering the fact that the most perfect way God revealed himself was through Christ, and since Christians identify themselves as Christ's followers, a prototype-based application should not only be theocentric but also Christocentric since it assumes that Christ is our main prototype. Hence, the ultimate goal of our belonging to the category of Christ's followers is similarity to its central prototype – namely, to Christ alone.

Surprisingly, this theocentric and Christocentric perspective also includes studying and learning from human biblical characters. The Bible describes numerous individuals who embody various Christlike qualities that should be emulated, and such individuals may function as exemplars. While emphasizing the importance of God as the main character of biblical revelation, preachers should not downplay human characters. However, when preachers analyze the lives and actions of these people, they should not do so in isolation but with respect to the immediate literary context, the context of salvation history, and the broadest theocentric context of God's revelation.[73] Actions

---

72. Froese and Bader, *America's Four Gods*, 13–36.

73. For more about reading narratives about biblical characters in various contexts that prevent an anthropocentric approach, see Szumorek, *Spotkanie z Wszechmocnym*, 25–56.

and choices of human characters who are regarded as exemplars must be seen in the context of the actions of God and his plan.

Therefore, the first step in developing prototype-based application is to recognize in what ways God and Christ are exemplars of a particular virtue or behaviour or how human exemplars embody these virtues and live them out in various situations.

5.1.3.2 Developing a New Understanding of Prototypes and Basic-Level Categories

As asserted in this book, Christian ethics is not based on rules but on prototypes, among which Christ is the most prominent prototype. However, developing prototype-based application does not end with presenting God and Christ as exemplars but also aims at showing prototypical biblical concepts and prototypical scenarios that often require using basic-level categories.

Most of our prototypes belong to the basic-level category of concepts such as a chair, a dog, love, justice, and so on. Numerous studies have shown that children learn concepts belonging to this category first and that adults recognize them quickest. Moreover, most human knowledge is organized on this level.[74] Consequently, the basic-level category is essential for teaching and should be used as a starting point for explaining more complex ideas.

Considering the fact that preaching nowadays takes place in increasingly secularized contexts and our listeners are not very biblically literate, preachers cannot assume that their listeners share their prototypes of basic concepts such as mercy, love, grace, faith, God, and so on. Therefore, when developing prototype-based application it is essential to establish an understanding of these basic-level categories, and this may also involve beginning by recognizing and questioning some cultural prototypes.

In my sermon "A Citizen or a Refugee?" I dealt with the issue of our Christian identity and began with a question: "What would you have left, if everything was taken from you?"[75] Even though contemporary listeners living in the Western world may find this question self-contradictory and abstract, this would have been a legitimate question for the Christians to whom Peter addressed his first epistle – those whom he calls strangers, aliens

---

74. Sanders, *Theology in the Flesh*, loc. 1721 of 5234, Kindle.
75. Szumorek, "Obywatel czy Uchodźca?"

or we could say refugees (παρεπιδήμοι).[76] So what did they have left? Who were they? How would they define their identity in such circumstances?

Before defining biblical prototypical ways of describing our identity, I had to challenge the prototypical cultural ways people construct their identities, and this was accomplished through an extended narrative image.

> Your friends invited you to their wedding anniversary. When you arrive, you discover that with the exception of a very few known faces, there are many strange people whom you do not know. Suddenly, the host comes to you and says, "You have to meet somebody. This is Andrew. Andrew is the bank president." A few minutes later you meet some more people: Anne who is a neurosurgeon and her husband, an English teacher, Tom who is a plumber, Justine a shop assistant, Mary – a lady from a bookstore, and Peter who is unemployed and who told you about his previous work for a big company and the fact that he was made to be nobody. Is not it surprising that when we are asked to introduce ourselves or others we define our identities by what we do, what we have accomplished or what we possess? But what would you have left, if everything was taken from you?[77]

Even though Peter writes to strangers or refugees, he addresses them as chosen by God who is their Father. They might not be wanted by the world, but they are wanted by God, who gives them a new sense of identity. Fred Craddock explains how this new identity shapes our perception of ourselves by telling the story of an older man who approached him in a restaurant while he and his wife were on vacation. When the man discovered that Craddock was a preacher, he related his own story of how a particular preacher from his childhood influenced his life.

This man had a difficult childhood because he was born out of wedlock and never knew who his father was. His classmates made fun of him, and people were talking behind his back as they tried to guess who his daddy was. As a teenager, he started going to a church, but he always tried to sneak out just before the end of the service. However, one Sunday, there were people

---

76. Balz, EDNT 3:38.
77. Szumorek, "Obywatel czy Uchodźca?"

blocking him in the aisle and he was unable to leave early. As he was trying to leave, he felt somebody's hand on his shoulder. It was the minister. He recalls this event:

> He turned his face around so he could see mine and seemed to be staring for a while. I knew what he was doing. He was going to make a guess as to who my father was. A moment later he said, "Well, boy, you're a child of . . ." and he paused there. I knew it was coming. I knew I would have my feelings hurt. I knew I would not go back again. He said, "Boy, you are a child of God. I see a striking resemblance, boy." Then he swatted me on the bottom and said, "Now, you go and claim your inheritance." I left the building a different person. In fact, that was really the beginning of my life.[78]

I return now to the question of ways in which we construct our identity and the question "What would you have left, if everything was taken from you?" The two extended narrative images described above challenge cultural prototypes of our identity and establish a new prototype that does not depend on occupation, status, or accomplishments. As in 1 Peter, those who have lost everything and are unwanted by the world are wanted and chosen by God, their Father. In the first chapter of his letter, Peter helps his readers to redefine their identity. On the one hand, he describes them as "aliens" and "scattered," but on the other hand, they are chosen by God the Father, sprinkled with Christ's blood, and recipients of God's grace and of an imperishable inheritance, and Peter calls them to be holy as God is holy. They are to live as "strangers" in this world, and this idea of being strangers is not only a description of their state but also becomes a metaphor depicting the nature of their Christian living in this world.

Consequently, when preaching, we cannot assume that people have the same prototypes of basic concepts that we do. Thus, we need to spend time defining biblical prototypes.

---

78. Craddock, *Craddock Stories*, 156–157.

5.1.3.3 Addressing Non-prototypical Situations and Developing New Frames

Defining prototypes also has another purpose since it prepares listeners to deal with non-prototypical situations. Although preachers cannot predict all possible situations and challenges their audiences might face, by presenting biblical prototypes, they give them a point of reference for moral reasoning in all kinds of ethically complex circumstances. Mark Johnson claims that "most of our reflective moral reasoning concerns *nonprototypical* cases" and that these cases can be addressed because there are "principles of extension (e.g. metaphor) from the central to noncentral members within a category".[79] Therefore, in the paragraphs that follow, I will explain how preachers can address non-prototypical situations that could be defined as situations that differ from the situation that is perceived as ideal. These situations are labelled as non-prototypical because they might be imperfect or, in some cases, even morally ambiguous. The purpose of addressing these non-prototypical situations is to help the listener to make moral choices that are based on their prototypes even in circumstances that are far from perfect.

For instance, having prototypical concepts and prototypical scenarios of love and forgiveness is a starting point for determining our behaviour in situations where something goes wrong or does not happen as expected. In his Sermon on the Mount, Jesus challenged common prototypical scenarios of adultery and murder, and our typical responses to those who hurt us, and presented numerous non-prototypical scenarios (Matthew 5–7). His listeners thought that adultery was about going to bed with somebody's spouse, that murder was about taking a person's life, and that if people hurt them, they were entitled to retaliate by following the "eye for an eye" principle. Jesus, however, changed these scenarios, defining adultery as lusting after somebody, murder as being angry, and instructing his followers, if they were slapped on one cheek, to turn the other one as well. He redefined prototypes and applied them to situations that would not be considered prototypical, thereby changing the framings of these situations. As people start perceiving such situations differently, they will, hopefully, also start acting differently. Jesus, as our ultimate prototype, modelled how to act in a highly non-prototypical situation when he experienced hatred, injustice, betrayal, suffering, and death.

---

79. Johnson, *Moral Imagination*, 190 (emphasis original).

Introducing new prototypes is closely related to changing our framings of situations. Understanding that forgiveness is an unconditional decision and that those who wrong us do not have to pay for it – even though they deserve to do so and even if they do not regret their actions – radically changes our responses towards those who wrong us. Thus, preachers should aim at changing their listeners' prototypes and helping them to imagine new framings of situations in order to develop new and transformed attitudes.

By using prototype-based applications, preachers present new prototypes that often change their listeners' frames. They may also give some examples of non-prototypical situations that encourage their listeners to reflect on how their prototypes affect their perception of these situations. But, ultimately, they leave it to listeners to decide how to live out those prototypical scenarios. Hence, while prototypes may change our frames, we may still be faced with the challenge of how to apply a given prototypical scenario to an existing situation. For example, by showing listeners that love is a commitment and not just feeling, preachers change their framing of relationships. On the other hand, preachers may sometimes face the challenge of helping listeners to deal with an existing situation – for example, a difficult relationship with an alcoholic father. The preacher's task is to show how the prototype of love applies to this situation and what it means to love such a person, and these expressions of love will be very different from those in other relationships.

Prototype-based application in preaching shows tension between the ideal and the real. In a sermon based on Esther 1–2, which I titled "When Life Is Not Black and White," I tried to show life in shades of grey.[80]

> In the book of Esther we read a very morally complicated story. Even though, some time earlier Cyrus issued his decree allowing Jews to return to their homeland, Esther and her family remained in the exile. Eventually, Esther ends up in a situation when she has to spend a night with a pagan king. Apparently, she does what she can to make him happy, because eventually he marries her and makes her the queen. Against God's law, she marries the pagan; she eats at his table, and blends so well with the culture of the royal court that nobody even knows

---

80. Szumorek, "Kiedy Życie nie jest Czarno-Białe."

that she is a Jewess. Her world is not ideal and she is not ideal either. How can she live out her calling to be obedient to God in such circumstances?

At times we face similar dilemmas because we live in shades of grey and we cannot do anything about it. My friend is a missionary in China. He has lived there with his family for over a decade, but when asked by the authorities about the purpose of his stay he says that they are tourists. Just living in the shades of grey. What does it mean to be obedient to God in such a situation?

Sometimes we live in shades of grey because we experience consequences of our own choices. A young man got married early, even though he was not ready for it. Soon, his son was born and not long after his marriage fell apart. Years later, he started a new family. This time he was more mature and it worked. He also attempted to be involved in bringing up his son from the first marriage, but he discovered that certain mistakes were irreparable and as hard as he might have tried, he would never be able to be a good father for him. It is simply impossible to be a good father when you see your kid every other weekend. He has no choice now. Just living in the shades of grey. What does it mean to be obedient to God in such a situation?[81]

Esther did not live in a perfect environment and she was not perfect herself, but in the most dramatic moment, when the lives of her people were in danger, she made a critical decision about being involved and became a part of God's larger story. When she was making her decision, she did not have this perspective because all she knew was the fact that she decided to risk her life to ask for saving lives of all the Jews (Esth. 4–7).

When we get stuck in our non-prototypical situations, we might not see the larger picture either. However, even in such situations God is able to work in us and through us to accomplish his purposes in us and in the world around us.

---

81. Szumorek.

The purpose of this sermon was to help listeners to start perceiving their lives, as complicated as they are, as part of God's larger story and to begin to act accordingly because this is the first step towards transformation and living in non-prototypical situations in the light of prototypical concepts.

5.1.2.4 Method: Employing Metaphors and Narratives

At this point, a question arises regarding a methodology for developing prototype-based application. As shown in the examples given above, prototype-based application often takes the form of a metaphor, a narrative, or a metaphor that is part of a larger narrative. Mark Johnson argues that "the chief imaginative dimension of moral understanding is metaphor."[82] Thus, as was demonstrated earlier, our conceptual system, including morality is largely metaphorical, and when we start talking about morality and values, we seem unable to do so without using metaphors. Johnson also points out that whenever we encounter non-prototypical cases that require making an extension from the prototype, we make this extension using metaphor.[83] So, taking so-called life lessons is possible because we are able to make metaphorical extensions. Johnson shows how we can take a specific past experience, learn some lessons from it and live out these lessons in a new situation. This is possible because we "grasp the metaphorical structure of the previous situation and apply to what we are encountering now."[84]

Thus, metaphors play an important role in preaching that employs prototype-based application. As John Sanders claims, in order to "help others to live the way God intends them to, it might be necessary to change the metaphors we use." In fact, he is convinced that we may need to employ a whole variety of metaphors "to describe one phenomenon because it is too complex to be captured by one conceptualization."[85]

Mark Scott preached a wedding sermon for his son in which he used three different metaphors to show different aspects of marriage. He said that, "1. Marriage Is a Partnership (Gen 2:18–25) – it works best in the context of friendship. 2. Marriage Is a Duet (Songs) – it never works as a trio. 3. Marriage

---

82. Johnson, *Moral Imagination*, 193.

83. Johnson, 194.

84. Johnson, 195.

85. Sanders, *Theology in the Flesh*, loc. 1543 of 5234, Kindle.

Is a Play (Eph 5:22–33) – the success of the play depends on how well each person plays his or her part."[86] It appears that some concepts are too complex to be presented using a single metaphor.

The choice of metaphors preachers make will affect greatly attitudes their listeners will have and actions they will take. This was demonstrated in a series of experiments where participants were given the same statistics about crime in a particular city. However, in the first report, crime was depicted as a wild beast, while in the other, it was described as a virus. Interestingly, those who read the first report suggested fighting crime by introducing stricter penalties for criminals. Those who read the report where crime was depicted as a virus proposed ways of healing the city by introducing various social programmes.[87]

Similarly, preachers will influence the kind of Christian communities they build by their choice of metaphors. A culturally isolated type of congregation may be the result of preaching that focuses on the church as a little flock, a holy remnant that is supposed to be separate from a world that is depicted as evil, and warns that any kind of friendship with the world is hostility towards God. In contrast, mission-driven congregations may be formed by stressing that Christians are followers of Jesus, who was known as a friend of sinners, loves the world, died for it, and now sends his followers as his missionaries to a world that is to be seen as their mission field.[88]

A prototype-based application in preaching does not rely only on metaphors but also on narratives, and it needs narratives to make abstractions more concrete. Prototypes and metaphors are built on basic-level categories that are general, whereas narratives require subordinate-level categories that are specific. Basic-level categories are helpful in organizing our knowledge of the world, but we do not experience the world in such a way. While walking on the street, we do not see just some general man with some general dog getting into some general car, but we see our neighbour, a grey-haired, retired professor who walks with a limp, with his old German Shepherd, getting into his silver Volkswagen Passat. Thus, if our preaching is to attempt to represent

---

86. Jones and Scott, *Letting the Text Win*, loc. 3050–3062 of 4226, Kindle.

87. Thibodeau and Boroditsky, "Metaphors We Think With," 1–11.

88. Stephen Wright writes more on preaching from a sociological perspective as an identity forming event. He argues that reinforcing or adjusting existing identities depends on preaching and metaphors that are used by preachers such as a family or pilgrim people. Wright, *Alive to the Word*, 63–64.

the way people experience reality, it also has to utilize subordinate-level descriptions to present prototype-based applications.

Mark Johnson argues that since our lives have a narrative structure, narratives are essential tools to convey sermon applications. We experience our lives as a story, and since our earliest years we are ethically shaped by narratives. As Martha Nussbaum rightly observes, a child "does not learn its society's conception of love, or of anger by sitting in an ethics class," but this learning takes place "long before any classes, in complex interactions with parents and society."[89] She insists that this happens through listening to stories that embody exemplars and prototypes that are valued by the society.

Therefore, as with metaphors, preachers need numerous stories to address a variety of non-prototypical situations. Even though, according to the Bible, lying is wrong, there are several biblical examples when people lie to fulfil God's purposes – for example, the Hebrew midwives lying to the kings about why they disobeyed his orders to kill newborn Jewish boys, saying that Hebrew women often gave birth to their children faster than expected (Exod 1:15–21); Rahab lying in order to hide the Jewish spies (Josh 2:4–5); or Samuel deceiving Saul about the real purpose of his visit to David (1 Sam 16:2). Even though none of these stories are about lying nor presents lying as a moral principle that God's people should follow, they show the dilemmas that people living in different periods of history had to face. These stories demonstrate how application of our prototypes might change in non-prototypical situations. Sanders argues that "by telling multiple stories that address the complexities of real life, the community learns how to employ various precepts in different situations and learn to navigate nontypical cases."[90]

Narratives as the means of application help accomplish one more purpose as far as non-prototypical cases are concerned. It can be said that human life is not only experienced as a story but also that most people want their lives to be a part of a larger narrative of some kind. Christian preaching may help listeners to make better choices in non-prototypical situations by transforming their prototypical view of life and history. Instead of perceiving their lives as short and meaningless episodes, they may begin to see themselves as created in the image of God, believing in Christ the perfect image of God, and

---

89. Nussbaum, *Love's Knowledge*, 293.
90. Sanders, *Theology in the Flesh*, loc 2776 of 5234, Kindle.

being transformed by the Holy Spirit into the image of Christ. Even difficult ethical choices are made differently when people realize that their lives are part of a larger story of salvation.

However, if our sermon applications are based on prototypes, we are faced with the problem of the role of rules in our ethical thinking and preaching. Stressing that our moral reasoning is based on prototypes does not mean that all rules are redundant. Mark Johnson argues that moral laws are "abstractions based on cultural prototypes" and adds that "such abstracted rules have their meaning and proper application only relative to the prototype."[91] This intricate relationship between rules and prototypes can be explained with an example of an interplay between rules and prototypes in giving up smoking and developing a healthy lifestyle.

While "No Smoking" signs are important to designate smoke-free areas and ensure the comfort of non-smokers, such signs have little value in convincing smokers to give up their addiction. What might convince smokers to stop smoking are prototypes expressed in positive images of a healthy person or negative ones, such as a person suffering from lung cancer. Smokers may think about prototypical situations such as being socially stigmatized for smoking, being out of fashion, saving money, or inconveniences caused by smoking as the number of areas designated for smokers decreases. These deeply ingrained images of who people want or do not want to become may push smokers to make certain ethical decisions. However, when they make these decisions based on their prototypes, these choices will be expressed in very practical and tangible actions, which include some rules. A person pursuing a healthier lifestyle by giving up smoking will have to change some habits, decide to spend money differently, make time for regular exercise, and start eating differently, which means that there are some rules, and some foods that can be eaten and others that are not allowed. Depending on a person, these external actions that express the internal prototypes, may look very different.

The same idea applies to prototype-based application in preaching, which is a novel concept in homiletics. As preachers, we should focus on helping our listeners to learn biblical prototypes and follow Christ, their ultimate prototype, by growing into his likeness. However, listeners will need to find their own answers to the question of how to apply these prototypes in their lives

---

91. Johnson, *Moral Imagination*, 192.

and translate these into specific moral choices and actions in both prototypical and non-prototypical situations. In this whole process, the moral imagination is key because it allows us to see connections between our prototypes and everyday situations that we face.

Therefore, Cognitive Linguistics, with its notion of prototypes, not only changes our approach to developing sermon applications but also provides preachers with specific guidelines for accomplishing this task. Moreover, it places the whole discussion on developing prototype-based application in the wider context of human cognition and communication, showing the connection between our internal prototypes and typical framings of situations, metaphors, and narratives. Analogically, as in the process of discovering listeners' prototypes, here metaphors and narratives are effective tools in shaping these prototypes.

5.2 Cognitive Linguistics and Preaching Biblical Texts, Images, and Metaphors

In this section, I will present a practical application of conceptual metaphor theory to preaching biblical texts in general and images and metaphors in particular. In the first part of this section, I will list strategies for reworking existing biblical metaphors for preaching purposes. Cognitive linguists have identified most of these strategies while analyzing the process of reworking conventional metaphors by forming novel ones. I have not only adopted their approach to preaching biblical metaphors but also supplemented this approach with several methods of my own.

In the second part of this section, I will devote some attention to ways of creating metaphors and images when preaching biblical texts in general, even where these texts are non-metaphorical.

In the final part, I will discuss methods by which preachers can employ metaphors and images as elements of a sermon structure that give their sermons coherence and unity.

5.2.1 Preaching Biblical Metaphors and Images

Numerous homileticians have undertaken the task of providing insights and practical guidelines regarding methods of preaching biblical metaphors and images. They also offer suggestions about entering the creative process of developing new metaphors that reflect the meaning of the biblical texts. For instance, Jennifer L. Lord urges preachers to make note of both biblical images and other images that come to mind while studying a passage. In the process of generating new images, Lord suggests using mind mapping, writing off the page, and daily journalling.[92] David Day suggests that a preacher should begin with expanding the image which is already in the Bible. By expanding images he means that one should "play free association with them, imagine what they might look like if you saw them or heard them, ransack the lexicon to see how these words are used in non-technical contexts."[93] Day believes that in order to initiate the generative process in our thinking, we need to learn to see things from different perspectives and that, to do so, we might try making forced connections between concepts, images, and stories. Paul Scott Wilson stresses the idea of teaching biblical truths by using comparison and contrast. He states that "contradiction works in the same way that metaphor works," allowing listeners to experience the tension created by by placing side by side two elements that are similar and dissimilar.[94]

Although Cognitive Linguistics is sometimes perceived as a theory that deals only with the simplest, everyday metaphors used in speech, cognitivists have effectively shown that their approach is also fruitful in analyzing complex poetic metaphors, indicating that these are all rooted in conventional metaphors. Moreover, when studying these poetic metaphors, they identified various strategies of reworking conventional metaphors into novel ones.

Considering that one of the key challenges that preachers face is the problem of how to present biblical metaphors to their listeners, I find the methods proposed by these cognitivists helpful and fruitful in preaching biblical metaphors in fresh and creative ways. In the process of working with biblical metaphors in my sermons, I have identified a few more methods for effectively communicating these metaphors. In the subsequent paragraphs, I will describe the following methods of presenting and reworking biblical metaphors and images: illustrating conventional metaphors, describing metaphors,

---

92. Lord, *Finding Language and Imagery*, 34–39.

93. Day, *Embodying the Word*, 70.

94. Wilson, *Setting Words on Fire*, 43, 47. See also Graves, *Fully Alive Preacher*, 19, 41, 47; Craddock, *As One without Authority*, 75–77; Buttrick, *Homiletic: Moves and Structures*, 123–133; Eslinger, *Narrative Imagination*, 166–171; Eslinger, *New Hearing*, 26–28; Rice, "Shaping Sermons," 104–105; Sheard, "Preaching in the Hear and Now," 140.

extending metaphors, elaborating metaphors, amplifying metaphors, paralleling metaphors, questioning metaphors, and combining metaphors.

5.2.1.1 Illustrating Conventional Metaphors

On the basis of my personal study of Cognitive Linguistics, I now introduce one of my own methods of conveying biblical metaphors that is based on identifying and illustrating conventional metaphors. The Bible has numerous examples of metaphors that may appear ambiguous to our listeners – for instance, Jesus's words to the Pharisees, accusing them of being spiritually blind, his call to his disciples to take up their cross and follow him, or the command to his followers to build their lives on the rock. In order to help listeners to comprehend these metaphorical expressions and relate these to their everyday experiences, it might be helpful to begin by identifying the conventional metaphors underlying these expressions these expressions, such as UNDERSTANDING IS SEEING, LIFE IS A JOURNEY, and LIFE IS A BUILDING. This task may not be easy, and these metaphors are not always effortlessly recognized. However, even though preachers may find it difficult to come up with a clear statement such as LIFE IS A JOURNEY, they may still ask questions about how life is portrayed in a given metaphorical expression and why it speaks about turns, bumpy roads, following the path, and so on. Moreover, preachers can benefit from indexes of common conceptual metaphors that include the most typical examples.[95]

Once conventional metaphors are identified, they can be illustrated with other commonly known linguistic examples to show how we conceptualize life using this particular metaphor. In order to do so, it is necessary not only to identify the conventional metaphors behind given metaphorical expressions but to see these expressions in the wider context of the whole discourse. For instance, in the Gospel of John, we find the story of the healing of a man born blind (John 9:1–41). At the end of this episode, Jesus made a shocking statement: "For judgment I came into this world, so that those who do not see may see, and that those who see may become blind" (9:39). When the Pharisees heard this, they wondered if Jesus had just called them blind. Jesus made himself even clearer, saying, "If you were blind, you would have no sin;

---

95. "Index of /lakoff/metaphors", www.lang.osaka-u.ac.jp/~sugimoto/MasterMetaphor List/metaphors/index.html, [Accessed 11th May, 2018].

but since you say, 'We see,' your sin remains" (9:41). In order to understand Jesus's argument, it is important to pay attention to the context of his words and the structure of this narrative. The story begins with the disciples seeing a man born blind and equating his blindness with sin – either his own or his parents' sin. This notion of equating blindness with sin is also confirmed by the Pharisees, who rejected the healed man's testimony, saying, "You were born entirely in sins, and are you teaching us?" (9:34). Jesus, however, rejected this idea by stating that the blind man was born this way "so that the works of God might be displayed in him" (9:3) and then healing him.

Thus, the story begins with the blind man not being able to see and being accused of sin but ends with the man seeing and Jesus pronouncing the Pharisees blind and guilty of sin. As the narrative unfolds, readers can see the progression in the healed man's perspective and understanding. First, he recovered his physical sight. Then, he stated that the man called Jesus opened his eyes. Next, he called Jesus a prophet and claimed that Jesus had to have come from God. Finally, he called Jesus "Lord," confessing that he believed in the Son of Man, and worshipped Jesus. The Pharisees, however, stated that Jesus could not be from God since he had healed the man on the Sabbath, and they urged the healed man to pronounce Jesus a sinner. So, while a blind man starts seeing and understanding more, Jesus's opponents seem to see and understand less. In narrating this episode, the apostle John employs a conventional metaphor – UNDERSTANDING IS SEEING – and without paying attention to and comprehending this metaphor, it is impossible to understand the final judgement Jesus pronounced on the Pharisees.

In a sermon, preachers can help listeners to understand these structural elements appearing in the story and explain Jesus's words in the wider context. They may also help them to grasp the various metaphorical expressions related to seeing and blindness that are used in the text by pointing out the conventional metaphor UNDERSTANDING IS SEEING that underlies them all and showing how this concept functions in everyday language. I have attempted to do so in my sermon on John 9:1–41.

> Jesus calls the Pharisees blind because he knows that the worst kind of blindness is the blindness to our own blindness. It is the conviction that what I see is enough and there is no more to see. We know it from our own experience that the most difficult

people to talk to are those who are convinced that they are right, they understand, and see everything as it is while refusing to acknowledge the fact that they actually might not see and understand everything. Since they are blind to their own blindness, they deprive themselves of any chance to change and grow.

That is the reason why Jesus uses in this story seeing as an image of understanding and we use it often too. We say, "Don't you see where this is going?" and we mean "Don't you understand the consequences?" We say, "He does not see how serious it is" and we mean that "He does not understand the gravity of the situation." Sometimes people say, "If you believe that she will keep her word, you must be blind" meaning "You need to understand that she is lying to you." We say those things, because we know that UNDERSTANDING IS SEEING and to understand something is to see something differently.

So, what should we see and understand? Since the worst kind of blindness is the blindness to our own blindness we need to see that it is only when, being aware of our own blindness, we turn to Jesus and allow him to open our eyes that we can see him differently and live differently. It is because those who see differently will live differently.

So, what can you see when you look at Jesus? If your answer is "My Lord and Saviour," this will change you and people around you will start seeing it in you too, because those who see differently, will live differently.[96]

By using examples from everyday language to illustrate how the metaphor UNDERSTANDING IS SEEING works, I attempted to help listeners to see that Jesus's teaching about seeing and being blind is not as abstract as some might think and that it is deeply rooted in our language and experience.

The same approach can be applied to other texts. To explain the idea of following Jesus and taking up our cross, preachers may begin by identifying the conventional metaphor LIFE IS A JOURNEY and illustrating it with well-known examples, such as "There is a long way to go before I finish working

---

96. Adam Szumorek, "Co Widzisz?"

on this," "This marriage is a bumpy road," or "I got lost in my choices and have no idea which way to go." A preacher may say something like this:

We like our journey to be smooth, comfortable, take place in good company, and have a great destination, but Jesus invites his followers to make a different kind of journey through life. His disciples are called to follow in his footsteps and, as they do so, they discover that he walks towards the cross to die. Their journey is not comfortable since they have to take up their cross as a constant reminder of their purpose – which is to die to their own life agenda.

Illustrating metaphors, even though very useful in conveying biblical metaphors and images, has its limits. It is not based on the idea of reworking biblical metaphors but, rather, allows listeners to experience the linguistic power of a biblical metaphorical expression by relating it to other contemporary metaphorical expressions that are developed on the basis of the same conventional metaphor. In some cases, however, it may be difficult to recognize the conventional metaphors underlying biblical metaphorical expressions. In such instances, it might be prudent to use another approach – namely, describing metaphors.

5.2.1.2 Describing

Describing metaphors is another method which I developed during my research. Even though describing metaphors does not qualify as a method of reworking ordinary metaphors into more creative ones, it may be useful in conveying biblical metaphors. Although some argue that it is impossible to explain a metaphor – just as it is not possible to explain a joke without losing its rhetorical impact – there are times when both metaphors and jokes have to be presented in simpler terms.

There were occasions during Jesus's ministry when his listeners had difficulty comprehending the metaphors and images he used. Jesus talked about seeds and different kinds of soil as an image of different responses to the word of God, he told his followers to eat his body and drink his blood, and he was called the Lamb of God. Some of these images were misunderstood during at the time of Jesus, just as they are now. In some cases, Jesus himself provided an explanation (Mark 4:10–20). Thus, it is not surprising that, today, a puzzled listener might ask the preacher about the meaning of some of these metaphors and images.

Instead of talking about explaining metaphors, I prefer to use the term "describing," which does not assume translating metaphors into propositional statements but, rather, showing interconnections between source and target domains, and stressing existing mappings with hiding and highlighting of certain elements. This description should take place with respect to the boundaries set by mappings, hiding and highlighting, and the context of the whole discourse.

For instance, in the New Testament, Jesus is described as the Lamb of God. In discussing this metaphor, Zoltán Kövecses points out that two frames can be identified here: the frame of the Old Testament and the frame of the New Testament.[97] I prefer to use more precise terminology and talk about two domains: the domain of the Old Testament law and sacrifices and the domain of Christ's sacrifice. In the Old Testament, when people sinned against God, they had to bring a lamb as a sacrifice for their sins. In the New Testament, Christ is the ultimate sacrifice for our sins. In both cases, people sin against God and death is the consequence of sin. Moreover, in both cases, there is an innocent sacrifice that is offered instead of the sinner. Thus, we can establish the following mappings between domains, as shown in this diagram that I have adopted and expanded.

Domain of the Old Testament sacrifices		Domains of Christ's sacrifice
God	→	God
Owner of the lamb	→	people
Sin by the owner of the lamb	→	sins of people
Death as a consequence of sin	→	death as a consequence of sin
Lamb	→	Jesus
Unblemished	→	perfect
Sacrificing the lamb for the owner's sin	→	Jesus dying for people's sins

Diagram 8. Old Testament sacrifices and Christ's sacrifice mappings[98]

When preaching on Jesus as the sacrificial Lamb of God, it is necessary to pay attention to both elements that are highlighted and elements that are hidden. Not every element of the source domain gets mapped into the

---

97. Kövecses, "Heart of the Matter," 93.

98. Kövecses, 94. A diagram adopted and expanded.

target. For instance, an animal was brought as a sacrifice; it was owned by the person who brought it; the animal did not choose to be sacrificed but was an unwilling sacrifice and, almost till the very end, was unaware of its fate; and its death meant the end if its existence and did not provide any lasting solution to the problem of sin. Understanding Christ as the Lamb of God requires us to reject or redefine many of these elements of the source image: Christian theology holds that Christ, as fully human and fully divine, willingly gave up his life to be sacrificed for the sins of people; we do not own Jesus; he knew the purpose of his coming, and his death redeemed people the world; furthermore, he conquered death, and his sacrifice did not mean the end of his life but, rather, allowed people to have eternal life.[99]

Thus, an analysis of highlighting and hiding in metaphors allows preachers to identify those elements that are essential to their understanding. While conducting this analysis, preachers can establish mappings, but they must also notice those elements that do not get mapped. In the case of Christ's sacrifice, even these non-mapped elements are important because they enable preachers to see the uniqueness of Christ's sacrifice in comparison to Old Testament sacrifices. The idea of hiding and highlighting helps us to notice the tension between the source and target domains since it does not only show similarity but also shocking dissimilarity – for instance, comparing the Son of God to an animal.

When describing metaphors in their sermons, preachers should refrain from using cognitive terminology that might be unfamiliar to their listeners and which would deprive the sermon of its rhetorical impact. Instead, they may employ a narrative description that includes describing metaphors.

> I remember this hot and sunny day when I stood by the Jordan River with a few other disciples of John the Baptist. Yes, you know me. My name is Andrew. We all listened as John addressed the crowd gathered. When suddenly, he saw a young rabbi called Jesus approaching and he said, "Behold, the Lamb of God who takes away the sin of the world!" Then, John testified that he saw the Spirit of God coming on this man and said

---

99. For a more extensive treatment of the New Testament metaphors depicting Jesus's death, studied from the perspective of Cognitive Linguistics, see Schröter, *From Jesus to the New Testament*, 185–203.

that he is the Son of God. But, for some reason his words "the Lamb of God who takes away the sin of the world" caught my attention and were still ringing in my ears. What does he mean by that? How can a person be a sacrificial lamb?

As a Jew I knew the Law and made many sacrifices in my life. While looking at Jesus my thoughts went to these numerous occasions when I was haunted by my own guilt because I knew I had done something that offended God. At those dreadful times I did what every pious Jew should do. I went to the temple bringing an animal – the best I had. The lamb was sometimes fighting for its life because neither people nor animals want to die. But there are times when someone has to. See, if the consequence of our sins is death, someone has to die. This is the reason why I was bringing those animals. I did not want it to be me. So, I brought my lamb to the priest who slaughtered it and spilled its blood on the altar. I could walk away free and forgiven. Till the next time. There was always the next time. But we learned in a painful way that every sin has its price.

On that day, I was looking at this new rabbi – Jesus – and I wondered how could he be the Lamb of God? God did not allow human sacrifices. So, how could this Jew pay for my sins? I understood it three years later. At that time, I was one of Jesus's disciples. He was talking something about giving his life for the sins of the world and about going to Jerusalem to die. And he went. We saw him captured. Then, he was flogged and nailed to the cross. It did not look like the sacrifices at the temple. It was more like an execution of a criminal.

It took us some time until we understood that John the Baptist was right. Jesus was the Lamb of God and died for our sins. He did for us what our lambs could never do, he willingly gave his life to remove all our sins forever. We were free and forgiven.[100]

---

100. A sermonic sample created for this study.

A preaching metaphor such as "Christ is the Lamb of God" is challenging because it is culturally remote, might be difficult for a contemporary audience to understand, and might be considered offensive by some. There are numerous strategies that could be employed in such cases, but the simplest is describing the metaphor by helping the listeners to see the domains and mappings without actually talking about domains and mappings. The purpose of doing this is not to iron out rough edges of a given metaphor and make it more acceptable but, rather, to make the metaphor more understandable in its own context.

5.2.1.3 Extending

One of the ways of extending a conventional conceptual metaphor is to create a novel metaphorical expression by adding a new unconventional element to the source domain.[101] Any given conventional metaphor does not map everything from the source domain to the target domain; thus, to extend a metaphor means to identify new mappings.[102] In Psalm 23, for instance, there is an extension of the conventional metaphor LIFE IS A JOURNEY. This metaphor is extended in several ways by adding new elements to enrich our understanding of walking through life. When reading this psalm, readers discover that there is a guide in this journey. Novelty in conceptualizing this journey is also based on introducing in the source domain an element that describes various locations people visit. In this psalm, the travellers go through the green pastures, dark valleys, and end up in the house of the Lord.

Another example of extending metaphors can be found in 1 Corinthians 12, where the apostle Paul talks about the church as the body of Christ. This novel metaphorical expression is based on the conventional metaphor ORGANIZATIONS ARE LIVING ORGANISMS. Typical understanding of this metaphor assumes that organizations grow like living organisms, and that they might be healthy or unhealthy, alive or dead. Paul extends this metaphor by providing his readers with an imaginary conversation between different parts of the body, with different parts using their own criteria to try to exclude

---

101. Kövecses, *Metaphor: A Practical Introduction*, 53.

102. Lakoff and Turner, *More than Cool Reason*, 67. Lakoff and Turner show how, in *Hamlet*, Shakespeare extends the conventional metaphor "death is sleep" by adding a new element to the source domain – namely, a possibility of dreaming.

each other from the body. Paul also states that while we treat different parts of the body differently – giving more attention to some parts because other parts do not require as much attention – all parts are needed and essential. All these elements are considered additions to the metaphor since they are not conventionally used in describing organizations and, in the case of Paul's letter, they are used to convey the new theological meaning that the church is the body of Christ.

Preachers can use a similar approach when preaching biblical metaphors. Paul's main idea behind the image of the church being the body of Christ is to show its subordination to Christ and its unity in the diversity of its gifts. Consequently, a preacher can extend this image by saying:

> Paul pictures the church as a healthy and unified body of Christ, but while growing up, I saw many churches – the local bodies of Christ – that were bruised or even crippled by conflicts, gossips, divisions, and ruptures in relationships. The problem with such a body is that it cannot do much and it cannot go anywhere.

In this case preachers, knowing how the human body functions and that it can be bruised or unhealthy, add this new element to a biblical metaphor of the church being the body of Christ by describing it as a bruised or crippled body. Moreover, knowing that healthy bodies are active, another element can be added – that of a church not being able to do anything or go anywhere because it is consumed with arguments about its different gifts instead of uniting to use these gifts.

Philip Yancey offers another example of extending this particular metaphor by comparing a local church to a disabled woman's body. He tells the story of Carolyn Martin, who was born with cerebral palsy. Yancey says that "it is the peculiar tragedy of her condition that its outward signs drooling, floppy arm movements, inarticulate speech, a bobbing head cause people who meet her to wonder if she is retarded."[103] Because of this common perception, she spent fifteen years in an institution for the mentally challenged. Yet, she managed to prove herself intelligent and capable of learning. She began her education and, finally, went to a Bible college. However, even there, people perceived Carolyn as "the disabled person" and many were uncomfortable

---

103. Yancey, *Disappointment with God*, 227.

around her. One day, Carolyn was asked to speak during a student chapel service. She typed her speech and her friend Josee read it for her since she was not able to speak clearly. Yancey writes:

> On the day of the chapel service, Carolyn sat slumped in her wheelchair on the left side of the platform. At times her arms jerked uncontrollably, her head lolled to one side so that it almost touched her shoulder, and a stream of saliva sometimes ran down her blouse. Beside her stood Josee, who read the mature and graceful prose Carolyn had composed, centred around this Bible text: "But we have this treasure in jars of clay to show that this all-surpassing power is from God but not from us."
>
> For the first time, some students saw Carolyn as a complete human being, like themselves. Before then her mind, a very good mind, had always been inhibited by a "disobedient" body, and difficulties with speech had masked her intelligence.[104]

Reflecting on Carolyn's story, Philip Yancey concludes by saying, "The New Testament image of Christ as head of the body took on a new meaning as I gained a sense of both the humiliation that Christ undergoes in his role as head, and also the exaltation that he allows us, the members of his body."[105] He also points out that even though the church has a perfect head – Christ – it often acts and behaves in ways that show little subordination to the head, similar to Paul's description of the church, where some parts tell other parts of the body that they are not needed.

The novelty of extending a metaphor is based on introducing a new element in the source domain – in this case, a brilliant mind in a paralyzed body is the foundation for the contrast between Christ, the perfect head of the church, and the church, which is his unperfected body that even argues about the gifts that have been given by Christ for the body's growth.

When extending metaphors, it is essential to be aware of the limits of reasonable extensions that remain faithful to the text and do not draw attention to themselves due to their artificial manner. Thus, when preaching the Pauline text on the church as the body of Christ, it is wise to recognize

---

104. Yancey, 227–228.
105. Yancey, 228.

its main focus – namely, diversity and unity of different parts of the body of Christ – and express this as the main idea of the sermon. In the process of defining this main idea, an analysis of mappings will be helpful to identify which elements of the source domain of the church as the body metaphor are highlighted and which are hidden. Understanding that metaphors function in the context of a wider discourse allows preachers to establish limits in their interpretation and communication. Consequently, preachers will not be able to talk about the church as a body that gets old, sweats, smells, needs to be dressed nicely, dances, or goes rock climbing since such extensions are not faithful to the context of the given metaphor and may sound forced or artificial. Context and metaphorical mappings limit the range of extensions, which must be in accord with the main idea of the text and its aim. Thus, the text itself and its main idea control the scope of extensions.

Another challenge in extending metaphors is the importance of being sensitive to the audience since some extensions may be perceived as offensive or hurtful, especially when they relate to disabilities. The preacher's task is to preach in such a way that people struggling with illness or disability do not feel excluded, offended, stigmatized, inferior, or put on the spot. When preaching a sermon on blindness, I was aware that one of our church members was sightless, but, with his permission, I used his example to show that even though he was visionless, there was a time when he saw what was most important – Christ as his Saviour. Even though he still cannot see, he sees more than many people he passes on the streets every day. Philip Yancey's example also shows how we can talk about disabilities and use a story about a disabled person in a sensitive and respectful way.[106]

5.2.1.4 Elaborating

Kövecses defines elaboration as being "different from extension, in that it elaborates on an existing element of the source in an unusual way."[107] Lakoff and Turner define this process as elaborating on schemas "by filling in slots

---

106. More insights on this subject can be found in Kathy Black's book, where she presents a biblical and theological perspective on the issue of suffering. In her work, she offers helpful reflections regarding ways of preaching on the key healing accounts from the Gospels in such a way that the preacher takes into consideration the needs and perspective of those who suffer from various disabilities. See Black, *Healing Homiletic*.

107. Kövecses, *Metaphor: A Practical Introduction*, 53.

in unusual ways rather than by extending the metaphor to map additional slots."[108] As an example of elaborating a conventional metaphor DEATH IS DEPARTURE, they quote Horace, who refers to death as the "eternal exile of the raft,"[109] thereby elaborating on an existing element of the source by providing a vehicle for the departure.

In Psalm 23, which utilizes the conventional metaphor LIFE IS A JOURNEY, a novel element is added as an extension, namely, the author's identification, at least in the first part of the psalm, of the travellers as sheep. Preachers can elaborate further on images employed in a text by making them even more specific. So, when preaching on Psalm 23, I might reflect on the brevity of life and the fact that this journey passes much quicker than we expect, and say:

> When I was young, I thought, there is a long way ahead of me and it is going to be a really slow walk through green pastures and dark valleys to the house of the Lord. I believed that I had plenty of time. However, now that I am nearer the end, I feel that it has not been a long walk but, rather, a fast train ride. It was much quicker than I expected. My memory is full of images – short glimpses through the window. Yes, I saw the green pastures and dark valleys. There were some stops along the way, but I have an impression that I did not stay long in any of these places. What I thought was supposed to be a long time of bliss or an exhausting period of turmoil turned out to be just a short stop on the way – just another station. Now I am heading to my final station, believing that it is not really going to be the final one but only the changing station on the way home.

In this sermon, I utilized a conventional metaphor employed by the psalmist – LIFE IS A JOURNEY – and elaborate on existing mappings of moving in time and space by adding a train as the vehicle used in this journey. I filled existing slots in a new and unconventional way. Another way of elaborating this conventional metaphor of life as a journey would be to depict different places visited on the way as train stations and to liken memories to glimpses through the windows along the way.

---

108. Lakoff and Turner, *More than Cool Reason*, 67.

109. Lakoff and Turner, 67.

While preaching my mother's funeral sermon, I quoted Psalm 23. Although home was always important, she was not always able to enjoy a real home, and so I chose to summarize her life as a journey home. Psalm 23 depicts this journey as walking through green pastures, by still waters, and passing through dark valleys – including the valley of death. However, the journey does not end in the valley but leads to the house of the Lord.

In my sermon, I utilized the metaphor LIFE IS A JOURNEY, which assumes that journeys have their destinations. In Psalm 23, the house of the Lord is the final destination. Against the background of the Old Testament understanding of the temple as a physical sign of God's presence and the knowledge that when we die we go to be with the Lord, I elaborated on this well-known text by saying that death is moving to our eternal home. Even though we are the temples of the Holy Spirit and experience his presence daily, there comes a time when we move to his presence. We go home. Thus, the novelty in conceptualizing life as a journey lies in the fact that this is a journey home – to a place where we can experience God's presence as never before.

It is interesting that Jesus himself elaborated on the idea of the house of the Lord when he told his disciples that he was leaving to prepare a place for them and that there were many rooms in his Father's house (John 14:2). Thus, by adding the idea of rooms, Jesus enriched this image and made it more precise. As they read the Gospels, preachers may discover that Jesus often employs elaboration. For instance, when he said that he was the true vine, his Father was the vinedresser, and his followers the branches, Jesus was elaborating on the Old Testament image of the vine as a reference to Israel (Isa 5:1–7; Jer 2:21). By doing so, Jesus claimed that he was the true Israel and that the only way of being a part of the vine is abiding in him. Jesus's elaboration includes elements such as the new identity of the vine, the vinedresser, branches, and fruits. He also extended this metaphor by adding new elements such as abiding in the vine, pruning the vine, and burning dry branches.

Again, a word of caution is needed when elaborating metaphors since it is possible to fill existing mappings in ways that are not supported by the text or with ideas that sound bizarre to listeners. In other cases, elaborating may border on allegorizing the text, especially when preachers are tempted to elaborate on their own elaborations and push them to extremes. When preaching on Psalm 23 and elaborating the conventional metaphor LIFE IS A JOURNEY, preachers may choose to compare life to a train ride, as was done in the example above. However, they may also be tempted to elaborate on their own elaboration and fill all the blank slots of this new image saying that on this ride, God is our engine driver, the train is the community of the people of God, God's grace is a ticket, and so on. Thus, while choosing ways of elaborating metaphors, preachers must make sure that they only elaborate on images in the text and not on their own images, and also that the images they create do not violate the message of the text. The purpose of elaboration is to awake listeners' imagination to help them see the connections between the text and their lives and to experience the force of biblical images but without replacing biblical images with contemporary ones. This challenge is difficult partially because this task of elaborating metaphors is based on the sensitivity of the particular preacher. There is always a danger that the preacher while attempting to elaborate on a biblical metaphor, may turn an evocative image into something banal.

5.2.1.5 Amplifying

As I reflected on extending and elaborating metaphors, I decided to create another strategy of reworking conventional metaphors, namely, amplifying them. If extending was based on adding new mappings and elaborating on filling in existing mappings in new ways, amplifying aims at detailing and amplifying existing mappings.

For instance, Paul writes that God "predestined us to adoption as sons through Jesus Christ to Himself, according to the kind intention of His will" (Eph 1:5) and depicts our relationship with God as that of being his adopted children. After identifying correspondences between adoption and entering into a relationship with God, preachers can amplify existing mappings by providing a more detailed description.

> In many cases, having no parents means that you are alone. There is nobody to care for you and protect you. To put it simply, even crudely – nobody wants you and you just do not belong anywhere. You may even wonder about the point of having a family name when you have no family. The name is just a re-minder of a happier past and a harbinger of an uncertain future.
>
> But then, one day, somebody shows up – and you discover that there is somebody who wants you, wants to give you a new

name, a new family, and new future. You are not alone any more.
You have a place to go because you are wanted. You are loved.

In this case, amplifying aims at helping listeners to see and feel the emotional force of the idea of adoption by contrasting it with being an orphan. Preachers can take a single concept and, by means of a description like this, show how it functions in real life.

The aim of amplifying is not to create a new metaphorical expression – unlike in the case of extending and elaborating but, rather, to help listeners to feel the weight of the original metaphor by showing how it describes real life situations. Since amplifying is about finding connections between a metaphor and life, it is a very helpful approach to developing a sermon application. However, when utilizing this approach, preachers will experience tension between the need to recreate the realities of a text and the need to create images that connect with their listeners' experiences. For instance, the process of adoption in ancient times looks different to such a process in modern times. Thus, while amplifying this image in the minds of listeners, it is wise to keep it general enough that we do not force contemporary ideas on the ancient text. However, there is another option that allows keeping both an explanation of ancient realities and a contemporary extended narrative metaphor – this option is called paralleling.

5.2.1.6 Paralleling

Paralleling is another strategy that I have introduced and developed. Although closely related to elaborating, paralleling elaborates on a metaphor by employing a narrative description whose main image corresponds to the image created by a metaphorical expression. Thus, this strategy is based on paralleling a biblical image with a short narrative that conveys and amplifies the image.

Stephen Wright seems to suggest a similar approach when he talks about parabolic paralleling in biblical interpretation. He says that the literal meaning of the word parable is "something thrown alongside." Thus, he suggests that "in a similar way, interpreters are called to 'throw' Scripture alongside historical occurrences in such a way as to provoke profound reflection and a sense of real, though provisional meaning."[110] He points out that just as

---

110. Wright, "Inhabiting the Story," 514–515.

Jesus did not usually feel obliged to show or explain the connections between parables and life, preachers can also "throw" stories alongside biblical texts without explaining explicitly connections between them.

Paralleling is a very useful approach to adopt when preaching difficult texts that seem very remote from our listeners' experience. For instance, Jesus defined being a disciple in terms of taking up one's cross and following him. This idea might sound foreign and strange for our listeners until they realize that even today, in many parts of the world, following Christ often means death. Hence, some recent reports about the persecution of Christians may help listeners to understand the consequences of this decision to follow Christ.[111] Similarly, there are also reports from the past that might help in grasping this idea of following Christ to death and daily dying to ourselves.

> During the Protestant Reformation, when Christians faced increasing persecution, there was a small seminary in Basel, providing training for future ministers. In those times, being a preacher was risky, and the number of Christian martyrs among pastors were skyrocketing. So, when students graduated from the seminary and were receiving their diplomas, their professors would tell them, "This is your death certificate," because they knew that it was usually just a matter of time before their students would be dead. Living with a death certificate means that somebody is officially dead. Following Christ has always meant both being ready for death and daily dying to ourselves.

In this case, paralleling employs not only a narrative but also an image since taking up one's cross is paralleled with an image of receiving a death certificate, which is much closer to our contemporary realm of experience.

The biggest difficulty with paralleling is selecting the right story, one that actually illustrates the same concepts as the biblical image. Preachers often choose stories that touch generally upon the same images as a biblical metaphor. However, on a closer examination, the story often goes in a different direction, stresses different concepts, and evokes different emotional responses. This may happen when preachers parallel metaphors conveying positive concepts and emotions with narratives containing negative examples – for

---

111. See OpenDoors, www.opendoorsuk.org [Accessed 11th May, 2018].

instance, teaching about the unity of a church by talking about how the citizens of one country united to attack people of another nation. In both cases, the preacher may talk about unity and acting together, but the purposes of that unity and the emotional responses evoked by these two images are completely different.

5.2.1.7 Questioning

Kövecses says that "in the poetic device of questioning, poets can call into question the very appropriateness of our common everyday metaphors,"[112] and he quotes a few lines from a poem as an example:

> Suns can set and return again,
> but when our brief light goes out,
> there's one perpetual night to be slept through.
> (Catullus 5)[113]

In this poem, Catullus employs the conventional metaphors A LIFETIME IS A DAY and DEATH IS NIGHT and shows their inadequacy and their incoherence with our experience. In everyday life, after a night always comes another day, but when somebody dies, "there's one perpetual night to be slept through."[114] According to the poet, there is no day coming after this night.

One of the key metaphors used by the prophet Jeremiah to depict the relationship between God and his people is the image of marriage. Through Jeremiah, God says to Judah, "I remember concerning you the devotion of your youth, The love of your betrothals" (Jer 2:2). However, when this metaphor became inappropriate due to the idolatry of God's people, it was replaced with images of adultery and divorce. The people of Judah had not repented even after seeing how Israel was sent into exile: "And I saw that for all the adulteries of faithless Israel, I had sent her away and given her a writ of divorce, yet her treacherous sister Judah did not fear; but she went and was a harlot also" (Jer 3:8). The Judeans believed that they were in a special relationship with God as close as marriage, Jeremiah had to confront them and question their metaphors replacing them with different ones.

---

112. Kövecses, *Metaphor: A Practical Introduction*, 54.

113. Quoted in Kövecses, *Metaphor: A Practical Introduction*, 54.

114. Kövecses, 54.

Preachers can follow a similar strategy in preaching by questioning the appropriateness of metaphors as applied to given people or situations or by showing their limits.

> We believe that the church is a family, but many people have completely different experiences of the church. If you asked them about their perception, they may describe the church as a very dysfunctional family. It turns out that even though Christians claim to be the children of God, they sometimes behave like spoiled brats and, at times, this family resembles a battlefield with the wounded being killed by their own companions. So, who are we?

By questioning this specific metaphor, preachers communicate that even though the church is the family of God, we Christians often fail to live out this calling and, as a result, people observing us from the outside have a completely different view of the church. In this case, questioning is confrontational since it is aimed at people who claim a certain kind of identity and use specific metaphors to describe themselves but have failed to notice that these metaphors are no longer applicable.

Questioning can also be more pastoral in nature, in terms of expressing listeners' doubts and questions regarding God, and as such, is an effective strategy for establishing common ground. Understanding that many people have experienced God's silence in various life situations, preachers may address this issue by questioning the biblical metaphor of God as shepherd. This may sound like this:

> If God is my shepherd, leading me through life, why do I feel lost most of the time and not know where to go? When I am at the crossroads, I have no idea where to turn, and there is no voice whispering directions in my ear. I am desperate to hear my shepherd, but he seems to be silent, and there are no green pastures and still waters in sight.

By questioning this biblical metaphor, preachers have the opportunity to move towards developing a more balanced biblical theology of suffering and God's involvement in the world. The purpose of questioning is not to negate biblical metaphors but, rather, to show that we all sometimes struggle with experiencing the reality they describe. Jeffrey Arthurs provides another example of questioning biblical metaphors by quoting the familiar proverb "You reap what you sow" that is reflected in Proverbs 22:8 and Galatians 6:7. Against the background of these biblical images of sowing and reaping, Arthurs asks provocatively, "What to do when you plant a carrot, but get an onion?"[115] His question shows that there are situations that seem to contradict the assumption that the kind of results we get always match the kind of actions we choose and demonstrate that, sometimes, our good deeds are rewarded with evil or vice versa.

Questioning is sometimes a useful method to recover the strangeness of a biblical text, which can be an effective way of grabbing listeners' attention. This can be accomplished by testing if metaphors found in a text actually reflect our experience of reality and are applicable to our lives. Walter Wangerin, reflecting on Psalm 23, writes:

> No, the Lord is *not* my shepherd. Neither am I a sheep. I am a man something over six feet when I stand up in socks (what sheep ever wore socks?), and my God is one whom I cannot directly describe at all.[116]

Next, Wangerin deepens the conflict by describing his encounters with sheep that in so many respects seemed to be so different from him, but in one respect they were just like him – they all need guidance.[117]

Finally, questioning can take the form of confronting culturally ingrained metaphors and images. As pointed out earlier, some concepts, such as life, love, happiness, and time, are so complex that it is impossible to conceptualize them using just one metaphor. Consequently, different metaphors capture different facets of a given concept, but these metaphors also express various, often conflicting, world views – this is seen, for example, in diverse attitudes people have towards money. In such cases, preachers can question some culturally ingrained metaphors that people accept as expressions of their world views.

---

115. Arthurs, *Preaching with Variety*, 141.
116. Wangerin, *Whole Prayer*, 55 (emphasis original).
117. Wangerin, 55–56.

For instance, TIME IS MONEY is one of the most commonly used conventional metaphors. However, for some, it is almost a life motto that fuels their actions and gives them a sense of direction. Here is an example that preachers can follow in order to recognize and question this metaphor.

> All of us, in one way or another, believe that TIME IS MONEY or at least talk about it as if we believed it. We talk about having time, spending time, saving time, giving more time, earning time, wasting time, living on borrowed time, or running out of time. We use these kinds of expressions because we believe that our time is precious and that how we use time is important. We know that, sooner or later, how we spend our time will determine the way we spend our whole lives.
>
> It would be great if we counted our days, hours, and minutes as meticulously as we count our money, but the problem is that some people – instead of counting their days, hours, and minutes – spend their days, hours, and minutes counting their money. They actually measure their time and their lives with coins and bills because their life motto is "time is money" and life is about accumulating coins and bills.
>
> But one day, when they have a lot of coins and bills, they discover that they wasted their time and their lives because they lost health, family, and friends. So, they start spending their money to get back their health, families, and friends because they have realized that there is something more important than coins and bills.
>
> If you define your life in terms of "time is money," when you run out of money, your life is deprived of substance, and death is the final failure because you cannot accumulate any more and have to part with what you have. So, if money is not a good way to define the meaning of life, and if coins are not a good means to measure time, is there a better way to define our lives and measure our time?

At this point, the preacher can move towards introducing an alternative vision of life by turning to biblical metaphors. In this case, questioning serves as a way of engaging with listeners' prototypes and metaphors and clears the ground for exhibiting new prototypes and metaphors.

However, when preachers begin questioning biblical and contemporary metaphors, they need to be able to find the right and satisfactory answers. It is easy to question a metaphor of God as the good shepherd by giving numerous examples of pain and suffering in life, but it might prove difficult to defend this metaphor at the end and convey it in such a way that listeners understand it and experience its force. Conversely, while questioning contemporary metaphors in order to show their inadequacy, the preacher might not be able to prove that the biblical perspective is actually more adequate.

In order to accomplish this task well, preachers need to study the text carefully enough to first identify the biblical world view and the biblical perspective. They can then move to recognizing those cultural prototypes, metaphors, and images the text argues against. Effective questioning must be rooted in the preacher's thorough understanding of the Bible and its perspective. Only then will their answers be convincing and have a transformational effect.

Thus, while trying to convey biblical metaphors by reworking them in new creative ways, it is essential to remember that all communication is based on an exchange of concepts and that this applies to single metaphors that explain one concept in terms of another as well as to whole units of text that convey their main concept. Even though defining this concept is only a human attempt to put in human words the message of the Bible, it is a helpful practice in communicating biblical passages. Since preachers must be consistent with the textual concept, recognizing the main concept of the text controls the ways in which, and the extent to which, they can rework biblical metaphors.

5.2.1.8 Combining

One of the features of poetic language that employs novel metaphorical expressions is that it takes advantage of several different conceptualizations of the same idea at the same time. For instance, the concept of life can be pictured in terms of a day, a journey, a precious possession, a play, a game, and in a number of other ways.[118] For example, chapter 4 of the book of Revelation contains various different metaphors and images that are used to convey the concept of God's royal splendour. Hence, when presenting complex concepts,

---

118. Lakoff and Turner, *More than Cool Reason*, 70.

preachers may want to combine several different metaphors to express various aspects of these concepts.

Jesus explained discipleship as a costly process that involves following him and carrying our crosses. Discipleship involves both a journey under Jesus's guidance and a denial of ourselves. This rich variety of textual images invite similar richness of imagery in sermons.

In one of my sermons on Psalm 23, I focused on the image of God as depicted by the psalmist. In order to convey this image to a contemporary audience, I employed two strategies of preaching metaphors, namely, paralleling and combining. I identified three key images in the Psalm that portray God. First, a shepherd who leads the psalmist to green pastures and provides nourishment. Second, the image of somebody who leads the psalmist through dangerous valleys and whose staff provides comfort. While the staff might refer to a shepherd's staff and thus suggest a continuation of the shepherd image, it is also possible to see here a picture of a guide who leads travellers and whose travelling staff is a means of defence. Finally, there is the image of a meal at the house of the Lord, with God being the one who invites the psalmist there. Hence, there are three images: the first focuses on provision and nourishment, the second on guidance and protection, and the last on fellowship and feasting. Therefore, the image of God as presented in this text is a combination of all these concepts.

In order to present these concepts to a contemporary audience, I "paralleled" biblical images with modern ones. I said that God is the chef who knows our needs and tastes; God is the guide who leads us and protects us in our journey through life and beyond; and, finally, God is the host who invites us to fellowship and feast with him.[119]

As I conclude this section on the methodology of preaching biblical metaphors, I must stress that while traditional homiletics has given some advice on this topics and preachers have often intuitively found ways of communicating biblical metaphors, Cognitive Linguistics offers a comprehensive theoretical foundation and a whole set of coherent strategies for reworking conventional metaphors. These strategies, when understood in the context of the cognitive approach and applied to biblical texts, provide preachers with a consistent and rational method that may enhance their creativity and

---

119. Szumorek, "Owce w Skarpetkach," 248–261.

offer them more direction in this area of their sermon preparation. As they become more familiar with these strategies, preachers will probably become more confident about choosing the most suitable strategies for conveying a particular biblical metaphor or image.

5.2.2 Creating Metaphors and Images to Convey the Meaning of the Text

In the previous section, I offered a methodology for reworking conventional metaphors that are behind biblical metaphorical expressions and incorporating these in sermons. However, preachers can not only rework existing metaphors but also create new ones to convey the meaning of texts, even non-metaphorical texts.[120] Thus, the purpose of this section is to take this next step and show how metaphors can be created as a means of presenting the meaning of the text.

This concept of developing images and metaphors to explain or illustrate the biblical text has been addressed in numerous publications. David Buttrick notes that traditionally, sermon illustrations have been mainly used as analogies or as proofs that lend support to the preacher's statements. In his opinion, however, this traditional approach does not do justice to the capacity of an image for bridging time and helping to cross the gap between the past and the present, the world of the Bible and the contemporary world.[121] He emphasizes that examples and illustrations can build models of consciousness in listeners' minds and says that "much like metaphor, illustrations can bring together images from different realms of experience, and by their juxtaposition break out surprising new meanings."[122] By stressing this he comes close to the understanding offered by Cognitive Linguistics, which talks about explaining one concept by another concept or experience. Buttrick also enumerates criteria for choosing suitable illustrations saying that:

> (1) There must be a clear analogy between an idea in sermon content and some aspect of the illustration; (2) There ought to

---

120. I use this term non-metaphorical with caution since, as was pointed out earlier, our language is largely metaphorical and even prepositional expressions are metaphorical in nature. Hence, I use this notion of non-metaphorical texts to refer to texts where these more developed metaphors and images that are traditionally classified as metaphorical do not appear.

121. Buttrick, *Homiletic*, 127.

122. Buttrick, 128.

be a parallel between the structure of content and the shape of an illustration; (3) The illustration should be "appropriate to the content."[123]

This means that the imagery that is presented "has much the same moral, aesthetic, or social value as the idea being presented."[124] Buttrick insists that even though illustrations may not reflect the structure of the idea in its entirety, there should be "an obvious point of similarity."[125] Again, by stressing structural similarity between the sermon content and an illustration, he employs an approach similar to conceptual metaphor theory.

Wayne McDill, speaking about a strategy for finding natural analogies, also begins with defining the idea that needs to be conveyed in an image form. His approach consists of the following steps: clearly state the sermon idea, generalize the concept using the subject/complement pattern, brainstorm natural analogies which can be found in the world around, and particularize the analogy by making it as specific as possible.[126] Therefore, he begins with the idea and finds analogies that reflect it in specific ways.

Kenton Anderson, presenting his approach for developing visionary sermons, compares sermons to paintings and points out that painters have to take two steps to create a picture – selecting the subject, since "every painting needs to have a 'big idea,'" and composing the scene, since a picture is a structured vision.[127] He then translates these steps into a preaching method that includes determining the vision and articulating the vision, which means that preachers have to decide what to show through their images and how to show it. Anderson emphasizes the fact that an image and a story can overlap in a sermon and that the preacher's task is to create a narrative vision in people's minds.[128]

Finally, Daniel Sheard, building on his own missionary experiences of using imagery in preaching to illiterate people in French-speaking settings, develops the idea of parabolic engagement and demonstrates how to convey

---

123. Buttrick, 133–134.
124. Buttrick, 133–134
125. Buttrick, 134.
126. McDill, *12 Essential Skills*, 208–214.
127. Anderson, *Choosing to Preach*, 214–219.
128. Anderson, 222–227.

biblical images in a three-step approach that includes: "(1) *analysis* or the defining subjects; (2) *analogy* using figured correspondence; (3) *extension* by employing contextual realities to expand material and control delivery method".[129] Sheard's method, since it stresses both defining subjects and finding correspondences, seems to be the closest to Buttrick's approach. Sheard is also concerned with ways of expanding images in a controlled way by seeing them in their context. Cognitive Linguistics provides tools to conduct this task in a more systematic way, both on a theoretical and practical level.

There are several features that are common to all these approaches, for instance, defining the idea that needs to be conveyed and establishing some kind of analogy between the image and the textual idea. Even though the notion of finding concepts in biblical texts is widely criticized especially when applied to metaphorical texts, as was shown earlier, numerous homileticians see defining the textual idea in some form as being necessary for interpreting and communicating the text.

The process of employing Cognitive Linguistics to create metaphors to convey meaning of the text has not been addressed by cognitive linguists or homileticians, but it is possible to distinguish some key principles that organize that process. Some of these principles to some degree overlap with approaches proposed in the previous section (5.2.1), but the uniqueness of these principles here is that they are utilized within a framework of Cognitive Linguistic theory, which makes the whole process more structured and coherent.

Consequently, my strategy for creating new metaphors to convey the textual meaning includes the following steps: identifying the key concepts, creating unifying metaphors, analyzing possible correspondences, employing personification, and developing extended narrative images.

5.2.2.1 Identifying the Key Concepts

The first step in creating new metaphors to communicate the textual meaning is identifying the key textual concepts. If communication is based on conveying and exchanging concepts and the main idea behind the biblical revelation is that God wanted to communicate with humans, then sermon preparation

---

129. Sheard, "Preaching in the Hear and Now," 132 (emphasis original). For a full description of his approach, see 132–184.

should include an attempt to recognize concepts or ideas in the biblical text. This process includes identifying the biblical concept of the whole textual unit, as well as subordinate concepts appearing in this unit, including concepts behind individual metaphors and images. As pointed out in an earlier section (5.2.1) on reworking and communicating biblical metaphors, understanding the textual idea sets limits to the ways in which preachers can rework conventional metaphors. This is necessary since the particular context in which metaphors appear is significant for their interpretation.

The notion of detecting textual ideas plays an even greater role in creating metaphors that express the meaning of non-metaphorical texts. When preachers use metaphors or create new metaphors and images, they must be specific about which ideas they are actually illustrating and communicating through these images. Images and metaphors have to be conceptually and emotionally coherent with concepts and emotions embodied in the biblical text in such a way that they express both the meaning and the mood of the text.

To some critics, the notion of identifying textual concepts may seem like an attempt to reduce all metaphors to concepts while ignoring emotive dimensions of the text. However, the idea of evoking textual mood and addressing listeners' emotions actually has its roots in Cognitive Linguistics, where most concepts are not dealt with in isolation but are conceptualized on the basis of our experience or embodiment. Not only do conceptual metaphors convey concepts related to emotions, they are born out of emotions and evoke emotions. As pointed out earlier, conceptual metaphors frequently come into existence when abstract concepts are explained in terms of tangible experiences, often experiences that are embodied. Thus, we may use an image of a pressurized container to talk about anger. We talk about being filled with anger, not being able to contain our feelings, exploding, or steam coming out of somebody's ears. We understand these expressions because we have experienced these emotions and because these statements not only describe our emotions but, as we hear them, also evoke emotions.

Researchers have shown that comprehension of a particular phrase that describes an action activates the parts of our brains that are responsible for performing such an action. For instance, when people hear a sentence about picking up a pen, functional magnetic resonance imaging studies show that not only are the parts of the brain responsible for linguistic understanding of this phrase activated but, additionally, those parts responsible for the motor processes of picking up a pen are also activated.[130] Thus, images and metaphors that people hear are highly evocative and affect not only their emotions but also their bodies.

Furthermore, when preachers look at metaphors from the even wider perspective of God's revelation, they discover that since God created people in their wholeness in his image and since his salvation addresses the whole human being, therefore preaching should also be holistic and take into consideration human emotions as well. Thus, I would argue that utilizing images and conceptual metaphors in preaching does not only serve the purpose of expressing concepts but also that of evoking the emotions of the text and addressing the emotions of listeners.

For instance, when preaching a sermon on Jesus's genealogy as found in Matthew 1:1–17, preachers should notice that in the context of the whole Gospel of Matthew – which presents Jesus as the true king of Israel – this passage shows that Jesus is a legitimate descendant of Abraham and David. The list of Jesus's ancestors in this passage shows his royal rights. Apart from male ancestors and the final mention of Mary, we also find four female characters who have complicated life stories: Tamar, Rahab, Ruth, and Bathsheba. Their inclusion in Jesus's genealogy, which might be regarded as unexpected, shows that when Christ came to this earth, he entered our complicated human history in order to redeem it.[131]

Thus, in preparing to preach on this text, we should identify key concepts, such as Jesus being a descendant of Abraham and David, his royal rights, and his ancestors and their complicated life stories. In a sermon, preachers may resort to a traditional explanation of concepts, or they may choose to use images that also evoke emotions. One of the images that could be employed is the image of this strange family of Jesus, which, in some respects, is just like our own families. In our families, we may have great ancestors whom we are proud of, but there may also be strange relatives who did not do well in their lives. To make a sermon more evocative, concrete, and emotionally closer to listeners' experiences, it is prudent to take into consideration the notion of embodiment and make concepts as tangible as possible.

---

130. Sanders, *Theology in the Flesh*, loc. 258 of 5234, Kindle.

131. For more on women in Jesus's genealogy, see Clements, *Mothers on the Margin?*

Thus, in the sermon, instead of discussing a list of names, preachers can take their listeners for a walk around an imaginary graveyard, stopping by various tombs of Jesus's family members. On the tombstones, there are names written, and behind each name is a story to tell. Some of these stories are inspiring, but others are frightening. There are also some tombs and stories of unexpected people who do not seem to fit in Jesus's family – like the handful of women mentioned by Matthew.

By employing this strategy, the preacher faithfully communicates the idea of the text which focuses on the fact of Jesus's royal ancestry while remaining sensitive to its form that is a list of names, and evokes emotions as listeners imagine walking through a cemetery and listening to stories about those who have passed away. Fred Craddock would warn his students, "When you're preaching from the biblical text, avoid the lists. They're deadly." Yet in his sermon based on Romans 16 "When the Roll is Called Down Here," he gives an example of using images to preach the greetings section at the end of Paul's letter.[132] This approach to preaching creates in listeners' minds concrete images that evoke emotions and encourage mental participation through the use of imagination.

Another example comes from my sermon titled "On the Margin of Relationships" ("Na Marginesie Relacji"), based on the Epistle to Philemon.[133] The whole epistle focuses on the idea of the need for Philemon to welcome back his runaway slave Onesimus, who was not only a fugitive but might also have caused some loss to Philemon's family. Thus, when applying this text to contemporary listeners, the preacher can address the problem of accepting and forgiving those who have wronged us even though it might be costly to do so. This idea will control the selection and use of metaphors and images.

The main image I used in this sermon is that of being on the margin of relationships. Since a conceptual metaphor is based on the idea of explaining one concept in terms of another, I explain the concept of accepting the wrongdoer back by an image of moving from the margin to the centre of our relational maps. While preaching this, I usually have a large white sheet of paper ready and explain that when we enter this world, we are like this clean white sheet of paper.

---

132. Craddock, "When the Roll Is Called."
133. Szumorek, "Na Marginesie Relacji."

We do not bring any relationships with us but discover the key people in our lives. (While explaining, I write on the paper – first, our parents, some of us have siblings, and we can add the names of our brothers and sisters, then friends, and later our spouse and children.) When we look at this paper, we discover a map of our relationships. Some of the names are closer to the centre because they are important. Some are a bit further from the centre because these people are not as close as the others. Unfortunately, there are also names that, for some reason, appear very far from the centre, maybe even on the margin of our lives. Some of these people might have been close to us in the past, but then something happened, and now they are on the periphery.

Philemon also had his map of relationships that included Apphia – who was probably his wife – Archippus – most likely his son – Paul – who might have led him to Christ – and, finally, the most important name – Jesus Christ. But there was one name, a man who had lived with him under his roof as his slave but, even though he was part of the household, had decided to run away and thus found himself on the margin of Philemon's life.

Onesimus also had his map of relationships. After he ran away, he thought that the name of Philemon would disappear forever, somewhere on the margin. However, while he was trying to enjoy his freedom, new names appeared on his map – first, the name of Paul and then, because of Paul, another name appeared there – the name of Jesus Christ. This last name changed everything in his life.

Now Paul writes to Philemon, urging him to rewrite his map of relationships and allow Onesimus to come back from the margin, closer to the centre. Paul says that Onesimus was separated for a while but can now come back; he was a slave, but now he has become a brother. He concludes by saying "if he has wronged you in any way or owes you anything, charge that to my account" because Paul knew that accepting somebody who has wronged us is usually a costly process (Phlm 15–19).

It is interesting that Paul, in his letter, makes several references to Christ as the ultimate reason why Philemon should show mercy to Onesimus. God also has his map of relationships and we – as humans made in his image – had a very special place on this map. But we moved to the margin because we sinned against God. However, now we can go back towards the centre because Christ was willing to pay for our sins. He said "charge that to my account" and went to the cross for us.

This sermon, because of its visual aspect, allows listeners to imagine people who happen to be on the margins of their lives and also shows that movement in the opposite direction, however costly, is possible. It utilizes the strategy of creating images that convey the main idea of the text – namely, accepting and welcoming back those who wronged us despite the cost of doing so. Helping people to imagine their own maps of relationships and all the movements that have taken place there can be a very emotional experience, which allows them to feel, at least to some extent, the tensions present in the text.[134]

5.2.2.2 Creating Unifying Metaphors and Images

Identifying key ideas and expressing them through images or metaphors can be done with regard to whole textual units or individual textual ideas, which should be labelled as subordinate ideas. When preachers manage to find a metaphor that conveys the idea of the whole text, this becomes the dominant or unifying image of a sermon. Both examples given above show how a single image can create coherence for the whole sermon – not just logical coherence but also conceptual and emotional coherence.

In the case of the sermon based on the Epistle to Philemon, there is a single image that is repeated five times, uniting the sermon and, at different stages, serving different functions as shown in the table below.

---

134. Even though I have created images of a map of relationships and being marginalized, there are other metaphors that appear in this text – such as MORALITY IS ACCOUNTING – that can also be developed in preaching.

Part of the sermon	Image	Function
Introduction	Listeners' maps of relationships and margins	Introducing the text, the main problem, and the textual image
The body	Philemon's map and margins	Exposition of the text
The body	Onesimus' map and margins	Exposition of the text
The body	God's map and margins	Theological analysis
Conclusion	Listeners' maps and margins	Application and conclusion

Diagram 9. Uniting images in the sermon based on the Epistle to Philemon

At the beginning of the sermon, the image of a map and the concept of margins help listeners to recognize the main problem presented in the sermon. Next, describing Philemon's and Onesimus's maps is a starting point for an exposition of the text and telling their stories. Then, the reference to God also having his map of relationships enables listeners to see their relationships and the choices they make in the wider theological context of salvation. This idea also serves the purpose of developing a prototype-based application since Christ who was willing to pay with his life to forgive our sins becomes our prototype. The sermon concludes by returning to listeners' maps and inviting them to reflect on people who are on the margins of their lives and consider possible actions they might take to bring these people back, closer to the centre. Therefore, this image of a sheet of paper with a map of relationships and people on the margins becomes the dominant image of the sermon and creates its conceptual and emotional coherence.

Another way of ensuring the sermon's coherence by finding uniting metaphors and images is to analyze image schemas that appear in the text. In chapter 3, I defined image schemas as the basic experiential structures that enable us to conceptualize ideas in terms of PATHS, LINKS, CONTAINERS, or basic orientations, such as UP-DOWN, BACK-FORTH, BIG-SMALL, PERIPHERY-CENTER, CLOSE-FAR, PART-WHOLE, and so on. In Paul's Epistle to Philemon, we can identify the image schema of CLOSE-FAR, and this could become the dominant metaphor for the whole sermon.

Another example of image schema can be found in Paul's Letter to the Philippians. In Philippians 2:1–11, Paul encourages believers to have the same attitude they see in Christ and then describes Christ's humility as being evident in the fact that despite being God, he became fully human. As a human, Christ lowered himself to be a bond-servant and, as a servant, was obedient to death, a most humiliating death by crucifixion. However, Paul states that "God highly exalted Him, and bestowed on Him the name which is above every name" (Phil 2:9). Thus, we can identify in this passage the image schema UP-DOWN. This basic image schema can become the dominant image for the whole sermon – if you follow Christ, the way up is always the way down. Many people are preoccupied with going up in their career, their social life, their income, and their influence, but Christ moved in the opposite direction and became a servant. However, this way down actually leads up since God acknowledges and exalts those who humbly serve.

Michael Quicke's sermon titled "Going up? Going down?" – based on Philippians 2:5–11 – is a good example of employing up and down orientations to structure the sermon and convey the meaning of the text. To make his sermon more visual and show the movement in the text, Quicke uses the metaphor of an escalator and talks about "the escalator of life," which goes up and down. Most people, when they get on this escalator of life, are interested in going up. However, Christ shows that the movement in the opposite direction is necessary to build a new kind of relationship and community.[135] Even though Quicke does not talk about image schemas, he utilizes them intuitively by identifying basic textual orientations. As will be shown in more detail later, image schemas, because of their general and schematic nature, are effective means to give a general structure to a sermon to make it more coherent.

5.2.2.3. Analyzing Correspondences

In the process of creating new metaphors and images to convey the meaning of the text, preachers must ensure that a particular metaphor not only conveys the textual idea well but also has some legitimate points of correspondence with this idea and with the text itself. As mentioned before, conceptual metaphors are based on mappings or correspondences in structure between the source domain and the target domain, which means that we, as humans, tend to understand a structure of complex abstract concepts by perceiving them

---

135. Michael Quicke "Going up? Going down?" in Peter K. Stevenson and Stephen I. Wright, Preaching the Incarnation (Louisville: Westminster John Knox, 2010), (location 2076–2151 of 3266).

in terms of the structure of other concepts, often very experiential ones such as fighting, flying, or counting.

Thus, in the sermon based on the Epistle to Philemon, there is the very abstract concept of accepting somebody back and restoring relationship, which is illustrated with the image of moving somebody from the margin of our lives to the centre. However, if this newly formed concept is to make any impact on the minds of listeners, they have to see clear correspondences between the concept of accepting somebody back and the concept of moving names from the margin towards the centre.

When studying this text, we notice several contrasts that describe Philemon's relationship with Onesimus. Paul stresses that Onesimus, whose name means "useful," was actually useless but then became useful again; he was distant and lost for a while, but now Philemon can have him back forever; he was a slave, but now he is a brother in Christ. All these statements describe a positive change in relationships.

One of the most common ways of describing relationships is by using the concept of closeness – the more intimate the relationship, the shorter the distance. Thus, when Paul talks about positive changes in Onesimus and positive results with regard to restoring this relationship, he is speaking about shortening the distance between Philemon and Onesimus. Essentially, he tells Philemon that although Onesimus was separated from him, he can now get him back. Consequently, it is justifiable to convey this text using the image of moving names from the margin to the centre and making those who were far away close again. However, this image becomes even more convincing and accurate when we identify correspondences between concepts.

As mentioned earlier, when analyzing correspondences, preachers should make sure that these correspondences are legitimate and are not forced on the text. This requires that preachers be clear about the concepts they want to convey through images. These concepts should come from the text itself, as for instance the idea of distance and closeness in relationships. When defining correspondences between textual concepts and created metaphors, it is important to reflect the textual characteristics of the given concept as closely as possible by noticing, for example, what the text actually says about distance and closeness in relationships and how changes in relationships occur. Moreover, preachers need to pay attention not only to elements that are highlighted in the image but also to those that are hidden.

A map of relationships		The listeners' relational experience
People in the center	→	People who are important in our lives
Physical closeness	→	Relational closeness
People away from the center	→	People who are not as close
Physical distance	→	Relational distance
People on the margin	→	People who hurt us – no close relationships
Moving from the margin to the center	→	Restoring relational closeness
Effort to move names from the margins	→	Effort to restore relationships
Restored physical closeness	→	Restored relational closeness (useful, returned, brother, forever)

Diagram 10. Correspondences between a relational map and listeners' relational experience

This question of paying attention to hiding and highlighting can be seen more clearly in the example given earlier about preaching Jesus's genealogy in terms of walking around a cemetery where Jesus's ancestors are buried. Not everything from the source domain gets mapped onto the target domain, and the key concept of the text enables preachers to determine which elements are highlighted and which are hidden. Hence, if preachers bear in mind that the aim of this text is to show that Jesus, as the true king, is a descendant of Abraham and David but, as someone truly human, also belongs to a real human family with a variety of imperfections, this will limit the extent to which they utilize the image of the cemetery. There is a lot that could be said about the idea of ancestry, genealogies, cemeteries, graves and their shapes, burial rituals, and ways of remembering the dead; but all these ideas, even though they belong to the source domain of walking around a cemetery, are not highlighted by the text and should not be included in the sermon.

To sum up, since, in understanding concepts, we use the structure of one concept to explain another, we should pay close attention to structural correspondences between the key concept of the text and the image that is used to convey this concept.

5.2.2.4 Employing Personification

Personification is another method of conveying the meaning of the text in the form of images . Lakoff and Turner define personification as "metaphors through which we understand other things as people."[136] Kövecses claims that personification "permits us to use knowledge about ourselves to comprehend other aspects of the world, such as time, death, natural forces, inanimate objects, etc. . . ."[137] In his discussion on personification, he agrees with Lakoff and Turner that personification is frequently based on the generic-level metaphor EVENTS ARE ACTIONS since we as humans often conceptualize external events as actions performed by the world or by some kind of an agent and these actions are beyond our control.[138] Hence, people talk about a new day coming, death coming and taking somebody, or joy indwelling somebody's house. In all these instances, we see results and attribute these results to some kind of human-like agent who has caused them.

In the Bible, personification is often employed to talk about God since we cannot comprehend God directly and can only attempt to do so by using human terms. Hence, personification serves the purpose of shortening the distance between far removed concepts and makes difficult ideas more comprehensible. In my opinion, the effectiveness of personification lies in the fact that it takes advantage of our embodiment. As humans, we find it easier to interact and comprehend the physical, tactile, and tangible instead of the abstract and the elusive. For this reason, we find ideas and concepts more accessible when they are embodied and conceptualized as persons. This might be why the Bible often employs personification when talking about God, who is incomprehensible to human beings. When we consider the progressiveness of God's revelation, it appears that when God wanted to enter a new level of relationship with humans, he not only described himself in human terms but truly became a human Therefore, I define personification as an act of embodying ideas.

In my sermon on Ecclesiastes 11 8–12:14, I used a unifying image of three important encounters that are, in most cases, unavoidable in our lives: the encounter with ageing, the encounter with death, and the encounter with

---

136. Lakoff and Turner, *More than Cool Reason*, 72.

137. Kövecses, *Metaphor: A Practical Introduction*, 56.

138. Kövecses, 56. See also Lakoff and Turner, *More than Cool Reason*, 72–80.

God. In the introduction, in order to show that some meetings are beyond our control and cannot be planned, I used personification.

> An elderly couple sits at the table and just finishes their sup-
> per. They have lived together for fifty years, brought up their
> kids, laughed and argued, but now old and weak they just live
> through the last years of their lives. Tonight they are alone,
> because they did not invite anybody and were not expecting
> any guests. However, they do not know that even though they
> thought they were alone, they have one unexpected visitor at
> their house – somebody they did not invite and did not wait
> for. It was death. She just sneaked in unnoticed and sat quietly
> somewhere in the corner waiting for her time. When the hands
> on the clock show the right hour, she will take this older man
> for a journey he will never return from, because today is the day
> of his meeting with death.[139]

Suddenly, in the minds of listeners, death stops being an abstract concept; it is embodied and becomes a person whom they, too, will have to meet one day. The abstract idea of dying one day in the future becomes a tangible meeting that is actually in their calendars, even though, in most cases, they did not put it there.

Another example of personification relates to a text about the Lord's Supper (1 Cor 11:17–34). In this text, Paul expresses his sadness about the way the Christians at Corinth were partaking in the Lord's Table, where everyone brought their own meal and, as a result, "one is hungry and another is drunk." Thus, the preacher might convey the meaning of this text using personification.

> If you were there at the church in Corinth and looked around
> at the faces at the Lord's Table, you would recognize, sitting
> among the members of the church, some unwelcome guests:
> Greed, Selfishness, Indifference, Quarrelling, Gossip, and Self-
> interest. However, if you looked more closely, you would notice
> that some faces were missing. Love was not there. Neither was
> Peace. Neither was Unity. Neither was Compassion. Neither

---

139. Szumorek, "Trzy Kluczowe Spotkania."

was Sharing nor Mercy nor Grace. They were all gone from that
church because there was no place for them at the Lord's Table.

Personification gives preachers an opportunity to awaken their listeners'
imagination and emotions. John Bunyan's *Pilgrim's Progress* is a classic example of employing personification in order to convey theological concepts.
In Bunyan's tale, remote notions – such as piety, hypocrisy, mercy, prudence,
and discretion – become more tangible and accessible through a process of
embodying ideas. Thus, creative utilization of personification in Christian
teaching has a long pedigree. Nevertheless, a word of caution is in order since
personification, when overused, could become tiresome, boring, and may end
up creating a greater distance between listeners and the text.

5.2.2.5 Developing an Extended Narrative Image

The final approach I propose for using images to convey the meaning of the
text is developing an extended narrative image. In this process, the main
principles that should be applied are identifying the key image or images of
the text and analyzing the correspondences.

This approach is especially helpful when applied to difficult texts or ones
that are very remote from the listener's experience. Moreover, it might be
helpful in creating narrative tension or developing the conflict. For instance,
when preaching on Ecclesiastes 3:1–22, I had to explain verses 18–21, where
the author says that "the fate of the sons of men and the fate of beasts is the
same" and continues, "as one dies so dies the other; indeed, they all have the
same breath and there is no advantage for man over beast." The idea behind
this small textual unit is that people and animals are mortal. Solomon finds
several correspondences between the deaths of human beings and animals –
they die, their life ends, and they turn into dust. Taking into consideration
the key idea of this text and its correspondences, I developed the following
extended narrative image:

> I do not know what inspired Solomon to write these words.
> Maybe it was a walk across the City of David. He had some
> important decisions to make, and so he decided to walk around
> the neighbourhood. Eventually, he came to that prominent place
> known as the Tomb of David. He liked coming here when he

had some thinking to do and some choices to make. But now he forgot about his worries and began thinking about his father.

In his youth, David had been a strong and courageous warrior whom whole nations had feared. When he led his army, he led it to victory. He was also attractive, and women liked him. Even Solomon's own mother, Bathsheba, lost her head over him and betrayed her husband to be with David.

But when David got old, he was not as strong as he used to be. He had some problems with blood circulation and would get cold at night. Solomon also remembered that night when servants came to his chamber and woke him up saying "It is now! You need to hurry!" Solomon had entered David's chamber and seen his father on his bed, breathing heavily, his eyes half-closed, hazy, kind of absent. When Solomon took David's half-cold hand, he had felt a gentle squeeze. He had been watching his father breathing heavily when, suddenly, he just stopped – stopped forever. The king was dead.

As he was standing by the Tomb of David and thinking about his father's death, Solomon recalled his first encounter with death. You do not forget things like that, especially when you are just a small kid. Solomon remembered a little puppy that had been wandering not far from the palace. Jewish boys did not play with dogs since these animals were considered unclean and dangerous. But this one caught Solomon's attention because it was small, funny, and playful. Solomon sometimes brought him something to eat, and the dog was not afraid of him. One day, the boy noticed that the dog was sleeping under a bush. He came closer and noticed that he was not moving and not even breathing. The dog was dead.

Suddenly, on this hot and sunny day, standing before his father's tomb, these two distant images merged. The great king had died and the dog had died. The king had stopped breathing and the dog had stopped breathing. The king's heart had stopped the same way as the dog's heart. One turned into dust just like the other. So, what is the difference? Is it true that we live like animals and die like animals?[140]

Instead of only explaining the text by pointing out the similarities between human death and the death of an animal, I decided to paint a picture that presents those similarities and allow listeners to feel the tension. Although a comparison between the death of the king and the death of a dog may sound offensive, there are enough similarities for the comparison to be accurate . Thus, by juxtaposing these two images, I created the conflict that needed to find its resolution in later parts of the sermon.

5.2.3 Levels of Schematicity in Sermons

Cognitive Linguistics is helpful not only in reworking and communicating biblical metaphors and images, and in creating new metaphors and images to express the meaning of the text, but also in developing the sermon structure. In chapter 3, I explained Kövecses's idea of levels of schematicity in metaphors. While arguing for a multilevel view of conceptual metaphor theory, Kövecses claims that image schemas, domains, frames, and blendings form four different levels of metaphor, beginning from the most schematic to the most specific.[141] As I reflected, I realized that since the same levels of schematicity can be employed in a sermon, Kövecses's approach was also applicable to preaching. Effective preaching that utilizes metaphors and images does so on different levels and uses imagery that ranges from the general to the specific. Kövecses's model can be utilized in preaching in a variety of ways. I propose employing it on a macro level – as a model for a sermon structure that shows the movement from the most general to the most specific – and on a micro level – at various stages of the sermon development as a means of conveying the meaning of smaller textual units. On the macro level, I do not claim that this is the only way in which this approach can be used, and I believe that some other applications are also possible.

In discussing levels of schematicity in a sermon, I identify four stages of sermon development: sketching, showing, engaging, and connecting. On the macro level, these four stages describe four stages of the sermon development. On the micro level, they can be applied individually, in different parts of the

---

140. Szumorek, "Carpe Diem," 328–330.
141. Levels of metaphors were explained in section 3.3.10.

sermon, to develop a single image. In the example given below, I present an interplay between the macro and micro levels and show how levels of schematicity can be used to develop both the sermon structure and a single image.

The first step in the development of a sermon structure is sketching, which aims to create the general and schematic conceptual foundation for the whole sermon that may result in identifying the unifying image as described earlier. At this stage, preachers focus listeners' attention on the subject by using very general images based on image schemas. The schematic nature of image schemas allows listeners to grasp general concepts that might convey the main themes of sermons or a sermon series – for example, "Big or Small?," "Upside Down," "Way Up," "Next Step," or "Come Back." Even when these themes or dominant images are used in titles, they can still play the role of conceptually uniting elements – for instance, the idea of being empty and being filled, moving, growing, or employing various contrasts and comparisons.

In the fall of 2017 our church had a sermon series based on the book of Joshua. Since the book's main theme is entering the promised land, the series was titled "Forward." Thus, employing this general image schema not only provided a conceptual framework and served as a unifying image for the whole series, it also became a starting point for developing imagery in individual message. Even though the notion of "forward" implies the idea of movement, it does not specify the kind of movement. Therefore, in my sermon, I had to move to the next level of specificity and apply different domains.

The next stage in sermon development is showing, which aims at particularizing general image schemas and making them more precise by utilizing domains and metaphors. At this stage, the preacher wants listeners to see a more detailed image. When preaching a sermon titled "Remembering What Is Important" based on Joshua 3–5 – which was about the Israelites crossing the Jordan River – I had to make this simple image schema of moving along the path more precise and develop it into the domain of a journey by using the metaphor LIFE IS A JOURNEY.[142] In Joshua 3–5, the idea of remembrance is one of the key motifs uniting these chapters. First, the ark of the covenant showed the way, and the Israelites were instructed to remember the way God had led them as well as his presence among them. After crossing the Jordan, they were told to build memorials made of twelve stones taken from

---

142. Szumorek, "Pamiętając o Tym co Ważne."

the river to help them remember how God had parted the waters to allow them to enter the promised land. Next, the Israelites had to circumcise the new generation so that they would remember the covenant that they were part of. Finally, the people celebrated the Passover to remember how God had led them out of Egypt.

Combining the idea of a journey and remembrance, this was the opening statement of my sermon: "While going through life, at some point we discover that we often cannot go forward if we forget about what was behind. We cannot face the future if we forget about our past." Here, the very general and schematic image schema of moving along the path – that found expression in the series title "Forward" – was developed into the metaphor LIFE IS A JOURNEY and took the form of a very specific metaphorical expression that talks about the importance, in our life journeys, of remembering our past in order to face our future. Making the transition from schematic image schemas to domains makes images more concrete and more evocative. At this stage, general image schemas are developed into particular metaphors.

The next step in sermon development – that is still part of the sermon introduction – is engaging, which involves making the general idea of the importance of remembering the past more specific and personal. At this stage, preachers engage with listeners' frames and the text – that is, they enter the world of the listeners and invite them to enter the world of the biblical text. The preacher's aim, at this stage, is to show understanding of the listeners and help them to understand the text. Thus, preachers must move from image schemas and domains to the next level, which is frames, beginning with the frame of the listeners. If preachers want the ideas presented in their sermons to be compelling for listeners, they must engage listeners and their experiences.

To make images more specific and more personal, I paralleled the concept of remembrance with a narrative image of a woman who attended her husband's funeral but, because she had Alzheimer's disease, no longer remembered her husband and did not know that this was his funeral. When we forget about the past, we may find it difficult to live in the present and face our future. This story, coupled with other examples, aimed at showing listeners that in many situations good memory is essential to define our identity and direction in life.

After I opened the frame of the listeners and their lives, I had to move to the frame of the biblical text itself, which is another dimension of engaging – namely, engaging listeners with the textual reality. This is accomplished through depicting the historical and cultural context and by textual analysis. In performing this task, preachers may also utilize the idea of schematicity in preaching on a micro level, using image schemas, domains, frames, and blendings as a means of conveying the meaning of smaller textual units. In the same way, preachers develop imagery for the whole sermon by moving along the levels of schematicity, beginning from schematic to specific, and may also develop a single textual or sermonic image.

Moreover, preachers may discover that different levels of schematicity can be used individually to convey some textual elements. In some cases, preachers will use image schemas, such as following the path shown by the ark of the covenant, before and after, the ark going before the people and the Israelites walking after, crossing through the river, and entering the new land. In other cases, they may want to employ domains and metaphors since there are more specific images in the text, such as the ark as the sign of God's presence, the memorial stones, circumcision, and the Passover meal. Preachers may also create their own metaphors and blendings that are very specific metaphorical actualizations, such as God being our guide and companion on the journey.

The final stage in relation to the macro level of the sermon structure is connecting, where preachers use images to blend the world of the text and the world of listeners by showing how to apply biblical ideas in everyday situations. Using images, preachers can show how remembering God's presence impacts the way we go through different life experiences and the way we respond to difficulties.

In explaining the meaning of the memorial stones, I wanted the sermon to be more personal, so I decided to employ paralleling and talk about my own stones and stone memorials, for example, receiving my first adult Bible, accepting Christ, serving as a volunteer at Christian camps, graduating from seminary, and, during my years of ministry, meeting friends who are God's gift to me. By utilizing paralleling, I blended the textual image of twelve stones with my own experience and, hopefully, helped listeners to think about their own life experiences that could be marked by memorial stones. Here, from a Cognitive Linguistics perspective, the domains of memorial stones and remembrance and the frames of listeners and the text find expression in conceptual blendings such as our own memorial stones or placing a stone to commemorate an event.

Another instance of blending the textual reality with the reality of the listeners and creating new conceptual blendings is a reference in the text to circumcision and the Passover. After the Israelites crossed the Jordan, they had to circumcise the new generation as the sign and reminder of the covenant. Afterwards, they celebrated the Passover as a reminder of God's rescue. For the same reason, we Christians can never forget our identity as God's covenant people, and we partake in Holy Communion as a reminder that we are saved because of the death of Christ. Thus, eating the bread and drinking the wine is a sign that helps us to remember who we are and what Christ did for us.

Accordingly, the idea of Kövecses's levels of metaphor is applicable to developing both a micro and macro sermon structure since it facilitates capturing the essential movement in the sermon from general to specific. This is illustrated by the table below, which shows different parts of the sermon, macro level sermon elements, levels of schematicity and their function, and levels of schematicity on a micro level.

Sermon part	Macro level	Levels of schematicity	Function	Levels of schematicity on micro level
Title	Sketching	Image schemas Domains	Generalizing Particularizing	Image schemas Domains
Introduction	Sketching Showing Engaging (the listeners' frame)	Image schemas Domains Frames	Generalizing Particularizing Understanding	Image schemas Domains Frames Blendings
Body	Engaging (the textual frame) Connecting	Frames Blendings	Understanding Applying	Image schemas Domains Frames Blendings
Conclusion	Connecting	Blendings	Applying	Image schemas Domains Frames Blendings

Diagram 11. Macro and micro level sermon structure.

At this point, however, a question arises regarding the correlation between this approach and more traditional notions of deductive and inductive preaching. Since deductive preaching assumes a movement in the sermon – from a general sermon idea to particular exegetical insights and instances of life application – it might appear that the idea of levels of schematicity follows the same path of reasoning and results in creating only deductive messages. Even worse, this may be perceived as deductive preaching disguised by new cognitive terminology.

The idea of applying levels of schematicity in preaching might sound contradictory to the basic presuppositions of inductive preaching as developed by Fred Craddock. Craddock's approach is based on movement in the opposite direction – namely, from particular questions, problems, life stories, and examples to a general conclusion at the end. By following this movement in their sermons, preachers retrace their own journey throughout the text to their conclusions and allow their listeners to do the same.[143] Thus, on the macro level of a sermon structure, Craddock argues for moving from the particular to the general, while on the micro level of individual stories, he encourages giving primary attention to "the specific and particular rather than the general" since life "is not experienced or known in general."[144]

However, it is worth noticing that both deductive and inductive sermon models are concerned with different ways of presenting the sermon idea. In the deductive model, the sermon idea is given at the beginning and then explained, proved, and applied, whereas in an inductive sermon, the sermon idea may appear as a conclusion at the end or may not be stated at all. The approach proposed in this book does not focus on ways of presenting the main idea of a sermon but, rather, on developing sermon imagery. Thus, in my method I also stress the importance of identifying textual and sermonic ideas and my method can be used effectively both in deductive and inductive messages. For instance, my sermon based on Joshua 3–5 was inductive and its main idea "It is important that we remember God, but it is more important that he remembers us – and don't forget it" came at the very end.

I am convinced that the novelty of my approach lies in the fact that it allows preachers to be more conscious in their movements along the levels of

---

143. Craddock, *As One without Authority*, 48.

144. Craddock, *Preaching*, 163.

schematicity in sermons. This approach stresses that in order to develop a sermon structure on a macro level, it is helpful to begin with schematic ideas that give listeners a basic mental structure and a sense of direction that then leads to more developed images. This does not mean that a sermon cannot begin with a particular story or end with a reminder of image schemas but only that the overall development of a sermon begins from the schematic and leads to the specific.

Considering that I argue about following the movement from the general and schematic to the particular and specific, my approach might appear to contradict Craddock's notion that preachers, when using individual stories as sermon illustrations, should pay attention to the particular over the general. However, I have also argued along the same lines when talking about focusing in our narrative descriptions on the subordinate-level categories (such as a Volvo, a German Shepherd, or an armchair) – instead of on the basic-level categories (such as a car, a dog, or a chair) since we experience reality on the subordinate level. Nevertheless, this does not exclude the value of employing some more schematic structures in sermons – for example, image schemas depicting basic orientations, especially when they come from the text itself and can serve purposes such as unifying text images. Thus, applying the idea of levels of schematicity in preaching does not exclude simultaneously employing existing traditional approaches but, rather, enriches their metaphoric and visual dimension and enables preachers to help their listeners to develop their mental images in a much more strategic and structured fashion.

5.3 Chapter Summary

In this chapter, I have shown how utilizing Cognitive Linguistics in preaching can actually impact the ways in which preachers understand their listeners, prepare their sermon, and develop the imagery and structure of these sermons. Thus, understanding the notion of prototypes as conceptual structures allows us to organize our knowledge of the world and also, as foundational elements of our ethical system, allows us to apply them to preaching as effective means of understanding the worldviews of our listeners. The notion of prototypes is also useful in developing a new approach to application, namely a prototype-based application that helps to shape the biblical values of listeners by changing their existing prototypes and introducing new ones. Therefore, the ultimate goal of preaching is transformation of the whole person of the listener, so that they may continue growing into the likeness of Christ.

In the second part of this chapter, I showed how Cognitive Linguistics can be applied to preaching biblical images and metaphors by conveying their meaning and reworking them more creatively. I also showed how to convey the meaning of the text by creating completely new metaphors and images. The novelty of this section was in applying Cognitive Linguistics' approach of reworking of conventional metaphors to homiletics and expanding it with my own new approaches. I also introduced an improved model that employs Cognitive Linguistics to convey the meaning of the text using metaphors and images.

I concluded this chapter with an example of an application of Kövecses's levels of schematicity idea to developing a sermon structure at the macro level and sermon images at a micro level. Again, this strategy is novel and helps to apply Kövecses's ides of a multilevel view of metaphor in preaching, thereby providing preachers with a practical guide for how to consciously develop images in their listeners' minds, moving from the most schematic structures to the most specific ones. Awareness of this process impacts the preacher's methodology for developing both the whole sermon structure and the individual images.

Conclusion

The purpose of this book is to demonstrate how Cognitive Linguistics, when applied in a theological context, can be productive in biblical preaching that employs metaphors and images and seeks to convey the meaning and mood of the biblical text by connecting with listeners' embodied minds, emotions, and imagination.

In this work, I have shown that since Cognitive Linguistics provides a unique perspective on human conceptualization, language, and communication, it can be effectively utilized in biblical interpretation and biblical preaching. However, in order to apply Cognitive Linguistics to Christian preaching, preachers need to be aware of both its limitations and its strengths.

Because Cognitive Linguistics is a secular and pragmatic science, it excludes any possibility of looking at reality from God's perspective – since this kind of all-knowing mind is not found in human beings. In this respect, Cognitive Linguistics and its its lack of consideration for God fits with what Christian theology has been saying, that people are not able to get to know God, to verify God's existence, or even to perceive reality from God's perspective on the basis of their mental faculties.

However, Cognitive Linguistics is also limited because of its narrow scope of research, which is restricted to human language, the human mind, and human perspectives. It does not take into consideration the idea of God's revelation, which – while still using human language and conceptual systems – enables humans to get to know God, enter into relationship with him, and perceive their lives in the context of his redemptive plan. Therefore, when applied to biblical interpretation and Christian preaching, Cognitive Linguistics as a secular and pragmatic science has to be utilized in the context of Christian theology, especially God's revelation as seen in creation, the inspiration of Scripture, and the incarnation.

In this theological context, Cognitive Linguistics can make a great contribution to hermeneutics and homiletics because it helps preachers to understand the mechanisms behind the conceptualization of theological ideas. Although cognitivists argue that we as humans do not have any special mental faculty or special language to talk about God, we do conceptualize God using the same cognitive system that we employ to conceptualize any other idea. Cognitivists claim that our language is mostly metaphorical, which means that, as human beings, we understand less accessible concepts in terms of more accessible ones. Thus, when people talk about God, they not only use their typical conceptual framework but must also resort to employing metaphors and images. This notion of using the human conceptual system to communicate about God is not limited to human communication about God but extends to God's communication about himself. This can be seen in the fact that God revealed himself through creating humans in his image, through the Bible, and through the act of the incarnation. Each of these ways of revelation is an example of God communicating with humans while using human conceptual systems based on metaphors and images – people who are created in the image of God, metaphors and images found in the Bible, and Christ as the image of the Father.

Moreover, when cognitivists explain the dynamics of human perception, they maintain that perception is shaped by our experience, which is largely grounded in the fact of our embodiment. The way we perceive the world depends on our senses and our bodies. The notion of embodiment helps to overcome traditional dichotomies between the mind and the body, and between the reason and emotions, showing a much more holistic and unified view of human beings. It also allows us to better appreciate the fact of the incarnation where God became a human in order to reveal himself using human terms. Moreover, the idea of embodiment plays an important role in analyzing biblical metaphors and images, and it has serious implications for understanding ways our listeners conceptualize ideas and develop their values.

Since Cognitive Linguistics integrates what we know about human perception, language, the mind, and communication with other scientific disciplines and shows that its principles agree with findings in other areas of knowledge it provides a comprehensive theoretical approach to studying biblical metaphors and images. This approach changes our perception of metaphors and their meaning because it stresses that they are not only linguistic phenomena but also cognitive ones and, as such, belong to the realm of concepts. Thus, meaning is construed when one concept is understood in terms of another.

Consequently, when Cognitive Linguistics is applied to biblical hermeneutics, it makes the whole process of analyzing biblical metaphors and images less intuitive and more systematized by placing it within a broader theoretical framework. This provides a much more unified and balanced view on the relationships between the implied author, the text, and the implied and contemporary readers, guarding against stressing the importance of one over the others. This also argues for a holistic understanding of all these three elements as parts of one process of communication when the encounter of minds takes place. Thus, while discussing the application of Cognitive Linguistics to hermeneutics, I concluded my section devoted for hermeneutics with a summary of a cognitive methodology for interpreting biblical metaphors and images.[1]

Cognitive Linguistics can also be transformative when utilized in preaching since it gives preachers deeper insights into ways people communicate and develop their ethical reasoning. It argues that ethical decision-making is not based on rules but on mental models called prototypes. This notion of prototypes is useful for preachers in their attempts to understand their audience and influences their approach to developing application that are prototype-based. In this section, I adopted and expanded Johnson's discussion on the elements of ethical reasoning in order to show how understanding the interrelationships between prototypes, frames, metaphors, and narratives can be employed to identify and change listeners' prototypes.[2]

When discussing the application of Cognitive Linguistics to homiletics, I proposed a number of strategies for communicating biblical metaphors in preaching. These strategies are based on adopted and expanded cognitive methods of reworking conventional metaphors. I also described a methodology of creating new metaphors and images to convey the meaning of biblical texts that are non-metaphorical. Finally, I employed Kövecses's notion of

---

1. See section 4.3.
2. See section 5.1.3.

levels of schematicity as a model for developing both a sermon structure and individual sermon images.

As I reflected on the usefulness of Cognitive Linguistics in preaching, I realized that the question arose about whether Cognitive Linguistics is more valuable in preaching as an analytical tool or as a creative tool. . In other words, to what extent does Cognitive Linguistics offer the preacher actual tools for use in sermon construction? And is it possible to accomplish similar results using other, more traditional, approaches without employing Cognitive Linguistics?

Before I answer this question about the usefulness of Cognitive Linguistics as an analytical and creative tool, I must affirm that Cognitive Linguistics, as a descriptive science, is based on an analysis of the cognitive processes that take place in the human mind and how these processess are expressed in the form of language. Thus, in many instances, Cognitive Linguistics does not seem to tell us anything new but simply confirms what we already intuitively do and know. This is because Cognitive Linguistics describes the mental processes that we are familiar with since we utilize these processes on a daily basis in order to conceptualize the surrounding world and communicate with others. This is one of the greatest strengths of this approach since it gives us deeper insights into our own thinking. There is no question that it is possible to engage in cognitive processes and communicate without any knowledge of Cognitive Linguistics. For instance, people may talk about a difficult lecture as being "hard to swallow" without ever knowing the metaphor IDEAS ARE FOOD. However, knowledge of Cognitive Linguistics enables us to communicate and use such metaphors with greater intentionality.

A vast body of literature devoted to Cognitive Linguistics shows its usefulness as an analytical tool to study language. In this book, I have demonstrated, with numerous examples, that this approach is also helpful when studying biblical texts. I also realize that Cognitive Linguistics is extremely helpful in analyzing contemporary sermons from a linguistic perspective.[3] Doing so gives us a deeper understanding of how metaphors are used in a sermon, how these metaphors are developed, and how preachers express their ideas

---

3. Marcin Kuczok employs Cognitive Linguistics to analyze conceptual metaphors for grace in the sermons of John Newman. See Kuczok, "'Amazing Grace,'" 257–267.

employing prototypes, image schema, conceptual blendings, and other elements of cognitive theory.

However, while I believe that Cognitive Linguistics is a helpful tool for sermon analysis, I am also convinced that it is an effective creative tool that enhances our intuition and other more intuitive approaches. Being aware of how human thinking and perception take place allows us to shape our sermons in ways that make communication clearer and more natural. Understanding image schema, the theory of conceptual metaphors, and ways of reworking existing metaphors and creating new ones gives us specific homiletical tools. Nevertheless, the greatest value of Cognitive Linguistics as a creative tool lies in the fact that it changes our perspective on human conceptualization and heightens our awareness of the whole process of conceptualization and communication.

Thus, in this book, I have demonstrated how Cognitive Linguistics can be fruitful when employed in biblical interpretation and how it can shape Christian preaching. The main advantage of this study is that it combines findings of Cognitive Linguistics – especially conceptual metaphor theory – with a wider theological reflection, a hermeneutical context, and homiletical rigour. This study not only shows how Cognitive Linguistics confirms and agrees with numerous assumptions of Christian theology, hermeneutics, and homiletics but also how it can be utilized to enhance our understanding of theology and enrich our hermeneutical and homiletical methodology. Hence, without Cognitive Linguistics, hermeneutics and homiletics would be deprived of useful tools for interpretation, understanding listeners, and communicating in ways that address the whole human person by speaking to listeners' embodied minds, emotions, and imagination.

As mentioned before, this book opens possibilities for future research. Even though there is a growing body of literature on employing Cognitive Linguistics in biblical interpretation, there is a need to explore this area more thoroughly by conducting further research on category operations, schemas, domains, frames, and blends in biblical texts. One essential issue that extends beyond the scope of this research is the question of the role and authority of extrabiblical sources pertaining to the cultural and historical context in preachers' attempts to understand the conceptual framework of the original audience.

As far as preaching is concerned, it is essential to continue studying the application of prototypes to preaching. In my book, I have argued that identifying prototypes plays a vital role in understanding our listeners. However, it is crucial to define more ways in which preachers can accomplish this task. The same applies to the notion of a prototype-based application. In this book, I have merely opened a door for future studies of a concept that can become a topic for a whole new research effort.

Nevertheless, I am convinced that I have shown how Cognitive Linguistics, placed in a wider theological framework, can be employed in preaching that uses metaphors and images to convey the meaning of biblical texts.

Bibliography

Akin, Daniel L. *A Theology for the Church*. Nashville: B&H Academic, 2007.

Allen, Ronald J. *Hearing the Sermon: Relationship, Content, Feeling*. St. Louis: Chalice Press, 2004.

———. "Listening to Listeners: The Beard Reflects Critically on the Study." *Encounter* 68.3 (2007): 69–84.

———. "The Turn Towards the Listener: A Selective Review of a Recent Trend in Preaching." *Encounter* 64 (2003): 165–194.

Allen, Ronald J., Mary Alice Mulligan, Diane Turner-Sharazz and Dawn Ottoni Wilhelm. *Believing in Preaching: What Listeners Hear in Sermons*. St. Louis: Lucas Park Books, 2014.

Alter, Robert. *The Art of Biblical Narrative*. New York: Basic Books, 2011.

Amant, Robert, Clayton T. Morrison, Yu-Han Chang, Paul R. Cohen, and Carole Beal. "An Image Schema Language." <www4.ncsu.edu/~stamant/papers/RSA-etal-iccm06.pdf.gz> [Accessed 30 May 2016].

Anderson, Kenton C. *Choosing to Preach: A Comprehensive Introduction to Sermon Options and Structures*. Grand Rapids: Zondervan, 2006.

Aquinas, Thomas. "Treatise on Human Nature." In *Summa Theologica*. Vol. 1. South Bend: St. Augustine's Press, 2010.

Aristotle. *Poetics*. Oxford: Oxford University Press, 2013.

Arthurs, Jeffrey D. *Preaching with Variety: How to Re-create the Dynamics of Biblical Genres*. Grand Rapids: Kregel, 2007.

Astley, Jeff. *Exploring God-Talk: Using Language in Religion*. London: Darton, Longman & Todd, 2004.

Austin, J. L. *How to Do Things with Words: The William James Lectures Delivered at Harvard University in 1955*. Edited by J. O. Urmson and Marina Sbisà. Oxford: Oxford Paperbacks, 1976.

Avis, Paul. *God and the Creative Imagination: Metaphor, Symbol and Myth in Religion and Theology*. London; New York: Routledge, 1999.

Balz, Horst, and Gerhard M. Schneider, eds. *Exegetical Dictionary of the New Testament*. 3 vols. Grand Rapids: Eerdmans, 1993.

Barr, James. *The Semantics of Biblical Language*. Eugene: Wipf & Stock, 1961, 2004.

Barrett, Justin L. Born Believers: The Science of Children's Religious Belief. New York: Free Press, 2012.

———. *Cognitive Science, Religion, and Theology: From Human Minds to Divine Minds*. West Conshohocken: Templeton Press, 2011.

———. *Why Would Anyone Believe in God?* Walnut Creek: AltaMira Press, 2004.

Barth, Karl. *The Doctrine of the Word of God*. Volume 1 of *Church Dogmatics*. Edited by G. W. Bromiley and T. F. Torrance. Translated by R. H. Fuller, Harold Knight, and J. K. S. Reid. Edinburgh: T&T Clark, 1936.

———. *The Doctrine of Creation*. Volume 3 of *Church Dogmatics*. Edited by G. W. Bromiley and T. F. Torrance. Translated by R. H. Fuller, Harold Knight, and J. K. S. Reid. Edinburgh: T&T Clark, 1936.

———. *Homiletics*. Translated by Donald E. Daniels and Geoffrey W. Bromiley. Louisville: Westminster John Knox, 1991.

———. *Revelation*. Edited by John Baillie and Hugh Martin. London: Faber and Faber, 1937.

Barthes, Roland. "The Death of the Author." In *Authorship: From Plato to the Postmodern*, edited by Sean Burke, 125–130. Edinburgh: Edinburgh University Press, 1995.

Beardsley, Monroe C. "The Metaphorical Twist." In *Philosophical Perspectives on Metaphor*, edited by Mark Johnson, 105–122. Minneapolis: University of Minnesota Press, 1981.

Berkouwer, G. C. *Man: The Image of God*. Grand Rapids: Eerdmans, 1962.

Bilezikian, Gilbert. "In God's Image." *Mutuality* 20 (2013): 8–11.

Bilsky, Manuel. "I. A. Richards' Theory of Metaphor." *Modern Philology* 50 (1952): 130–137.

Black, Kathy. *A Healing Homiletic: Preaching and Disability*. Nashville: Abingdon, 1996.

Black, Max. "Metaphor." In *Philosophical Perspectives on Metaphor*, edited by Mark Johnson, 63–82. Minneapolis: University of Minnesota Press, 1981.

Botterweck, Johannes. *Theological Dictionary of the Old Testament*, XII, 15 vols. Grand Rapids: Eerdmans, 2003.

Boyer, Pascal. *Religion Explained: The Evolutionary Origins of Religious Thought*. New York: Basic Books, 2001.

Brettler, Marc Zvi. *God Is King: Understanding an Israelite Metaphor*. Sheffield: Sheffield Academic, 2009.

———. "Incompatible Metaphors for YHWH in Isaiah 40–66." *Journal for the Study of the Old Testament* 78 (1998): 97–120.

Brown, Jeannine K. *Scripture as Communication: Introducing Biblical Hermeneutics*. Grand Rapids: Baker Academic, 2007.

Brown, Rosalind. *Can Words Express Our Wonder?* Norwich: Canterbury Press, 2009.

Bruce, Kathrine. "The Vital Importance of the Imagination in the Contemporary Preaching Event." PhD thesis, Durham University, 2013. <www.etheses.dur.ac.uk/9399/> [Accessed 28 March 2017].

Brueggemann, Walter. *Cadences of Home: Preaching among Exiles.* Louisville: Westminster John Knox, 2007.

———. *Finally Comes the Poet: Daring Speech for Proclamation.* Minneapolis: Fortress, 1989.

———. *Hopeful Imagination: Prophetic Voices in Exile.* Minneapolis: Augsburg Fortress, 1986.

———. *The Practice of Prophetic Imagination: Preaching an Emancipating Word.* Minneapolis: Fortress, 2012.

Brunner, Emil. *The Christian Doctrine of Creation and Redemption.* London: Lutterworth, 1952.

———. *Man in Revolt.* Philadelphia: Westminster, 1947.

Buber, Martin. *I And Thou.* New York: Touchstone, 1971.

Burghardt, Walter J. *Preaching: The Art and the Craft.* New York: Paulist, 1987.

Burke, Sean. *The Death and Return of the Author: Criticism and Subjectivity in Barthes, Foucault and Derrida.* Edinburgh: Edinburgh University Press, 2008.

Buttrick, David. *Homiletic: Moves and Structures.* Philadelphia: Fortress Press, 1987.

Campbell, Charles L. *Preaching Jesus: The New Directions for Homiletics in Hans Frei's Postliberal Theology.* Eugene Wipf & Stock, 2006.

Cazeaux, Clive. *Metaphor and Continental Philosophy: From Kant to Derrida.* New York: Routledge, 2009.

Chapell, Bryan. *Christ-Centered Preaching: Redeeming the Expository Sermon*, 2nd ed. Grand Rapids: Baker Academic, 2005.

Cicero. "On the Character of the Orator", in *Cicero on Oratory and Orators*, ed. by J.S. Watson. Carbondale: Southern Illinois University, 1970, 3.38.156-39.157

Cienki, Alan. "Frames, Idealized Cognitive Models, and Domains" In *The Oxford Handbook of Cognitive Linguistics,* edited by Dirk Geeraerts and Hubert Cuyckens, 170–187. Oxford; New York: Oxford University Press, 2010.

Clements, Elizabeth Anne. *Mothers on the Margin? The Significance of the Women in Matthew's Genealogy.* Eugene: Wipf & Stock, 2014.

Clines, David J. A. *The Bible and the Modern World.* Sheffield: Sheffield Phoenix, 2005. First published 1997 by Sheffield Academic (Sheffield). Page references to 2005 edition.

Cook, Michael L. "Revelation as Metaphoric Process." *Theological Studies* 47 (1986): 388–411.

Coulson, Seana. "Metaphor Comprehension and the Brain." In *The Cambridge Handbook of Metaphor and Thought*, edited by Raymond W. Gibbs, 177–194. New York: Cambridge University Press, 2008.

———. Semantic Leaps: Frame-Shifting and Conceptual Blending in Meaning Construction. Cambridge: Cambridge University Press, 2006.

Craddock, Fred B. *As One Without Authority*. Rev. ed. St. Louis: Chalice Press, 2001.

———. *Craddock on the Craft of Preaching*. Edited by Lee Sparks and Kathryn Hayes Sparks. St. Louis: Chalice Press, 2011.

———. *Craddock Stories*. Edited by Michael Graves and Richard Ward. St. Louis: Chalice Press, 2001.

———. *Overhearing the Gospel*. Rev. and enl. ed. St. Louis: Chalice Press, 2002.

———. *Preaching*. Nashville: Abingdon, 2010.

———. "When the Roll Is Called Down Here." https://cepreaching.org/audio-sermons/when-the-roll-is-called-down-here/ [Accessed 2 June 2023].

Croft, William, and D. Alan Cruse. *Cognitive Linguistics*. Cambridge; New York: Cambridge University Press, 2004.

Cutrer, Michelle. "Time and Tense in Narrative and in Everyday Language." PhD thesis, University of California, 1994.

Davidson, Donald. "What Metaphors Mean." In *Philosophical Perspectives on Metaphor*, edited by Mark Johnson, 200–220. Minneapolis: University of Minnesota Press, 1981.

Davies, Brian. *An Introduction to the Philosophy of Religion*. 3rd Ed. Oxford; New York: Oxford University Press, 2004.

Davis, H. *Design for Preaching*. Philadelphia: Fortress, 1958.

Day, David. *Embodying the Word*. London: SPCK, 2005.

Decker, Rodney J. "May Evangelicals Dispense with Propositional Revelation? Challenges to a Traditional Evangelical Doctrine." A Paper Presented at the 53rd Annual Meeting of the Evangelical Theological Society Colorado Springs, 2001. <www.semanticscholar.org/paper/May-Evangelicals-Dispense-with-Propositional-to-a-Decker-Seminary/4cadf5359e1388c67f715b65f8a8f8 4673725a74> [Accessed 21 June 2023].

Derrida, Jacques. *Of Grammatology*. Baltimore: Johns Hopkins University, 1997.

———. *Writing and Difference*. London: Routledge, 2001.

DesCamp, Mary Therese, and Eve E. Sweetser. "Metaphors for God: Why and How Do Our Choices Matter for Humans? The Application of Contemporary Cognitive Linguistics Research to the Debate on God and Metaphor." *Pastoral Psychology* 53 (2005): 207–238.

Dewell, Robert B. "Over Again: Image-Schema Transformations in Semantic Analysis." *Cognitive Linguistics* 5 (1994): 351–380.

Dilthey, Wilhelm. *Selected Works: Hermeneutics and the Study of History, IV*. Edited by Rudolf A. Makkreel and Frithjof Rodi. New Jersey: Princeton University Press, 2010.

Dinsmore, John. *Partitioned Representations: A Study in Mental Representation, Language Understanding and Linguistic Structure*. New York: Springer Science and Business Media, 1991.

Dirven, René, and Gunter Radden. "The Cognitive Basis of Language: Language and Thought." In *Cognitive Exploration of Language and Linguistics*, edited by Rene Dirven and Marjolijn Verspoor, 1–23. Amsterdam: John Benjamins Publishing, 2004.

Drummond, Lewis A. *Reaching Generation Next: Effective Evangelism in Today's Culture*. Grand Rapids: Baker Books, 2002.

Duduit, Michael. *Handbook of Contemporary Preaching*. Nashville: B&H Academic, 1993.

Eco, Umberto. *The Role of the Reader: Explorations in the Semiotics of Texts*. Bloomington: Indiana University Press, 1979.

Elliott, Mark Barger. *Creative Styles of Preaching*. Louisville: Westminster John Knox, 2004.

Enns, Peter. Inspiration and Incarnation: Evangelicals and the Problem of the Old Testament. Grand Rapids: Baker Academic, 2005.

Erickson, Millard J. *Christian Theology*. Grand Rapids: Baker Books, 1986.

Erickson, Millard J., and James L. Heflin. *Old Wine in New Wineskins: Doctrinal Preaching in a Changing World*. Grand Rapids: Baker Books, 1997.

Erussard, Laurence. "From SALT to SALT: Cognitive Metaphor and Religious Language." *Cuadernos de Filología Inglesa* 6.2 (1997): 197–212.

Eslinger, Richard L. *Narrative Imagination: Reaching the Worlds That Shape Us*. Minneapolis: Fortress, 1995.

———. *A New Hearing: Living Options in Homiletic Method*. Nashville: Abingdon, 1987.

Fauconnier, Gilles. "Cognitive Linguistics." In *Encyclopedia of Cognitive Science*, edited by Lynn Nadel. New York: Nature, 2003.

———. *Mappings in Thought and Language*. Cambridge: Cambridge University Press, 1997.

———. "Mental Spaces." In *The Oxford Handbook of Cognitive Linguistics*, edited by Dirk Geeraerts and Hubert Cuyckens, 351–376. Oxford; New York: Oxford University Press, 2010.

Fauconnier, Gilles, and George Lakoff "On Metaphor and Blending." *Cognitive Semiotics* (2014): 393–399. <http://www.cogsci.ucsd.edu/~coulson/spaces/GG-final-1.pdf> [Accessed 30 June 2016].

Fauconnier, Gilles. *Mental Spaces: Aspects of Meaning Construction in Natural Language*. Cambridge: Cambridge University Press, 1994.

Fauconnier, Gilles, and Mark Turner. "Rethinking Metaphor." In *The Cambridge Handbook of Metaphor and Thought*, edited by Raymond W. Gibbs, 53–66. New York: Cambridge University Press, 2008.

———. *The Way We Think: Conceptual Blending and the Mind's Hidden Complexities*. New York: Basic Books, 2003.

Fee, Gordon D. *Listening to the Spirit in the Text*. Grand Rapids: Eerdmans, 2000.

———. *Pauline Christology: An Exegetical-Theological Study*. Peabody: Hendrickson, 2007.

Feinberg, John S. "Literary Forms and Inspiration." In *Cracking Old Testament Codes: A Guide to Interpreting Literary Genres of the Old Testament*, edited by D. Brent Sandy and Ronald L. Giese, 45–67. Nashville: Broadman and Holman, 1995.

Fillmore, Charles J. "Frame Semantics." In *Linguistics in the Morning Calm*, edited by the Linguistic Society of Korea, 110–137. Seoul: Hanshin, 1982.

Fischer, Kathleen. *The Inner Rainbow: Imagination in Christian Life*. New York: Paulist Press International, 1983.

Fish, Stanley. *Doing What Comes Naturally: Change, Rhetoric, and the Practice of Theory in Literary and Legal Studies*. Durham: Duke University Press, 1989

Frei, Hans W. "Theology and the Interpretation of Narrative: Some Hermeneutical Considerations." In *Theology and Narrative: Selected Essays*, edited by George Hunsinger and William C. Placher, 94–116. New York: Oxford University Press, 1993.

———. *Types of Christian Theology*. New Haven: Yale University Press, 1994.

Froese, Paul, and Christopher Bader. *America's Four Gods: What We Say about God and What That Says about Us*. Oxford: Oxford University Press, 2015.

Gadamer, Hans-Georg. *Truth and Method*. Translated by Joel Weinsheimer and Donald G. Marshall. 2nd ed. New York: Continuum, 2004.

Galli, Mark, and Craig Brian Larson. *Preaching That Connects: Using Techniques of Journalists to Add Impact*. Grand Rapids: Zondervan, 1994.

Gardner, Howard. *Frames of Mind: The Theory of Multiple Intelligences*. New York: Basic Books, 2011.

Geeraerts, Dirk. "Introduction: A Rough Guide to Cognitive Linguistics." In *Cognitive Linguistics: Basic Readings*, edited by Dirk Geeraerts, 1–28. Berlin; New York: de Gruyter, 2006.

Gentner, Dedre, and Brian Bowdle. "Metaphors and Structure-Mapping." In *The Cambridge Handbook of Metaphor and Thought*, edited by Raymond W. Gibbs, 109–128. New York: Cambridge University Press, 2008.

Gibbs, Raymond W., and Herbert L. Colston. "The Cognitive Psychological Reality of Image Schemas and Their Transformations." *Cognitive Linguistics* 6 (1995): 347–378.

Gibbs, Raymond W., and Gerard J. Steen, eds. *Metaphor in Cognitive Linguistics: Selected Papers from the 5th International Cognitive Linguistics Conference, Amsterdam, 1997*, edited by Raymond W. Gibbs Jr. and Gerard J. Steen. Amsterdam; Philadelphia: John Benjamins Publishing, 1999.

Gibson, J. C. L. *Language and Imagery in the Old Testament*. London: SPCK, 1998.

Glancy, Jennifer A. *Slavery in Early Christianity*. Minneapolis: Fortress Press, 2006.

Glucksberg, Sam. "How Metaphors Create Categories – Quickly." In *The Cambridge Handbook of Metaphor and Thought*, edited by Raymond W. Gibbs, 67–83. Cambridge: Cambridge University Press, 2008.

Gorman, Michael J. *Elements of Biblical Exegesis: A Basic Guide for Students and Ministers*. Peabody: Hendrickson, 2009.

Grady, Joseph E. "Foundations of Meaning: Primary Metaphors and Primary Scenes." Unpublished PhD dissertation, University of California, 1997.

———. "Metaphor" In *The Oxford Handbook of Cognitive Linguistics*, edited by Dirk Geeraerts and Hubert Cuyckens, 188–213. Oxford; New York: Oxford University Press, 2010.

Grady, Joseph E., Todd Oakley, and Seana Coulson. "Blending and Metaphor." In *Metaphor in Cognitive Linguistics: Selected Papers from the 5th International Cognitive Linguistics Conference, Amsterdam, 1997*, edited by Raymond W. Gibbs Jr. and Gerard J. Steen, 101–124. Amsterdam; Philadelphia: John Benjamins Publishing, 1999.

Graves, Mike. *The Fully Alive Preacher: Recovering from a Homiletical Burnout*. Louisville; London: Westminster John Knox, 2006.

Green, Garrett. *Imagining God: Theology and Christian Imagination*. San Francisco: Harper & Row, 1987.

———. *Imagining God: Theology and Religious Imagination*. San Francisco: Harper & Row, 1989.

———. *Theology, Hermeneutics, and Imagination: The Crisis of Interpretation at the End of Modernity*. Cambridge: Cambridge University Press, 1999.

Greidanus, Sidney. *The Modern Preacher and the Ancient Text: Interpreting and Preaching Biblical Literature*. Grand Rapids: Eerdmans, 1989.

———. *Preaching Christ from the Old Testament: A Contemporary Hermeneutical Method*. Grand Rapids: Eerdmans, 1999.

Grelot, Pierre. *The Language of Symbolism: Biblical Theology, Semantics, and Exegesis*. Peabody: Hendrickson Publishers, 2006.

Grenz, Stanley J. *Created for Community: Connecting Christian Belief with Christian Living*. Grand Rapids: Baker Academic, 1998.

———. *The Moral Quest*. Leicester: Apollos, 1998.

———. *Theology for the Community of God*. Grand Rapids: Eerdmans, 2000.

Gupta, Nijay K. "Towards a Set of Principles for Identifying and Interpreting Metaphors in Paul: Prosagōgē (Romans 5:2) as a Test Case." *Restoration Quarterly* 51 (2009): 169–181.

Hamilton, Victor P. *The Book of Genesis 1–17*. NICOT 1. Grand Rapids: Eerdmans, 1990.

Hampe, Beate. "Image Schemas in Cognitive Linguistics: Introduction." In *From Perception to Meaning. Image Schemas in Cognitive Linguistics*, edited by Beate Hampe and Joseph E. Grady, 1–12. Berlin: de Gruyter, 2005.

Harrill, J. Albert. *Slaves in the New Testament: Literary, Social, and Moral Dimensions*. Minneapolis: Augsburg Fortress, 2006.

Hauerwas, Stanley. "Character, Narrative, and Growth in the Christian Life." In *The Hauerwas Reader*, edited by John Berkman and Michael Cartwright, 221–254. Durham: Duke University Press, 2001.

Hays, Richard B. *The Moral Vision of the New Testament: Community, Cross, New Creation, A Contemporary Introduction to New Testament Ethics*. San Francisco: HarperOne, 1996.

Hebblethwaite, Brian. *Philosophical Theology and Christian Doctrine*. Malden: Wiley-Blackwell, 2005.

Heywood, David. *Transforming Preaching: The Sermon as a Channel for God's Word*. London: SPCK Publishing, 2013.

Hick, John. *The Metaphor of God Incarnate: Christology in a Pluralistic Age*. Louisville: Westminster John Knox, 1993.

———. *Philosophy of Religion*. Englewood Cliffs: Pearson, 1989.

Hilkert, Mary Catherine. *Naming Grace: Preaching and the Sacramental Imagination*. New York: Bloomsbury Academic, 1997.

Hirsch, E. D. *Validity in Interpretation*. New Haven: Yale University Press, 1967.

Hobbes, Thomas. *Leviathan*. Oxford: Oxford University Press, 2008.

Hoekema, A. Anthony. *Created in God's Image*. Grand Rapids: Eerdmans, 1986.

Howe, Bonnie. *Because You Bear This Name: Conceptual Metaphor and the Moral Meaning of 1 Peter*. Atlanta: Society of Biblical Literature, 2008.

Howe, Bonnie, and Joel B. Green, eds. *Cognitive Linguistic Explorations in Biblical Studies*. Berlin: de Gruyter, 2014.

Iser, Wolfgang. *The Act of Reading: A Theory of Aesthetic Response*. Baltimore: Johns Hopkins University Press, 1980.

Jäkel, Olaf. "Hypotheses Revisited: The Cognitive Theory of Metaphor Applied to Religious Texts," *Metaphorik.de* 2 (2002), 20–42. www.metaphorik.de/de/journal/02/hypotheses-revisited-cognitive-theory-metaphor-applied-religious-texts.html [Accessed 25 May 2016].

Jauss, Hans Robert. *Toward an Aesthetic of Reception*. Minneapolis: University of Minnesota Press, 1982.

Jensen, Richard A. *Envisioning the Word: The Use of Visual Images in Preaching.* Minneapolis: Fortress, 2005.

Jindo, Job Y. "Biblical Metaphor Reconsidered: A Cognitive Approach to Poetic Prophecy in Jeremiah 1–24." <www.academia.edu/953461/Biblical_Metaphor_Reconsidered_A_Cognitive_Approach_to_Poetic_Prophecy_in_Jeremiah_1-24> [Accessed 21 September 2015].

———. "Toward a Poetics of the Biblical Mind: Language, Culture, and Cognition." *Vetus Testamentum* 59:2 (2009): 222–243.

Johnson, Darrell W. *The Glory of Preaching: Participating in God's Transformation of the World.* Downers Grove: InterVarsity Press, 2009. Kindle.

Johnson, Mark. *The Body in the Mind: The Bodily Basis of Meaning, Imagination, and Reason.* Chicago: University of Chicago Press, 1990.

———. "Metaphor in the Philosophical Tradition." In *Philosophical Perspectives on Metaphor*, 3–47. Minneapolis: University of Minnesota Press, 1981.

———. *Moral Imagination: Implications of Cognitive Science for Ethics.* Chicago: University of Chicago Press, 1994.

Johnson, Trygve David. "The Preacher as Artist: Metaphor, Identity, and the Vicarious Humanity of Christ." PhD thesis, University of St. Andrews, 2010. www.research-repository.st-andrews.ac.uk/handle/10023/944 [Accessed 28 March 2017].

Jones, J. K., and Mark Scott. *Letting the Text Win.* Joplin: College Press, 2014. Kindle.

Kant, Immanuel. *Critique of Judgment.* New York: Hafner Press, 1951.

Keller, Timothy. *Preaching: Communicating Faith in an Age of Scepticism.* New York: Penguin Books, 2017.

———. "Preaching Morality in an Amoral Age." In *The Art and Craft of Biblical Preaching: A Comprehensive Resource for Today's Communicators*, edited by Craig Brian Larson and Haddon W. Robinson, 24–29. Grand Rapids: Zondervan, 2005.

———. *The Reason for God.* London: Hodder & Stoughton, 2009.

Kern, R. Trembath. "Our Knowledge of God According to Karl Rahner." *Evangelical Quarterly* 59.4 (1987): 329–341.

Kilby, Karen. "Perichoresis." In *The Cambridge Dictionary of Christian Theology*, edited by Ian A. McFarland David A. S. Fergusson, Karen Kilby and Iain R. Torrance, 383. Cambridge: Cambridge University Press, 2014.

Kittel, Gerhard, ed. *Theological Dictionary of the New Testament.* Vol. 2. Translated by Geoffrey W, Bromiley. Grand Rapids: Eerdmans, 1964.

Klein, William W., Craig L. Blomberg and Robert I. Hubbard Jr. *Introduction to Biblical Interpretation.* Nashville: Thomas Nelson, 2004.

Knowles, Murray, and Rosamund Moon. *Introducing Metaphor.* London; New York: Routledge, 2005.

Kohlenberger, John, III, and Swanson, James A., eds. *The Hebrew-English Concordance to the Old Testament*. Grand Rapids: Zondervan, 1998.

Kövecses, Zoltán. "The Biblical Story Retold: Symbols in Action: A Cognitive Linguistic Perspective." In *Cognitive Linguistics: Convergence and Expansion*, edited by Mario Brdar, Stefan Th. Gries and Milena Žic Fuchs, 325–354. Amsterdam; Philadelphia: John Benjamins Publishing Company, 2011. <www.researchgate.net/publication/237624691_THE_BIBLICAL_STORY_RETOLD_SYMBOLS_IN_ACTION_A_cognitive_linguistic_perspective1> [Accessed 30 May 2016]

———. *Emotion Concepts*. New York: Springer, 2011.

———. "The Heart of the Matter: A Matter of the Heart. The Crucifixion of Jesus from a Cognitive Semantic Perspective." *Review of Cognitive Linguistics* 20:1 (2022): 91–103.

———. *Language, Mind, and Culture: A Practical Introduction*. New York: Oxford University Press, 2006.

———. *The Language of Love: The Semantics of Passion in Conversational English*. Lewisburg: Bucknell University Press, 1988.

———. "Levels of Metaphor." An unpublished article.

———. *Metaphor: A Practical Introduction*. Oxford; New York: Oxford University Press, 2010.

———. *Metaphor and Emotion: Language, Culture, and Body in Human Feeling*. Cambridge: Cambridge University Press, 2000.

———. "Metaphor and Poetic Creativity: A Cognitive Linguistic Account." *Philologica* (2009): 181–196.

———. *Metaphor in Culture: Universality and Variation*. Cambridge: Cambridge University Press, 2006.

———. "Universality and Variation in the Use of Metaphor." Selected Papers from the 2006 and 2007 Stockholm MetaphorFestivals, editors N.-L. Johannesson & D.C. Minugh, Stockholm: Stockholm University, 2007. 51–74 <www.remat.amu.edu.pl/wp-content/uploads/2014/04/Kovecses_Universality-and-Variation-in-the-Use-of-Metaphor.pdf> [Accessed 31 March 2017]

———. *Where Metaphors Come From: Reconsidering Context in Metaphor*. New York: Oxford University Press, 2015.

Kuczok, Marcin. "'Amazing Grace That Saved a Wretch Like Me': Conceptual Metaphors for Grace in Christian Discourse (on the Basis of John Newman's Sermons)." *Acta Neophilologica* (2017): 257–267.

Labahn, Antje. "Fire from Above: Metaphors and Images of God's Actions in Lamentations 2:1–9." *Journal for the Study of the Old Testament* 31 (2006): 239–256.

Lakoff, George. "The Contemporary Theory of Metaphor." In *Metaphor and Thought*, edited by Andrew Ortony 202–251. Cambridge; New York: Cambridge University Press, 1993.

———. *Don't Think of an Elephant!: Know Your Values and Frame the Debate*. White River Junction: Chelsea Green, 2004.

——— "How the Body Shapes Thought: Thinking with an All-Too-Human Brain." In *The Nature and Limits of Human Understanding*, edited by Anthony J. Sanford, 49–74. New York; London: T&T Clark, 2003.

———. *Moral Politics: How Liberals and Conservatives Think*. 2nd ed. Chicago: University of Chicago Press, 2002.

———. "The Neural Theory of Metaphor." In *The Cambridge Handbook of Metaphor and Thought*, edited by Raymond W. Gibbs, 17–38. New York: Cambridge University Press, 2008.

———. *Women, Fire, and Dangerous Things*. Chicago: University of Chicago Press, 1990.

Lakoff, George, and Mark Johnson. *Metaphors We Live By*. Chicago: University of Chicago Press, 2003.

———. *Philosophy in the Flesh: The Embodied Mind and Its Challenge to Western Thought*. version. New York: Basic Books, 1999. iBooks.

Lakoff, George, and Mark Turner. *More than Cool Reason: A Field Guide to Poetic Metaphor*. Chicago: University of Chicago Press, 1989.

Langacker, Ronald W. *Cognitive Grammar: A Basic Introduction*. Oxford: Oxford University Press, 2008.

———. *The Foundations of Cognitive Grammar, I: Theoretical Prerequisites*. Stanford: Stanford University Press, 1999.

Laughery, Gregory J. "Language at the Frontiers of Language." In *After Pentecost: Language and Biblical Interpretation*, edited by Craig Bartholomew, Colin Greene, and Karl Moller, 171–194. Vol. 2 of *Scripture and Hermeneutics Series*. Grand Rapids: Zondervan, 2001

Lewandowska-Tomaszczyk, Barbara. "Polysemy, Prototypes, and Radial Categories." In *The Oxford Handbook of Cognitive Linguistics*, edited by Dirk Geeraerts and Hubert Cuyckens, 139–169. Oxford; New York: Oxford University Press, 2010.

Lewis, C. S. *Mere Christianity*. London: Simon & Schuster, 1996.

Lewis, Gordon R. "Is Propositional Revelation Essential to Evangelical Spiritual Formation?" *JETS* (2003): 269–298. <www.etsjets.org/files/JETS-PDFs/46/46-2/46-2-pp269-298_JETS.pdf> [Accessed 31 March 2014].

Lindbeck, George A. *The Nature of Doctrine: Religion and Theology in a Postliberal Age*. Louisville: Westminster John Knox, 2009.

Lischer, Richard. "Imagining a Sermon." In *A Reader on Preaching: Making Connections*, edited by David Day, Jeff Astley, and Leslie J. Francis, 179–184. Aldershot: Ashgate, 2005.

Long, Thomas G. *The Witness of Preaching*. Louisville: Westminster John Knox, 2005.

Lord, Jennifer L. Finding Language and Imagery: Words for Holy Speech. Minneapolis: Fortress, 2009.

Lowry, Eugene L. *Doing Time in the Pulpit: The Relationship between Narrative and Preaching*. Nashville: Abingdon, 1985.

———. *The Homiletical Beat: Why All Sermons Are Narrative*. Nashville: Abingdon, 2012.

———. *The Homiletical Plot: The Sermon as Narrative Art Form*. Louisville: Westminster John Knox, 2000.

———. *How to Preach a Parable: Designs for Narrative Sermons*. Nashville: Abingdon, 1989.

———. *The Sermon: Dancing the Edge of Mystery*. Nashville: Abingdon, 1997.

Lowry, Noelle Z. "The Image of God in Humanity: Fleshing Out the Bare Bones of Marital Oneness." *Priscilla Papers* 26 (2012): 13–15. <www.search.ebscohost.com/login.aspx?direct=true&db=rlh&AN=83720908&site=ehost-live> [Accessed 11 September 2014].

MacKey, James P. "The Preacher, the Theologian, and the Trinity." *Theology Today* 54 (1997): 347–366.

Marczak, Mirosław. "The Significance of Peak and Frontground in Discourse Analysis and Translation: A Case Study in Acts 19–26." PhD thesis, University of Wrocław, 2004.

Mavrodes, George I. *Revelation in Religious Belief*. Philadelphia: Temple University Press, 1988.

McClendon, James William, Jr. *Ethics: Systematic Theology* Vol. 1. Nashville: Abingdon, 2002.

McClure, John S., Ronald J. Allen, Dale P. Andrews, L. Susan Bond, Dan P. Moseley, and G. Lee Ramsey Jr. *Listening to Listeners: Homiletical Case Studies*. St. Louis: Chalice Press, 2004.

McDill, Wayne. *The 12 Essential Skills for Great Preaching*. Nashville: B&H, 1994.

McGlone, Matthew S. "What Is the Explanatory Value of a Conceptual Metaphor?" *Language and Communication* 27 (2007), 109–126.

McGrath, Alister E. *Christian Theology: An Introduction*. West Sussex: Wiley-Blackwell, 2010.

Meeks, Wayne A. "A Hermeneutics of Social Embodiment." *Harvard Theological Review*, 79 no.1/3 (1986): 176–186.

Middleton, J. Richard. "The Liberating Image? Interpreting the Imago Dei in Context." *Christian Scholars Review* 24.1 (1994): 8–25.

Miller, Calvin. *Marketplace Preaching: How to Return the Sermon to Where It Belongs*. Grand Rapids: Baker Books, 1995.

Mitchell, Henry H. *Celebration and Experience in Preaching*. Nashville: Abingdon, 2008.

Mitchell, Jolyon P. *Visually Speaking: Radio and the Renaissance of Preaching*. Louisville: Westminster John Knox, 1999.

Mulligan, Mary Alice, and Ronald J. Allen. *Make the Word Come Alive: Lessons from Laity*. St. Louis: Chalice Press, 2005.

Myers, Isabel Briggs, and Peter B. Myers. *Gifts Differing: Understanding Personality Type*. London: Nicholas Brealey, 1995.

Narayanan, Srinivas. "Karma: Knowledge-Based Action Representations for Metaphor and Aspect." PhD thesis, University of California, 1997.

Nevin, Michael. "Analogy: Aquinas and Pannenberg." In *The Nature of Religious Language: A Colloquium*, edited by Stanley E. Porter, 201–211. Sheffield: Sheffield Academic, 1996.

Newbigin, Lesslie. *The Gospel in a Pluralist Society*. London: SPCK, 1989.

———. *The Light Has Come: An Exposition of the Fourth Gospel*. Grand Rapids: Eerdmans, 1982.

Nussbaum, Martha C. *Love's Knowledge: Essays on Philosophy and Literature*. New York: Oxford University Press 1993.

Oakley, Todd. "Image Schemas." In *The Oxford Handbook of Cognitive Linguistics*, edited by Dirk Geeraerts and Hubert Cuyckens, 214–235. Oxford; New York: Oxford University Press, 2010.

Ong, Walter J. *Orality and Literacy: The Technologizing of the Word*. 2nd ed. London; New York: Routledge, 2002.

Ott, Craig. "The Power of Biblical Metaphors for the Contextualized Communication of the Gospel." *Missiology* 42.4 (2014): 357–374.

Otto, Rudolf. *The Idea of the Holy*. Oxford: Oxford University Press, 1958.

Pannenberg, Wolfhart. *Revelation as History*. London: Sheed and Ward, 1969.

Pannenberg, Wolfhart, and Duane A. Priebe. *What Is Man? Contemporary Anthropology in Theological Perspective*. Philadelphia: Fortress, 1970.

Park, Yoon-Man. *Mark's Memory Resources and the Controversy Stories (Mark 2:1–3:6): An Application of the Frame Theory of Cognitive Science to the Markan Oral-Aural Narrative*. Boston: Brill, 2010.

Pasquarello, Mike, III. *Christian Preaching: A Trinitarian Theology of Proclamation*. Eugene: Wipf and Stock, 2011.

———. *Sacred Rhetoric: Preaching as a Theological and Pastoral Practice of the Church*. Eugene: Wipf & Stock, 2012.

Paul, Ian. "Metaphor." In *Dictionary for Theological Interpretation of the Bible*, edited by Kevin J. Vanhoozer and Craig Bartholomew, 507–510. Grand Rapids: Baker Academic, 2005.

————. "Metaphor and Exegesis." In *After Pentecost: Language and Biblical Interpretation*, edited by Craig Bartholomew, Colin Greene, and Karl Moller, 387–402. Vol. 2 of *Scripture and Hermeneutics Series*. Grand Rapids: Zondervan, 2001.

————. "The Value of Paul Ricoeur's Hermeneutic of Metaphor in Interpreting the Symbolism of Revelation Chapters 12 and 13." PhD thesis, St. John's College, 1998.

Petersen, Philip B. "Garden, Park, Glen, and Meadow: The Effect of Metaphor on Proclamation Today." Paper presented at the Evangelical Homiletics Society, 13–15 October 2005.

Peterson, Eugene H., trans. *The Message: The Bible in Contemporary Language*. Colorado Springs: NavPress, 2005.

Peterson, Gregory R., Michael Spezio, James A. Van Slyke, Kevin Reimer, and Warren Brown. "Rationality of Ultimate Concern: Moral Exemplars, Theological Ethics, and the Science of Moral Cognition." *Theology and Science* 8.2 (2010): 139–161.

Pinnock, Clark H. *Biblical Revelation: The Foundation of Christian Theology*. Chicago: Moody, 1971.

Piper, John. "The Image of God." Desiring God, 1971 <www.desiringgod.org/articles/the-image-of-god> [Accessed 27 August 2014].

————. "What I Mean by Preaching." Desiring God, 2009 <www.desiringgod.org/articles/what-i-mean-by-preaching> [Accessed 21 March 2017].

Pollard, Frank. "Preparing the Preacher." In *Handbook of Contemporary Preaching*, edited by Michael Duduit. Nashville: B&H Academic, 1993.

Postman, Neil. *Amusing Ourselves to Death: Public Discourse in the Age of Show Business*. New York: Viking Penguin, 1985.

Powell, Mark Allan. *What Do They Hear?: Bridging the Gap between Pulpit and Pew*. Nashville: Abingdon, 2007.

Pratt, Richard L. *He Gave Us Stories: The Bible Student's Guide to Interpreting Old Testament Narratives*. Phillipsburg: P&R, 1993.

Prickett, Stephen. *Words and The Word: Language, Poetics and Biblical Interpretation*. Repr. ed. Cambridge: Cambridge University Press, 1988.

Quicke, Michael J. *360-Degree Preaching: Hearing, Speaking, and Living the Word*. Grand Rapids: Baker Academic, 2003.

Radford, Shawn D. "The Sermon as Illustration: Confirming Biblical Texts in Concrete Expressions." Paper presented at Evangelical Homiletics Society, 13–15 October 2005. <www.ehomiletics.com/papers/05/Radford2005.pdf> [Accessed 21 September 2013].

Rahner, Karl. *Theological Investigations, XVIII: God and Revelation*. Translated by Edward Quinn. New York: Crossroad, 1983.

Regier, Terry. *The Human Semantic Potential: Spatial Language and Constrained Connectionism*. Cambridge: A Bradford Book, 1996.

———. "A Model of the Human Capacity for Categorizing Spatial Relations." *Cognitive Linguistics* 6 (1995): 63–88.

Reid, Barbara E. "Unleashing Inner Power." *America: The National Catholic Weekly* (2011): 37.

Rice, Charles. "Shaping Sermons by the Interplay of Text and Metaphor." In *Preaching Biblically: Creating Sermons in the Shape of Scripture*, edited by Don M. Wardlaw, 104–105. Philadelphia: Westminster, 1983.

Richards, I. A. "The Philosophy of Rhetoric." In *Philosophical Perspectives on Metaphor*, edited by Mark Johnson, 48–62. Minneapolis: University of Minnesota Press, 1981.

Ricoeur, Paul. *Freud and Philosophy: An Essay on Interpretation*. Yale: Yale University Press, 1970.

———. *Interpretation Theory: Discourse and the Surplus of Meaning*. Fort Worth: Texas Christian University Press, 1976.

———. "Metaphor and the Central Problem of Hermeneutics." In *Hermeneutics and the Human Sciences: Essays on Language, Action and Interpretation*, edited by John B. Thompson, 165–181. Cambridge: Cambridge University Press, 1981.

———. "The Metaphorical Process as Cognition, Imagination, and Feeling." *Critical Inquiry* 5 (1978): 143–159.

———. *The Rule of Metaphor: The Creation of Meaning in Language*. London; New York: Routledge, 2003.

Robinette, S.J. "Looking Beyond the Tree Jeremiah 17:5–8." In *Cognitive Linguistic Explorations in Biblical Studies*, edited by Bonnie Howe and Joel B. Green, 25–46. Berlin: de Gruyter, 2014.

Robinson, Haddon W. *Biblical Preaching: The Development and Delivery of Expository Messages*. Grand Rapids: Baker Academic, 2001.

———. "Convictions of Biblical Preaching." In *The Art and Craft of Biblical Preaching: A Comprehensive Resource for Today's Communicators*, edited by Craig Brian Larson and Haddon W. Robinson, 23–24. Grand Rapids: Zondervan, 2005.

———. "The Heresy of Application" In *The Art and Craft of Biblical Preaching: A Comprehensive Resource for Today's Communicators*, edited by Craig Brian Larson and Haddon W. Robinson, 306–311. Grand Rapids: Zondervan, 2005.

Rohrer, Tim. "Embodiment and Experientialism." In *The Oxford Handbook of Cognitive Linguistics*, edited by Dirk Geeraerts and Hubert Cuyckens, 25–47. Oxford; New York: Oxford University Press, 2010.

Rosch, Eleanor. "Principles of Categorization." In *Cognition and Categorization*, edited by Eleanor Rosch and Barbara B. Lloyd, 27–48. Hillsdale: Lawrence Erlbaum, 1978.

Runia, Klaas. "The Hermeneutics of the Reformers." *Calvin Theological Journal* 19 (1984): 121–151.

Ryken, Leland. *How to Read the Bible as Literature*. Grand Rapids: Zondervan, 1985.

———. *The Literature of the Bible*. Grand Rapids: Zondervan, 1974.

Sackett, Chuck. "Illusive Illustration: Letting the Text Win." Paper presented at Evangelical Homiletics Society, 13–15 October 2005.

Sanders, John. *Theology in the Flesh: How Embodiment and Culture Shape the Way We Think about Truth, Morality, and God*. Minneapolis: Fortress, 2016. Kindle.

Sanford, Anthony, ed. *The Nature and Limits of Human Understanding*. London; New York: T&T Clark, 2003.

Scharf, Greg R. "'Double Listening' Revisited: Hearing Listeners without Compromising Faithfulness to the Biblical Text." *Trinity Journal* 33.2 (2012): 181–197.

Schlafer, David J. *Surviving the Sermon: A Guide to Preaching for Those Who Have to Listen*. Cambridge: Cowley, 1992.

Schleiermacher, Friedrich. *The Christian Faith*. Berkeley: Apocryphile, 2011.

———. *Schleiermacher: Hermeneutics and Criticism: And Other Writings*. Edited by Andrew Bowie. Cambridge: Cambridge University Press, 1998.

Schröter, Jens. *From Jesus to the New Testament*. Waco: Baylor University Press, 2013.

Scotus, John Duns, *Duns Scotus – Philosophical Writings: A Selection*. Translated by Allan B. Wolter. Indianapolis: Hackett, 1987.

Searle, John R. *Expression and Meaning: Studies in the Theory of Speech Acts*. Cambridge: Cambridge University Press, 1985.

———. "Metaphor." In *Philosophical Perspectives on Metaphor*, edited by Mark Johnson, 248–285. Minneapolis: University of Minnesota Press, 1981.

———. *Speech Acts: An Essay in the Philosophy of Language*. Cambridge: Cambridge University Press, 1969.

Sheard, Daniel W. "Preaching in the Hear and Now: Justification, Development, and Assessment of 'Parabolic Engagement' Pedagogy in French-Speaking Missionary Settings." PhD thesis, University of Wales, 2005.

Silva, Moisés, ed. *New International Dictionary of New Testament Theology and Exegesis*. 2nd ed. 5 vols. Grand Rapids: Zondervan, 2014.

Smith, Argile. "Rethinking the Value of Metaphors in Listener-Sensitive Homiletics." Paper presented at Evangelical Homiletics Society, 2002.

Soskice, Janet Martin. *Metaphor and Religious Language.* Oxford: Oxford University Press, 1987.

———. *The Kindness of God: Metaphor, Gender, and Religious Language.* Oxford: Oxford University Press, 2008.

Sprinkle, Joe M. "Clean, Unclean." In *Evangelical Dictionary of Theology*, edited by Walter A. Elwell. Grand Rapids: Baker Academic, 1997. <www.biblestudytools.com/dictionaries/bakers-evangelical-dictionary/clean-unclean.html> [Accessed 9 March 2016].

Stączek, Marek. *Prezentacja Publiczna.* Warszawa: EdisonTeam, 2011.

Standing, Roger. "Mediated Preaching: Homiletics in Contemporary British Culture." In *The Future of Preaching*, edited by Geoffrey Stevenson, 9–26. London: SCM Press, 2010.

Stanley, Andy, and Jones Lane. *Communicating for a Change: Seven Keys to Irresistible Communication.* Sisters: Multnomah, 2006.

Steimle, Edmund A., Morris J. Niedenthal, and Charles L. Rice. *Preaching the Story.* Eugene: Wipf & Stock, 2003.

Sternberg, Meir. *The Poetics of Biblical Narrative: Ideological Literature and the Drama of Reading.* Bloomington: Indiana University Press, 1987.

Stevenson, Geoffrey. *Future of Preaching.* Norwich: SCM, 2010.

Stevenson, Peter K., and Stephen I. Wright. *Preaching the Incarnation.* Louisville: Westminster John Knox, 2010.

Stiver, Dan R. *The Philosophy of Religious Language: Sign, Symbol and Story.* Oxford: Blackwell Publishers, 1996.

Stockitt, Robin. *Imagination and the Playfulness of God: The Theological Implications of Samuel Taylor Coleridge's Definition of the Human Imagination.* Eugene: Wipf & Stock, 2011.

Stott, John. *Between Two Worlds: The Art of Preaching in the Twentieth Century.* Grand Rapids: Eerdmans, 1982.

———. *The Contemporary Christian: An Urgent Plea for Double Listening.* Leicester: IVP, 1992.

———. "A Definition of Biblical Preaching." In *The Art and Craft of Biblical Preaching: A Comprehensive Resource for Today's Communicators*, edited by Craig Brian Larson and Haddon W. Robinson, 24–29. Grand Rapids: Zondervan, 2005.

———. *I Believe in Preaching.* London: Hodder & Stoughton, 2014.

———. *The Preacher's Portrait: Five New Testament Word Studies.* Carlisle: Langham Preaching Resources, 2016.

Sullivan, Karen. *Frames and Constructions in Metaphoric Language.* Amsterdam; Philadelphia: John Benjamins Publishing, 2013.

Sweetser, Eve. "Blended Spaces and Performativity." *Cognitive Linguistics* 11 (2001): 305–333.

———. "The Definition of Lie: An Examination of the Folk Models Underlying a Semantic Prototype." In *Cultural Models in Language and Thought*, edited by Dorothy Holland and Naomi Quinn, 43–66. Cambridge: Cambridge University Press, 1987.

Sweetser, Eve, and Mary Therese DesCamp. "Motivating Biblical Metaphors for God: Refining the Cognitive Model" In *Cognitive Linguistic Explorations in Biblical Studies*, edited by Bonnie Howe and Joel B. Green, 7–24 Berlin: de Gruyter, 2014.

Szumorek, Adam. "Carpe Diem – Korzystaj z Dnia – Kaznodziei Salomona 3:1–22." In *Na Bezdrożach Starego Testamentu: Jak Wędrować, by Do Domu Wrócić*, 324–341. Ustroń: Wydawnictwo Szaron, 2017.

———. "Co Widzisz? Jana 9:1–41." Unpublished sermon. Tomaszów Mazowiecki, 2017.

———. "Droga do domu." Unpublished funeral sermon. Warszawa, 2016.

———. "Kiedy Życie Nie jest Czarno-Białe – Estery 1–2." Unpublished sermon. Tomaszów Mazowiecki, 2016.

———. "Na Marginesie Relacji – List do Filemona." Unpublished sermon. Tomaszów Mazowiecki, 2013.

———. "Obywatel czy Uchodźca? – 1 Piotra 1:1–12." Unpublished sermon. Tomaszów Mazowiecki, 2016.

———. "Owce w Skarpetkach – Psalm 23." In *Na Bezdrożach Starego Testamentu: Jak Wędrować, by do Domu Wrócić*, 248–261. Ustroń: Wydawnictwo Szaron, 2017.

———. "Pamiętając o Tym co Ważne – Jozuego 3–5." Unpublished sermon. Tomaszów Mazowiecki, 2017.

———. *Spotkanie z Wszechmocnym. Jak Głosić Kazania na Podstawie Historii Starego Testamentu*. Katowice: Wydawnictwo Credo, 2005.

———. "Trzy Kluczowe Spotkania – Kaznodziei Salomona 11:8–12:14." Unpublished sermon. Tomaszów Mazowiecki, 2017.

Talmy, Leonard. "How Language Structures Space." In *Spatial Orientation: Theory, Research, and Application*, edited by Herbert L. Pick Jr. and Linda P. Acredolo, 225–282. New York: Plenum Press, 1983.

Taylor, Barbara Brown. *The Preaching Life: Living Out Your Vocation*. Norwich: Canterbury Press, 2013.

Taylor, John R. "Categories and Concepts." In *Job 28: Cognition in Context*, edited by Ellen van Wolde, 163–178. Boston: Brill, 2003.

Thibodeau, Paul H., and Lera Boroditsky. "Metaphors We Think With: The Role of Metaphor in Reasoning." *PLOS ONE* 6 (2011): 1–11.

Thiselton, Anthony C. *Hermeneutics: An Introduction*. Grand Rapids, Eerdmans, 2009.

———. *New Horizons in Hermeneutics*. Grand Rapids: Zondervan, 1997.

Torrance, James B. *Worship, Community and the Triune God of Grace*. Carlisle: Paternoster, 1996.

Tracy, David. *The Analogical Imagination: Christian Theology and the Culture of Pluralism*. New York: Independent Publishers Group, 1998.

Troeger, Thomas H. *Creating Fresh Images for Preaching: New Rungs for Jacob's Ladder*. Valley Forge: Judson, 1982.

———. *Imagining a Sermon*. Nashville: Abingdon, 1990.

Tuggy, David. "Schematicity." In *The Oxford Handbook of Cognitive Linguistics*, edited by Dirk Geeraerts and Hubert Cuyckens, 82–116. Oxford; New York: Oxford University Press, 2010.

Turner, Mark. *The Origin of Ideas: Blending, Creativity, and the Human Spark*. Oxford; New York: Oxford University Press, 2014.

Valeš, Jan. "Wolfhart Pannenberg's *imago Dei* Doctrine as Interpreted by F. LeRon Shults and Kam Ming Wong." *European Journal of Theology* 23 (2014): 43–56.

Vanhoozer, Kevin J. First Theology: God, Scripture and Hermeneutics. Downers Grove; Leicester: IVP Academic, 2002.

———. *Is There a Meaning in This Text?: The Bible, the Reader, and the Morality of Literary Knowledge*. Grand Rapids: Zondervan, 2009.

Vanhoozer, Kevin J., and Craig Bartholomew, eds. *Dictionary for Theological Interpretation of the Bible*. Grand Rapids: Baker Academic, 2005.

Varner, William. "A Discourse Analysis of Matthew's Nativity Narrative." *Tyndale Bulletin* 58 (2007): 209–228.

Vine, W. E., and Merrill F. Unger. *Vine's Complete Expository Dictionary of Old and New Testament Words: With Topical Index*. Nashville: Thomas Nelson, 1996.

von Rad, Gerhard. *Genesis: A Commentary*. Translated by John H. Marks. Philadelphia: Westminster, 1961.

———. "The Prohibition of Images in the Old Testament." In *Theological Dictionary of the New Testament*, edited by Gerhard Kittel, 2:381–383. Translated by Geoffrey W. Bromiley, Grand Rapids: Eerdmans, 1964.

———. ""εἰκών." In *Theological Dictionary of the New Testament*, edited by Gerhard Kittel, 2:388. Translated by Geoffrey W. Bromiley. Grand Rapids: Eerdmans, 1964.

Waltke, Bruce K. *An Old Testament Theology: An Exegetical, Canonical, and Thematic Approach*. Grand Rapids: Zondervan, 2007.

Wangerin, Walter, Jr. *Whole Prayer*. Grand Rapids: Zondervan, 2001.

Wansbrough, Henry. "Made and Remade in the Image of God – the New Testament Evidence." In *Growing into God: A Collection of Papers Resulting from a Study Process Conducted by Churches Together in Britain and Ireland, Which Included Three Special Consultations*, edited by Jean Mayland. London: Churches Together in Britain and Ireland, 2003.

Webber, Robert E. *Ancient-Future Faith: Rethinking Evangelicalism for a Postmodern World*. Grand Rapids: Baker Academic, 1999.

Weber, Hans-Ruedi. "Interpreting Biblical Images." *Ecumenical Review* 34 (1982): 210–220.

Webster, John. *Holy Scripture: A Dogmatic Sketch*. Cambridge: Cambridge University Press, 2003.

Weiss, Meir. *The Bible from Within: The Method of Total Interpretation*. Translated by R. Levy and B. Schwartz. Jerusalem: Magnes, 1984.

Wheelwright, Philip. *Metaphor and Reality*. Bloomington: Indiana University Press, 1962.

Wiersbe, Warren W. *Preaching and Teaching with Imagination: The Quest for Biblical Ministry*. Repr. ed. Grand Rapids: Baker Books, 1997.

Wierzbicka, Anna. "Everyday Conceptions of Emotion: A Semantic Perspective." In *Everyday Conceptions of Emotion: An Introduction to the Psychology, Anthropology and Linguistics of Emotion*, edited by James A. Russel, José-Miguel Fernández-Dols, Anthony S. R. Manstead, and Jane C. Wellenkamp, 17–47. Dordrecht: Kluwer, 1995.

Willimon, William H. *The Intrusive Word: Preaching to the Unbaptized*. Eugene: Wipf & Stock, 2002.

Willimon, William H., and Stanley Hauerwas. *Preaching to Strangers: Evangelism in Today's World*. Louisville: Westminster John Knox, 1992.

Wilson, Paul Scott. *Imagination of the Heart: New Understandings in Preaching*. Nashville: Abingdon, 1988.

———. *The Practice of Preaching*. Nashville: Abingdon, 2007.

———. *Setting Words on Fire: Putting God at the Center of the Sermon*. Eugene: Wipf & Stock, 2016.

Wilson-Kastner, Patricia. *Imagery for Preaching*. Minneapolis: Fortress, 1989.

Wimsatt, William K., and Monroe C. Beardsley. "The Intentional Fallacy." In *On Literary Intention*, edited by David Newton-de Molina, 1–13. Edinburgh: Edinburgh University Press, 1976.

Wittgenstein, Ludwig. *Philosophical Investigations*. Translated by G. E. M. Anscombe. New York: Macmillan, 1953.

Wolde, Ellen van. "Cognitive Grammar at Work in Sodom and Gomorrah." In *Cognitive Linguistic Explorations in Biblical Studies*, edited by Bonnie Howe and Joel B. Green, 193–222. Berlin: de Gruyter, 2014.

———. "Wisdom, Who Can Find It? A Non-cognitive and Cognitive Study of Job 28:1–11." In *Job 28: Cognition in Context*, edited by Ellen van Wolde, 1–36. Boston: Brill, 2003.

Wright, Christopher J. H. *The Mission of God: Unlocking the Bible's Grand Narrative*. Nottingham: Inter-Varsity Press, 2006.

Wright, G. Ernest. *God Who Acts: Biblical Theology as Recital*. London: SCM, 1952.

Wright, Stephen I. *Alive to the Word: A Practical Theology of Preaching for the Whole Church*. London: SCM, 2010.

———. "An Experiment in Biblical Criticism: Aesthetic Encounter in Reading and Preaching Scripture." In *Renewing Biblical Interpretation*, edited by Craig Bartholomew, Colin Greene, and Karl Moller, 241–267. Grand Rapids: Zondervan 2000.

———. "Inhabiting the Story: The Use of the Bible in the Interpretation of History." In *"Behind" the Text: History and Biblical Interpretation*, edited by Craig Bartholomew, C. Stephen Evans, Mary Healy and Murray Rae, 492–519. Grand Rapids: Zondervan, 2003.

———. "The Phrase 'Image of God' in the New Testament." In *Growing into God: A Collection of Papers Resulting from a Study Process Conducted by Churches Together in Britain and Ireland, Which Included Three Special Consultations*, edited by Jean Mayland. London: Church House Publishing, 2003.

———. "The Voice of Jesus in Six Parables and Their Interpreters." PhD thesis, University of Durham, 1997.

———. "Words of Power: Biblical Language and Literary Criticism with Reference to Stephen Prickett's *Words and the Word* and Mark 1:21–28." In *After Pentecost: Language and Biblical Interpretation*, edited by Craig Bartholomew, Colin Greene, and Karl Moller, 224–240. Vol. 2 of *Scripture and Hermeneutics Series*. Grand Rapids: Zondervan, 2001.

Van Harn, Roger E. *Preacher, Can You Hear Us Listening?* Grand Rapids: Eerdmans, 2005.

Yancey, Philip. *Disappointment with God*. Grand Rapids: Zondervan, 1988.

Yu, Ning. "Metaphor from Body and Culture." In *The Cambridge Handbook of Metaphor and Thought*, edited by Raymond W. Gibbs, 247–261. New York: Cambridge University Press, 2008

Zagzebski, Linda. *Divine Motivation Theory*. Cambridge: Cambridge University Press, 2004.

———. "Exemplarist Virtue Theory." *Metaphilosophy* 41 January, 1996): 41–57.

———. "Moral Authority of Exemplars." In *Theology and the Science of Moral Action: Virtue Ethics, Exemplarity, and Cognitive Neuroscience* edited by James A. Van Slyke, Gregory Peterson, Warren S. Brown, Kevin S. Reimer, Michael Spezio, 117–129. New York: Routledge, 2013.

———. *Virtues of the Mind: An Inquiry into the Nature of Virtue and the Ethical Foundations of Knowledge*. New York: Cambridge University Press, 1996.

Langham
PARTNERSHIP

Langham Literature, with its publishing work, is a ministry of Langham Partnership.

Langham Partnership is a global fellowship working in pursuit of the vision God entrusted to its founder John Stott –

> *to facilitate the growth of the church in maturity and Christ-likeness through raising the standards of biblical preaching and teaching.*

Our vision is to see churches in the Majority World equipped for mission and growing to maturity in Christ through the ministry of pastors and leaders who believe, teach and live by the word of God.

Our mission is to strengthen the ministry of the word of God through:
- nurturing national movements for biblical preaching
- fostering the creation and distribution of evangelical literature
- enhancing evangelical theological education

especially in countries where churches are under-resourced.

Our ministry

Langham Preaching partners with national leaders to nurture indigenous biblical preaching movements for pastors and lay preachers all around the world. With the support of a team of trainers from many countries, a multi-level programme of seminars provides practical training, and is followed by a programme for training local facilitators. Local preachers' groups and national and regional networks ensure continuity and ongoing development, seeking to build vigorous movements committed to Bible exposition.

Langham Literature provides Majority World preachers, scholars and seminary libraries with evangelical books and electronic resources through publishing and distribution, grants and discounts. The programme also fosters the creation of indigenous evangelical books in many languages, through writer's grants, strengthening local evangelical publishing houses, and investment in major regional literature projects, such as one volume Bible commentaries like the *Africa Bible Commentary* and the *South Asia Bible Commentary*.

Langham Scholars provides financial support for evangelical doctoral students from the Majority World so that, when they return home, they may train pastors and other Christian leaders with sound, biblical and theological teaching. This programme equips those who equip others. Langham Scholars also works in partnership with Majority World seminaries in strengthening evangelical theological education. A growing number of Langham Scholars study in high quality doctoral programmes in the Majority World itself. As well as teaching the next generation of pastors, graduated Langham Scholars exercise significant influence through their writing and leadership.

To learn more about Langham Partnership and the work we do visit **langham.org**

Milton Keynes UK
Ingram Content Group UK Ltd.
UKHW020817171123
432750UK00018B/966

9 781839 737930